秦皇岛馆藏文物精品集

COLLECTIONS OF CULTURAL RELICS IN QINHUANGDAO MUSEUMS

闫乐耕 主编

燕山大学出版社
·秦皇岛·

《秦皇岛馆藏文物精品集》编辑委员会

序

根深者叶茂，源浚者流长，中华民族文明史亦然。

秦皇岛位于河北省东北部，北枕燕山，南襟渤海，自古便是华北进入东北的大通道，是民族交流、交往、交融的必经之路。这片广袤美丽的土地，孕育着丰富多彩的历史文化，抒写着波澜壮阔的璀璨华章。早在15000年前的旧石器时代晚期，人类就在这里繁衍生息。5000余载岁月长河，书写了夷齐采薇、秦皇求仙、汉武巡幸、唐宗驻跸、姜女寻夫等众多历史掌故，留下了秦皇行宫遗址、辽金源影寺塔、天下第一关、近代名人别墅等不可移动的人文景观，同时也留下了大量可移动的文物资源。秦皇岛所属区县文物保管所、博物馆文物收藏厚实，现有文物藏品5000余件，其中一、二级文物500余件，这是中华文明发展进程中最为坚实的见证，也为后世子孙留下了丰富的文化遗产。

习近平总书记指出："让收藏在博物馆里的文物、陈列在广阔大地上的遗产、书写在古籍里的文字都活起来。"党的十八大以来，秦皇岛文博事业发展迅猛，成绩斐然，覆盖城乡的综合博物馆、专题博物馆、企业博物馆及私立博物馆，类型丰富、主体多元，普惠均等的现代博物馆体系基本形成。博物馆拉近了文物与人的距离，"到博物馆看展览"已经成为群众喜爱的新生活方式和新社会风尚。秦皇岛文博人牢记习总书记嘱托，凝心聚力，共启征程，努力创建全市博物馆文化工程，把曾深藏在库房里的文物瑰宝"请"出来，利用现代科学技术手段进行宣传展示，阐释文物的历史价值、艺术价值、科学价值，把文物最神秘、最吸引人的那一面生动地呈现给大众，使人们走进历史，触摸历史，感悟蕴含在文物中的深刻哲理，让闪耀着祖先智慧光芒的文物"飞入寻常百姓家"。

"以古人之规矩，开自己之生面。"编纂一部涵盖全市文保所、博物馆馆藏文物精品的图书，既是对文物的研究与鉴赏，又是对优秀传统文化的传承与保护。经过数年的不懈努力，全市文博工作者甄别梳理，孜孜以求，《秦皇岛馆藏文物精品集》终于付梓，令人欣慰。本书收录文物精品270余件，按照历史时间顺序及种类进行著录，系统介绍了文物信息，解读了文物背后的故事。其中有抚宁邴各庄村出土的新石器时代的石磨盘、石磨棒、石镞等，表明当时大气磅礴的史前文化进程，进入了以农业为主导、畜牧渔猎并存的社会形态发达时期，让我们聆听到渤海湾远古人类走向文明、叩响大地的回声；有北戴河秦行宫遗址出土的卷云夹贝纹大圆瓦当、夔纹大瓦当、"建阳"铭文陶鉴等器物，其携带的历史信息使人联想到"千古一帝"秦始皇一统华夏卓著的功绩，也证实了"秦皇岛"城市名称的来历；有抚宁出土的洗、壶、簋、鼎、匜等造型质朴、铸工精细的铜质器皿，为研究汉代骊城社会经济发展及青铜器铸造工艺提供了实物依据；有青龙出土的铧、锤、釜、勺、碗、瓶等器物，涵盖了辽金时期生产生活的方方面面，彰显了满族厚重的历史文化底蕴；有明长城上的多种形制兵器，它们与守军一起相伴雄关险隘，见证朝代兴衰；有明清时期的碗、盘、瓶、尊等青花彩瓷，特别是北戴河文保所收藏的清代官窑瓷器，完整记录了清代瓷器发展史的辉煌成就，脉络清晰，弥足珍贵；还有造型丰富的佛教造像、工艺精湛的铜镜玉器、“明四家”之首沈周的书法《杨梅传》、近代杰出画家李可染的画作《五牛图》……

辑录的是文物精华珍品，凝聚的是不尽历史文化。

让文物活起来，就是要让更多文物“出圈”，焕发光彩，用文物之光穿透历史长河，汇聚先人智慧，弘扬时代精神，坚定文化自信。

文物所承载的中华民族文化精神，始终滋养着我们。赓续灿烂的历史文化，保护好文化遗产成为全社会共同的事业。让我们在历史文化的精神家园中汲取力量，在新时代伟大奋斗中创建新伟业，一起砥砺前行！

文物——记录过去，映照当下，启迪未来。

是为序。

秦皇岛市旅游和文化广电局党组书记、局长

乔树荣

2024-02-30

PREFACE

Those who have deep sources have long streams, while those who have deep roots have lush leaves, so is the history of Chinese civilization.

Qinhuangdao is located in the northeast of Hebei Province, bordered by the Yanshan Mountains to the north and the Bohai Sea to the south. Since ancient times, it has been a major channel for North China to enter the northeast. It is a necessary path for ethnic association, communication and integration. This vast and beautiful land, gives birth to a rich and colorful history and culture, and describes the magnificent and brilliant chapter of China. As early as 15000 years ago, in the late Upper Paleolithic period, human beings multiplied and lived here. Over five thousand years history has written numerous historical allusions such as "Yi and Qi picking wild vegetables", "The First Emperor of Qin seeking immortality", "Emperor Wu of Han going on an inspection tour", "Emperor Taizong of Tang stopping over", "Lady Mengjiang looking for her husband", and left immovable cultural relics such as the Beidaihe Qin Dynasty Palace Ruins, Yuanyingsi Pagoda (Liao and Jin Dynasty), the First Pass Under Heaven, modern celebrity villas, as well as a large number of movable cultural relics resources. The cultural relics storage centers and museums of the districts and counties under Qinhuangdao have a solid collection of over 5000 cultural relics, including over 500 first and second grade cultural relics, which is the most solid witness to the development process of the Chinese civilization for thousands of years, and has also left a rich cultural heritage for future generations.

General Secretary Xi Jinping pointed out: "Let the cultural relics collected in museums, the heritage displayed on vast land, and the words written in ancient books come alive". Since the 18th National Congress of the Communist Party of China, the cultural and museum industry in Qinhuangdao has developed rapidly and achieved remarkable results. A modern museum system covering urban and rural areas, including comprehensive museums, thematic museums, corporate museums, and private museums, with rich types, diversified subjects and universal equality, has been basically formed. Museums have brought cultural relics closer to people, and "visiting museums for exhibitions" has become a new lifestyle and social trend that is deeply loved by the public today. Qinhuangdao cultural and museum personnel should keep the instructions of General Secretary Xi Jinping in mind, unite our hearts, embark on a journey together, and strive to create a comprehensive museum in the city, "bringing out" the cultural relics treasures once deeply hidden in the warehouse, and utilizing various modern scientific and technological means for publicity and display. We would like to explain the historical, artistic, and scientific value of cultural relics, to present the most mysterious and attractive side of cultural relics to the public in a real and vivid way, allowing people to enter history, feel history, and comprehend the profound philosophical principles contained in cultural relics. Let cultural relics shine with the wisdom of our ancestors, "fly into the homes of ordinary people".

"According to the rules of the ancients, open up our own fresh outlook." Compiling a book that covers the collection of fine cultural relics in cultural preservation institutions and museums throughout the city is not only the study and appreciation of cultural relics, but also the inheritance and protection of excellent traditional culture. After years of unremitting efforts, the city's cultural and museum workers have screened and sorted out, diligently seeking, the *Collections of Cultural Relics in Qinhuangdao*

Museums has finally been published, which is gratifying. This book includes over 270 pieces of high quality cultural relics which are described in chronological order and types. It systematically introduces the information of cultural relics and interprets the stories behind cultural relics. Among them, the Neolithic Stone Saddle-Quern, Frotton, etc. unearthed in Binggezhuang Village, Funing, indicate that the grand prehistoric cultural process at that time entered a period of developed social form dominated by agriculture and coexistence of animal husbandry, fishing and hunting, allowing us to hear the echo of ancient human beings in Bohai Bay moving towards civilization and knock on the earth. The historical information carried by "round eaves tile with scallop on cirrus cloud pattern", "Eaves tile with Kui pattern", and pottery Basin (Jian) with "Jianyang" inscriptions pottery and other artifacts unearthed from the Beidaihe Qin Dynasty Palace Ruins remind people of the immortal merit of the first Emperor of Qin in unifying China through the ages, and also confirms the origin of the city name "Qinhuangdao". There are simple and finely crafted utensils such as Washbasins, Pots, Gui, and Ding unearthed in Funing, providing a physical basis for studying the social and economic development of Licheng in the Han Dynasty and the casting process of bronze ware. The unearthed tools such as Hua, Cauldrons, Spoons, Bowls, and Vases in Qinglong cover all aspects of production and life during the Liao and Jin Dynasty, highlighting the rich historical and cultural heritage of the Manchu people. There are a variety of weapons of different shapes used by the Great Wall of the Ming Dynasty. They are accompanied by the guards in the magnificent and dangerous pass, witnessing the rise and fall of the dynasty. There are blue-and-white colored porcelain from the Ming and Qing dynasties, such as Bowls, Plates, Vases, and Zun, especially the Qing Dynasty official kiln porcelain collected by Beidaihe Cultural Relics Protection and Management Institute, which fully records the glorious achievements of the development history of Qing Dynasty porcelain, with a clear and precious context. There are also Buddhist statues with rich shapes, exquisite copper mirrors and jade wares, the "Biography of Waxberry" written by Shen Zhou, the top of "the four masters of the Ming Dynasty", and "Five Oxen" drawn by Li Keran and so on.

It compiles the essence and treasures of cultural relics and condenses the endless history and culture.

Let cultural relics come to life is to make more cultural relics "go out of the fixed circle" and shine brightly. Use the light of cultural relics to penetrate the long river of history, gather the wisdom of ancestors, carry forward the spirit of the times, and strengthen cultural confidence.

The cultural spirit of the Chinese nation carried by cultural relics has always been nourishing us. Continuing the splendid history and culture, and protecting cultural heritage has become a common cause of the whole society. Let us wander in the spiritual home of history and culture, draw strength, create new great achievements in the great struggle of the new era, and work together to forge ahead!

Cultural relics — record the past, reflect the present, and enlighten the future.

Here is a preface.

Secretary of the Leading Party Members' Group,
Director of Tourism, Culture, Radio and Television
Bureau of Qinhuangdao

Qiao Shurong

2024-02-30

目　录

1 石核 旧石器时代 …… 1
2 石磨盘、磨棒 新石器时代 …… 2
3 石镞 新石器时代 …… 2
4 石斧 新石器时代 …… 3
5 石斧 新石器时代 …… 3
6 五角石纺轮 新石器时代 …… 3
7 尖状石器 新石器时代 …… 4
8 环首翘尾小铜刀 商 …… 4
9 木桶（一对） 商 …… 5
10 木锤 商 …… 5
11 高领四鋬陶罐 商 …… 6
12 陶鬲 商周 …… 7
13 三足铜甗 西周 …… 7
14 蟠虺纹青铜罍 春秋 …… 8
15 青铜啄斧 春秋 …… 9
16 直内青铜戈 战国 …… 9
17 错金银镶嵌绿松石铜带钩 战国 …… 10
18 球腹陶豆 战国 …… 10
19 泥质灰陶子母口豆 战国 …… 11
20 带盖陶豆 战国 …… 11
21 陶鉴 秦 …… 12
22 夔纹大瓦当 秦 …… 13
23 卷云夹贝纹大圆瓦当 秦 …… 13
24 鎏金铜蒜头壶 汉 …… 14
25 铜壶 汉 …… 15
26 铜钫 汉 …… 15
27 圆环耳兽足铜卣 汉 …… 16
28 铜匜 汉 …… 16
29 四神铜温酒炉 汉 …… 17
30 铜剑 汉 …… 18
31 双胡铜戈 汉 …… 18

32 铜鎏金威烈将军印 汉 …… 19
33 兽面铺首衔环铜壶 东汉 …… 20
34 兽面铺首衔铁环铜簋 东汉 …… 21
35 宝鼎山水纹铜洗 东汉 …… 22
36 双鱼龙凤纹铜洗 东汉 …… 23
37 凤鸟登鼎纹铜洗 东汉 …… 24
38 大吉利铜鼎 东汉 …… 25
39 军司马印铜印 东汉 …… 26
40 三扁平足铁釜 辽金 …… 27
41 六鋬铁釜 辽金 …… 27
42 六鋬铁釜 辽金 …… 28
43 双耳三足铁铛 辽金 …… 28
44 铁漏勺 辽金 …… 29
45 铁犁铧 辽金 …… 29
46 铁马蹬 辽金 …… 29
47 铁门铃 辽金 …… 30
48 铁鐎斗 辽金 …… 30
49 镂空团龙铜饰件 辽金 …… 30
50 三足铜釜 辽金 …… 31
51 铜熨斗 辽金 …… 32
52 铜熨斗 金 …… 32
53 铜熨斗 辽金 …… 33
54 铜印 辽金 …… 34
55 行军副统所铜印 金 …… 34
56 行军副统所印铜印 金 …… 35
57 西京皇甫铜权 辽金 …… 36
58 南京皇甫铜权 辽金 …… 36
59 象骨算筹 辽金 …… 37
60 六鋬铜釜 元 …… 37
61 京运铜子母铳 明·隆庆四年 …… 38
62 石炮 明 …… 39
63 石炮 明 …… 39
64 铜安边神炮 明·天启三年 …… 40
65 三箍平尾铁炮 明 …… 40
66 “崇祯十六年”大铁炮 明·崇祯十六年 …… 41
67 陷马陶筒 明 …… 41
68 二龙戏珠纹石药斗 明 …… 42

69 明长城年号砖 明 · 万历十二年 …… 42
70 燕尾形铁榫 明 …… 43
71 三兽足铜火盆 明 …… 43
72 张仓卧佛铜鎏金像 明 …… 44
73 铜胎掐丝珐琅太平有象 清 · 乾隆 …… 45
74 铜胎掐丝珐琅镂空开光云龙纹天球瓶 清 · 乾隆 …… 46
75 船形铜盒 清 …… 46
76 三足铜火盆 清 …… 47
77 覆斗形铜印 清 …… 47
78 微刻牛角印 清 …… 48
79 天汇缠枝花纹金簪 清 …… 48
80 五山纹铜镜 战国 …… 49
81 四神博局纹铜镜 汉 …… 50
82 鼍龙铜镜 唐 …… 51
83 真子飞霜铜镜 唐 …… 51
84 四瑞兽葡萄纹铜镜 唐 …… 52
85 婴戏图直柄铜镜 辽金 …… 53
86 双鱼纹铜镜 辽金 …… 53
87 祥云双鹤铜镜 辽金 …… 54
88 海马丹凤纹铜镜 辽金 …… 54
89 百鸟朝凤纹铜镜 辽金 …… 55
90 二龙戏珠卷叶纹铜镜 金 …… 56
91 五子登科铜镜 明 …… 57
92 五子登科铜镜 明 …… 57
93 观音菩萨石造立像 唐 …… 58
94 释迦牟尼佛铜立像 金 …… 59
95 普贤菩萨坐象鎏金彩绘铜像 明 …… 60
96 释迦牟尼佛鎏金彩绘铜坐像 明 …… 61
97 释迦牟尼佛铜坐像 明 …… 61
98 阿难尊者铜立像 明 …… 62
99 迦叶尊者泥金铜立像 明 …… 63
100 释迦牟尼佛石造坐像 明 …… 64
101 释迦牟尼佛泥金铜坐像 明 …… 64
102 观音铜坐像 明 …… 64
103 释迦牟尼佛鎏金铜坐像 清 …… 65
104 释袈牟尼佛鎏金彩绘铜坐像 清 …… 65
105 尊胜佛母鎏金铜造像 清 …… 66

106 绿度母鎏金铜坐像 清 …… 67
107 释迦牟尼佛鎏金铜坐像 清 …… 67
108 大势至菩萨舟形背光鎏金铜坐像 清 …… 68
109 送子观音石像 清 …… 68
110 道士铜立像 清 …… 69
111 白水晶道人坐像 清 …… 69
112 蟾形玉饰 战国 …… 70
113 龙形玉饰 战国 …… 70
114 白玉龙纹绔尾带板 唐 …… 71
115 青玉苍龙教子带钩 明 …… 71
116 青白玉苍龙教子带钩 明 …… 72
117 白玉镂雕双獾佩 明 …… 72
118 福寿白玉佩 清 …… 73
119 青玉浮雕梅花如意瓦 清 …… 73
120 青玉透雕重环转心佩 清 …… 74
121 青白玉大吉双夔龙佩 清 …… 74
122 白玉童子持莲抚狗坠 清 …… 74
123 翡翠苍龙教子带钩 清 …… 75
124 翡翠如意首带钩 清 …… 75
125 青白玉羊角龙首带钩 清 …… 75
126 白玉透雕双喜佩 清 …… 76
127 白玉螭纹指环 清·乾隆 …… 76
128 透雕瓜蝶纹玉佩 清 …… 76
129 白玉莲蓬菱角坠 清 …… 77
130 玛瑙兽头铺首耳鼻烟壶 清 …… 77
131 玛瑙鸟兽纹鼻烟壶 清 …… 78
132 玛瑙素面鼻烟壶 清 …… 78
133 蚌螺钿人物字纹鼻烟壶 清 …… 79
134 缠丝玛瑙鼻烟壶 清 …… 79
135 白玉浮雕花卉纹鼻烟壶 清 …… 79
136 珊瑚翡翠串珠项链 清 …… 80
137 褐釉三足陶奁 东汉 …… 81
138 黄釉绿彩兽形三足罐 唐 …… 81
139 龙泉窑青釉刻花大盘 宋 …… 82
140 酱釉鸡腿瓶 辽金 …… 83
141 黑褐色鸾凤和鸣四系瓶 辽金 …… 84
142 云龙纹四系瓶 辽金 …… 85

143 褐色卷茎大叶草四系瓶 辽金 85
144 褐色草叶纹四系瓶 辽金 86
145 褐色草叶纹四系瓶 金 86
146 青釉四系橄榄瓶 辽金 86
147 黑釉双系瓷樽 辽金 87
148 酱釉双系罐 辽金 87
149 酱釉竖条纹双系罐 金 88
150 黑釉敞口双系罐 金 89
151 钧釉双系罐 金 89
152 白釉广圈足大碗 辽 90
153 白釉深腹碗 辽 90
154 白釉深腹小碗 辽 91
155 磁州窑双弦纹碗 辽金 91
156 黑白釉瓷碗 辽金 92
157 磁州窑白釉大碗 宋 92
158 定窑模印荷塘鱼跃盘 宋 93
159 定窑模印莲花盘 辽金 94
160 定窑模印莲花碗 辽金 95
161 白釉圈足盘 辽 95
162 黑釉大瓷坛 辽金 96
163 黑釉葫芦瓶 辽金 96
164 三彩刻画花卉碗 辽 97
165 绿釉香炉 辽金 97
166 钧釉天蓝瓷碟 宋 98
167 钧窑天蓝釉红斑碗 元 98
168 钧窑天蓝釉深腹碗 元 99
169 钧窑天蓝釉浅腹盘 元 99
170 钧窑天青釉直腹杯 元 100
171 钧窑天蓝釉直腹杯 元 100
172 白釉雕塑二甲传胪尊 明·成化款 101
173 青花龙凤纹小缸 明·成化款 102
174 青釉刻花碗 明 102
175 青釉回纹大碗 明 103
176 青白釉高足碗 明 103
177 白釉高足碗 明 104
178 五彩凤凰牡丹纹小罐 明 104
179 珐华彩鹭鸶莲池纹罐 明 105

180 青花缠枝莲纹罐 明·崇祯 …… 106
181 青花人物罐 明·崇祯 …… 106
182 青花山水纹大盘 清·康熙款 …… 107
183 黄釉绿彩桃树鸟纹碗 清·康熙款 …… 108
184 青花地黄彩二龙赶珠纹碗 清·康熙款 …… 109
185 孔雀蓝釉鸽子 清·康熙 …… 110
186 霁红釉花觚 清·康熙 …… 110
187 青花百蝠纹盘 清·雍正款 …… 111
188 霁兰釉小盘 清·雍正款 …… 112
189 粉青釉四方八卦琮式瓶 清·雍正款 …… 112
190 粉彩花蝶纹笔筒 清·雍正款 …… 113
191 青花小筒子瓶 清·雍正 …… 113
192 粉彩凤尾花觚 清·雍正 …… 114
193 粉彩凤尾花觚 清·雍正 …… 114
194 青花冰梅盖罐 清·雍正 …… 114
195 青花狮子穿花将军罐 清·雍正 …… 115
196 青花梵文高足碗 清·乾隆款 …… 116
197 青花三果碗 清·乾隆款 …… 117
198 青花矾红彩宝相花小碗 清·乾隆款 …… 117
199 青花留白海水红彩龙纹盘 清·乾隆款 …… 118
200 黄地绿彩龙纹菊瓣口盘 清·乾隆款 …… 119
201 斗彩团花缠枝莲纹小缸 清·乾隆款 …… 120
202 霁红罐 清·乾隆款 …… 120
203 青花象鼻耳樽 清·乾隆款 …… 121
204 青花花卉罐 清·乾隆 …… 122
205 豆青釉红斑兽耳罐 清·乾隆 …… 122
206 窑变釉宝石红锥把瓶 清·乾隆 …… 123
207 红釉天球瓶 清·乾隆 …… 124
208 仿嘉靖款五彩游龙戏珠筒子瓶 清·乾隆 …… 124
209 粉彩八宝小碗 清·嘉庆款 …… 125
210 绿地粉彩宝相花直壁洗 清·嘉庆款 …… 125
211 青花鸾凤云纹盘 清·嘉庆款 …… 126
212 豆青青花象耳洗口瓶 清·嘉庆 …… 127
213 仿成化款青花花觚 清·嘉庆 …… 127
214 青花加白松乔之寿贯耳瓶 清·嘉道 …… 128
215 青花夔凤穿莲纹碗 清·道光款 …… 129
216 斗彩暗八仙束腰碗 清·道光款 …… 130

217 茶叶末釉荸荠瓶 清 · 道光款 …… 131
218 霁蓝釉碗 清 · 道光款 …… 132
219 窑变红釉天球瓶 清 · 道光 …… 133
220 青花冰梅瓶 清 · 道光 …… 134
221 仿康熙款哥窑铁锈花龙鹤纹瓶 清 · 道光 …… 134
222 五彩凤凰牡丹象腿瓶 清 · 道光 …… 135
223 仿雍正款豆青釉剔花龙纹天球瓶 清 · 道光 …… 136
224 仿乾隆款青花富贵白头花鸟纹帽筒 清 · 道光 …… 136
225 青花竹石芭蕉纹玉壶春瓶 清 · 同治款 …… 137
226 青花竹石芭蕉纹玉壶春瓶 清 · 同治款 …… 138
227 冰梅莲花口六连瓶 清 · 同治 …… 138
228 青花纸槌瓶 清 · 同治 …… 139
229 仿康熙款淡描红彩蝴蝶探花罐 清 · 同治 …… 140
230 仿乾隆款粉彩开光六棱小瓶 清 · 同治 …… 141
231 仿乾隆款黄地墨彩什锦碗 清 · 同治 …… 141
232 青花云龙赶珠纹盘 清 · 光绪款 …… 142
233 白地粉彩百蝶纹赏瓶 清 · 光绪款 …… 143
234 粉彩百蝠二龙戏珠纹赏瓶 清 · 光绪款 …… 144
235 白地粉彩夔凤穿莲纹碗 清 · 光绪款 …… 145
236 黄绿釉暗龙纹碗 清 · 光绪款 …… 145
237 黄地三彩二龙戏珠纹胆式瓶 清 · 光绪款 …… 146
238 黄地粉彩开光“万寿无疆”壶 清 · 光绪款 …… 147
239 青花开光八卦碗 清 · 光绪款 …… 148
240 宝石蓝釉描金麋鹿山水纹赏瓶 清 · 光绪 …… 149
241 窑变釉蒜头口瓶 清 · 光绪 …… 150
242 哥瓷铁锈花干枝梅小瓶 清 · 光绪 …… 150
243 墨地三彩梅竹石纹方瓶 清 · 光绪 …… 150
244 黄地粉彩万福万寿纹绣墩 清 · 光绪 …… 151
245 绿地三彩喜鹊登梅盖罐 清 · 光绪 …… 151
246 粉彩暗八仙碗 清 · 光绪 …… 151
247 豆青釉堆白花卉长颈瓶 清 · 光绪 …… 152
248 仿康熙款青花应龙衔莲纹罐 清 · 光绪 …… 153
249 仿康熙款青花云龙赶珠纹碗 清 · 光绪 …… 153
250 仿康熙款绿釉地紫彩蛟龙赶珠纹碗 清 · 光绪 …… 154
251 仿康熙款霁蓝釉瓷盘 清 · 光绪 …… 154
252 仿雍正款淡描青花竹纹碗 清 · 光绪 …… 155
253 仿雍正款白釉杯 清 · 光绪 …… 155

254 仿雍正款淡蓝釉四方瓶 清·光绪 …… 156
255 仿乾隆款白釉绿彩赶珠纹龙盘 清·光绪 …… 157
256 仿乾隆款青花地红绿彩二龙戏珠纹赏瓶 清·光绪 …… 158
257 仿乾隆款红彩应龙纹天鸡高足盖碗 清·光绪 …… 159
258 仿乾隆款粉青釉螭龙耳鹿头樽 清·光绪 …… 160
259 仿乾隆款粉彩二龙戏珠纹鼻烟壶 清·光绪 …… 160
260 仿乾隆款绿地凸雕三彩四方笔筒 清·光绪 …… 161
261 杨梅传 明 沈周 …… 162
262 溪溪山水图 明 张凤翔 …… 164
263 墨竹图 清 潘定澜 …… 165
264 鲤鱼图 清 宋紫山 …… 166
265 晨虎图 清 耕石 …… 167
266 工笔花鸟图 清 恽冰 …… 168
267 竹石图 清·光绪 墨禅 …… 169
268 梅花图 清 胡峻 …… 170
269 松下牡丹图 现代 陈半丁 …… 171
270 梅花鸳鸯图 现代 何香凝（款） …… 172
271 荷花图 现代 于非厂 …… 173
272 《北戴河》行书七言诗 现代 郭沫若 …… 174
273 高士图 现代 溥心畬 …… 175
274 五牛图 现代 李可染 …… 176
275 鸽子图 现代 吴作人 …… 177

图版说明 …… 179

DIRECTORY

1 Stone Cores
Paleolithic Age 1

2 Stone Saddle-quern, Frotton
Neolithic Age 2

3 Stone Arrowhead
Neolithic Age 2

4 Stone Axe
Neolithic Age 3

5 Stone Axe
Neolithic Age 3

6 Pentagram Stone Spinning Wheel
Neolithic Age 3

7 Cuspidate Stone Tool
Neolithic Age 4

8 Copper Knife with Ring Head and Warped Tail
Shang Dynasty 4

9 A Pair of Wooden Barrels
Shang Dynasty 5

10 Wooden Mallet
Shang Dynasty 5

11 High Neck Pottery Jar with Four Handles (Pan)
Shang Dynasty 6

12 Pottery Pot (Li)
Shang and Zhou Dynasty 7

13 Tripod Copper Vessel (Yan)
Western Zhou Dynasty 7

14 Bronze Urn-shaped Vessel (Lei) with Coiling Snake Patterns
Spring and Autumn Period 8

15 Bronze Hatchet
Spring and Autumn Period 9

16 Straight Bronze Dagger-axe (Ge)
Warring States Period 9

17 Gold and Silver Inlaid Turquoise Copper Band Hook
Warring States Period 10

18 Pottery Food Container with Ball-shaped Belly
Warring States Period 10

19 Clay Grey Pottery Food Container (Dou)
Warring States Period 11

20 Covered Pottery Food Container
Warring States Period 11

21 Pottery Basin (Jian)
Qin Dynasty 12

22 Eaves Tile with Kui-dragon Pattern
Qin Dynasty 13

23 Round Eaves Tile with Scallop on Cirrus Cloud Pattern
Qin Dynasty 13

24 Gilded Copper Garlic-shaped Pot
Han Dynasty 14

25 Copper Pot
Han Dynasty 15

26 Copper Square Pot (Fang)
Han Dynasty 15

27 Ring-Handled Copper Ewer (You) with Hoof-shaped Feet
Han Dynasty 16

28 Copper Gourd-shaped Ladle (Yi)
Han dynasty 16

29 Copper Wine-warming Burner with Four Divine Beasts
Han Dynasty 17

30 Copper Sword
Han Dynasty 18

31 Double Hu Dagger-axe (Ge)
Han Dynasty 18

32 Copper Gilded Seal of General Weilie
Han Dynasty 19

33 Copper Kettle with Animal Head Appliques Holding Rings
Eastern Han Dynasty 20

34 Copper Food Vessel (Gui) with Animal Head Appliques Holding Rings
Eastern Han Dynasty 21

35 Copper Washbasin with Treasure Tripod (Ding) and Mountain and River Pattern
Eastern Han Dynasty 22

36 Copper Washbasin with Double Fish Pattern and Dragon-phoenix Pattern
Eastern Han Dynasty 23

37 Copper Washbasin with Phoenix Climbing Tripod Pattern
Eastern Han Dynasty 24

38 Copper Tripod (Ding) of Good Luck
Eastern Han Dynasty 25

39 Copper Seal of Minister of War in Ancient China
Eastern Han Dynasty 26

40 Iron Cauldron (Fu) with Triple Flat Feet
Liao and Jin Dynasty 27

41 Six-handled (Pan) Iron Cauldron (Fu)
Liao and Jin Dynasty 27

42 Six-handled (Pan) Iron Cauldron (Fu)
Liao and Jin Dynasty 28

43 Iron Tripod Cauldron with Two Handles
Liao and Jin Dynasty 28

44 Iron Strainer
Liao and Jin Dynasty 29

45 Iron Plowshare
Liao and Jin Dynasty 29

46 Iron Horse Pedal
Liao and Jin Dynasty 29

47 Iron Ring Bell
Liao and Jin Dynasty 30

48 Iron Ladle
Liao and Jin Dynasty 30

49 Copper Round Hollow Ornaments with Encircling Dragons
Liao and Jin Dynasty 30

50 Copper Tripod Cauldron (Fu)
Liao and Jin Dynasty 31

51 Copper Iron
Liao and Jin Dynasty 32

52 Copper Iron
Jin Dynasty 32

53 Copper Iron
Liao and Jin Dynasty 33

54 Copper Seal
Liao and Jin Dynasty 34

55 Copper Seal of Vice Marching Control
Jin Dynasty 34

56 Copper Seal of Vice Marching Control
Jin Dynasty 35

57 Copper Sliding Weight (Quan) with Xijing and Huangfu
Liao and Jin Dynasty 36

58 Copper Sliding Weight (Quan) with Nanjing and Huangfu
Liao and Jin Dynasty 36

59 Elephant Bone Counting Rod
Liao and Jin Dynasty 37

60 Six-handled (Pan) Copper Cauldron (Fu)
Yuan Dynasty 37

61 Jingyun Copper Blunderbuss
Forth Year of Longqing , Ming Dynasty 38

62 Stone Cannon
Ming Dynasty 39

63 Stone Cannon
Ming Dynasty 39

64 Copper Anbian Divine Cannon
Third Year of Tianqi, Ming Dynasty 40

65 Three Hoop Flat Tail Iron Cannon
Ming Dynasty 40

66 Iron Cannon of "The Sixteenth Year of Chongzhen Period"
Sixteenth Year of Chongzhen, Ming Dynasty 41

67 Pottery Barrel for Trapping Horse
Ming Dynasty 41

68 Two Dragons Play with a Pearl Pattern Stone Medicine Cup
Ming Dynasty 42

69 The Great Wall Brick "Made by Yanhe Road in the Twelfth Year of Wanli"
Twelfth Year of Wanli, Ming Dynasty 42

70 Iron Dovetail Tenon
Ming Dynasty 43

71 Copper Fire-pan with Three Hoof-shaped Feet
Ming Dynasty 43

72 Gild-copper of Zhangcang Reclining Buddha
Ming Dynasty 44

73 Elephant-shaped Cloisonne with Meaning of Peace and Ceremony
Qianlong Reign, Qing Dynasty 45

74 Cloisonne Hollowed-out Globular Vase with Kaiguang Cloud Dragon Pattern
Qianlong Reign, Qing Dynasty 46

75 Copper Box in the Shape of Ship
Qing Dynasty 46

76 Copper Tripod Fire-pan
Qing Dynasty 47

77 Bucket Shaped Copper Seal
Qing Dynasty 47

78 Micro Carving Ox Horn Seal
Qing Dynasty 48

79 Golden Hairpin with Tianhui Interlocking Branches Pattern
Qing Dynasty 48

80 Copper Mirror with Five Mountain Character Pattern
Warring States Period 49
81 Copper Bo-ju Mirrors with Four Divine Beasts Designs
Han Dynasty 50
82 Copper Mirror with Chinese Alligator Pattern
Tang Dynasty 51
83 Copper Mirror with "Zhenzi Feishuang" Pattern
Tang Dynasty 51
84 Copper Mirror with Four Auspicious Animals and Grapes Pattern
Tang dynasty 52
85 Straight Handled Copper Mirror with Children Playing Pattern
Liao and Jin Dynasty 53
86 Copper Mirror with Double Fishes Pattern
Liao and Jin Dynasty 53
87 Copper Mirror with Two Cranes among Auspicious Clouds Pattern
Liao and Jin Dynasty 54
88 Copper Mirror with Mythical Animal in the Ocean and Phoenix Pattern
Liao and Jin Dynasty 54
89 Copper Mirror with Hundred Birds Pay Homage to the Phoenix Pattern
Liao and Jin Dynasty 55
90 Copper Mirror with Two Dragons Play with a Pearl and Curly Leaves Pattern
Jin Dynasty 56
91 Copper Mirror of "Wu Zi Deng Ke"
Ming Dynasty 57
92 Copper Mirror of "Wu Zi Deng Ke"
Ming Dynasty 57
93 Stone Statue of Avalokitesvara (Guanyin Bodhisattva)
Tang Dynasty 58
94 Copper Statue of Sakyamuni
Jin Dynasty 59
95 Gild-copper and Colored Decoration Statue of Samantabhadra Sitting on Elephant
Ming Dynasty 60
96 Gild-copper and Colored Seated Statue of Sakyamuni
Ming Dynasty 61
97 Copper Seated Statue of Sakyamuni
Ming Dynasty 61
98 Copper Statue of Ananda
Ming Dynasty 62
99 Copper Statue of Maha Kasyapa Coated by Powdered Gold
Ming Dynasty 63
100 Stone Seated Statue of Sakyamuni
Ming Dynasty 64
101 Gold Coating Copper Seated Statue of Sakyamuni
Ming Dynasty 64
102 Copper Seated Statue of Avalokitesvara (Guanyin Bodhisattva)
Ming Dynasty 64
103 Gild-copper Seated Statue of Sakyamuni
Qing Dynasty 65
104 Gild-copper and Colored Seated Statue of Sakyamuni
Qing Dynasty 65
105 Gild-copper Figure of Ushnishavijaya
Qing Dynasty 66
106 Gild-copper Seated Statue of Green Tara Buddha
Qing Dynasty 67
107 Gild-copper Seated Statue of Sakyamuni
Qing Dynasty 67

108 Gild-copper Seated Statue of Mahasthamaprapta with Boat-shaped Mandorla
Qing Dynasty 68
109 Stone Statue of Songzi Avalokitesvara
Qing Dynasty 68
110 Copper Statue of Taoist
Qing Dynasty 69
111 White Crystal Sitting Statue of Taoist
Qing Dynasty 69
112 Toad-shaped Jade Ornament
Warring States Period 70
113 Dragon-shaped Jade Ornament
Warring States Period 70
114 White Jade Decoration Belt Plate of Dragon Tail Pattern
Tang Dynasty 71
115 Green Jade Belt Hook in the Shape of Dragon Head and a Small Dragon
Ming Dynasty 71
116 Light Green Jade Belt Hook in the Shape of Dragon Head and a Small Dragon
Ming Dynasty 72
117 White Jade Hollow Double Badger Pendant
Ming Dynasty 72
118 White Jade Pendant of Happiness and Longevity
Qing Dynasty 73
119 Green Jade Embossed Plum Blossom Ruyi Tile
Qing Dynasty 73
120 Green Jade Pendant Carved in Concentric Circle Shape with a Rotating Hub
Qing Dynasty 74
121 Light Green Jade Pendant with Auspicious Double Kui-dragon Design
Qing Dynasty 74
122 White Jade Pendant in the Shape of Child Holding Lotus and Petting Dog
Qing Dynasty 74
123 Jadeite Belt Hook in the Shape of Dragon Head and a Small Dragon
Qing Dynasty 75
124 Jadeite Belt Hook in the Shape of Ruyi
Qing Dynasty 75
125 Light Green Jade Belt Hook in the Shape of Dragon Head and Ram's Horns
Qing Dynasty 75
126 White Jade Hollow Double Happiness Pendant
Qing Dynasty 76
127 White Jade Chi-dragon Pattern Ring
Qianlong Reign, Qing Dynasty 76
128 Jade Pendant with Hollow Melon and Butterfly Patterns
Qing Dynasty 76
129 White Jade Lotus Seedpod and Water Chestnut Pendant
Qing Dynasty 77
130 Agate Snuff Bottle with Handles in Animal Head Applique Shaped
Qing Dynasty 77
131 Agate Snuff Bottle with Bird and Beast Pattern
Qing Dynasty 78
132 Agate Snuff Bottle with Plain Surface
Qing Dynasty 78
133 Mother-of-pearl Snuff Bottle with Portrait and Characters Pattern
Qing Dynasty 79
134 Sardonyx Snuff Bottle
Qing Dynasty 79
135 White Jade Embossed Floral Snuff Bottle
Qing Dynasty 79

136 Coral Emerald Beaded Necklace
Qing Dynasty 80

137 Three-feet Pottery Dresser Set Box with Brown Glaze
Eastern Han Dynasty 81

138 Yellow Ground Glazed and Green Colored Jar with Three Animal-shaped Legs
Tang Dynasty 81

139 Cyan Glazed Plate with Incised Decoration of Longquan Kiln
Song Dynasty 82

140 Dark Brown Glazed Vase in the Shape of Chicken Leg
Liao and Jin Dynasty 83

141 Four-handled Vase with the Design of Black Colored Phoenixes
Liao and Jin Dynasty 84

142 Four-handled Vase with the Design of Black Colored Dragon among Clouds
Liao and Jin Dynasty 85

143 Four-handled Vase with the Brown Colored and Large Leaf Pattern Curled Stems
Liao and Jin Dynasty 85

144 Four-handled Vase with the Brown Colored Grass and Leaf Pattern
Liao and Jin Dynasty 86

145 Four-handled Vase with the Brown Colored Grass and Leaf Pattern
Jin Dynasty 86

146 Four-handled Olive-shaped Vase with Yellowish Green Glaze
Liao and Jin Dynasty 86

147 Two-handled Vessel (Zun) with Black Glazed
Liao and Jin Dynasty 87

148 Dark Brown Glazed Two-handled Jar
Liao and Jin Dynasty 87

149 Dark Brown Glazed Two-handled Jar with Vertical Stripes
Jin Dynasty 88

150 Two-handled Jar with Black Glazed
Jin Dynasty 89

151 Two-handled Jar of Jun Kiln
Jin Dynasty 89

152 Wide Round Foot Large Bowl with White Glaze
Liao Dynasty 90

153 Deep Belly Bowl with White Glaze
Liao Dynasty 90

154 Deep Belly Small Bowl with White Glaze
Liao Dynasty 91

155 Double Circle Pattern Bowl of Cizhou Kiln
Liao and Jin Dynasty 91

156 Black and White Glazed Bowl
Liao and Jin Dynasty 92

157 White Glazed Large Bowl of Cizhou Kiln
Song Dynasty 92

158 IDing Kiln Mold Printing Plate with Lotus Pond Fish Jumping
Song Dynasty 93

159 Ding Kiln Mold Printing Plate with Lotus
Liao and Jin Dynasty 94

160 IDing Kiln Mold Printing Plate with Lotus
Liao and Jin Dynasty 95

161 Round Foot Plate with White Glaze
Liao Dynasty 95

162 Black Glazed Porcelain Jar
Liao and Jin Dynasty 96

163 Black Glazed Gourd-shaped Vase
Liao and Jin Dynasty 96

164 Tri-color Bowl with Engraved Floral Pattern
Liao Dynasty 97

165 Green Glazed Censer
Liao and Jin Dynasty 97

166 Azure Glazed Dish of Jun Kiln
Song Dynasty 98

167 Azure Glazed Bowl with Red Colored Patch of Jun Kiln
Yuan Dynasty 98

168 Azure Glazed Bowl with Deep Belly of Jun Kiln
Yuan Dynasty 99

169 Azure Glazed Dish with Shallow Belly of Jun Kiln
Yuan Dynasty 99

170 Azure Glazed Cup with Straight Belly of Jun Kiln
Yuan Dynasty 100

171 Azure Glazed Cup with Straight Belly of Jun Kiln
Yuan Dynasty 100

172 White Glazed Sculpture Vessel (Zun) of Two Crabs Delivering Reed
Chenghua Reign, Ming Dynasty 101

173 Blue-and-white Glazed Small Mortar Jar with the Design of Dragon and Phoenix
Chenghua Reign, Ming Dynasty 102

174 Cyan Glazed Bowl with Incised Floral Pattern
Ming Dynasty 102

175 Cyan Glazed Bowl with Hui Pattern
Ming Dynasty 103

176 Azure Glazed Bowl with High Foot
Ming Dynasty 103

177 White Glazed High Foot Bowl
Ming Dynasty 104

178 Small Porcelain Jar with the Design of Polychrome Phoenix and Peony Pattern
Ming Dynasty 104

179 Fahua Color Jar with Lotus Pond and Egret Design
Ming Dynasty 105

180 Blue-and-white Glazed Jar with the Design of Interlocking Branches of Lotus
Chongzhen Reign, Ming Dynasty 106

181 Blue-and-white Glazed Jar with the Design of Figures
Chongzhen Reign, Ming Dynasty 106

182 Blue-and-white Glazed Plate with the Design of Landscape Pattern
Kangxi Reign, Qing Dynasty 107

183 Yellow Glazed Bowl with Green Colored Peach Trees and Birds Patterns
Kangxi Reign, Qing Dynasty 108

184 Bowl with the Design of Two Yellow-colored Dragons Chasing a Pearl on Blue-and-white Ground Glaze
Kangxi Reign, Qing Dynasty 109

185 Peacock-blue Glazed Pigeon
Kangxi Reign, Qing Dynasty 110

186 Sacrificial-red-glazed Beaker Vase
Kangxi Reign, Qing Dynasty 110

187 Blue-and-white Dish with the Design of Hundred Bats
Yongzheng Reign, Qing Dynasty 111

188 Sacrificial-blue-glazed Plate
Yongzheng Reign, Qing Dynasty 112

189 Light Greenish-blue Glazed Cong-shaped Vase with the Design of the Eight Diagrams
Yongzheng Reign, Qing Dynasty 112

190 Famille-rose Glazed Brush Holder with the Design of Flower and Butterfly
Yongzheng Reign, Qing Dynasty 113

191 Blue-and-white Glazed Bobbin-shaped Vase
Yongzheng Reign, Qing Dynasty 113

192 Famille-rose Beaker Vase with the Design of Phoenix-tail
Yongzheng Reign, Qing Dynasty 114

193 Famille-rose Beaker Vase with the Design of Phoenix-tail
Yongzheng Reign, Qing Dynasty 114

194 Blue-and-white Glazed Covered Jar with Plum Pattern
Yongzheng Reign, Qing Dynasty 114

195 Blue-and-white Glazed General Jar with the Design of Lions Playing among Flowers
Yongzheng Reign, Qing Dynasty 115

196 Blue-and-white Glazed High-footed Bowl with the Design of Sanskrit Inscriptions
Qianlong Reign, Qing Dynasty 116

197 Blue-and-white Glazed Bowl with Three Fruits Pattern
Qianlong Reign, Qing Dynasty 117

198 Blue-and-white and Alum Red-colored Glaze Small Bowl with Baoxiang Flowers Pattern
Qianlong Reign, Qing Dynasty 117

199 Blue-and-white Glazed Dish with the Design of Red Dragon Crossing the Ocean in Blank
Qianlong Reign, Qing Dynasty 118

200 Yellow Ground Glaze Chrysanthemum Petal-shaped Dish with the Design of Green-colored Dragon
Qianlong Reign, Qing Dynasty 119

201 Doucai (Contrasting-colors) Jar with Flowers and Interlocking Lotus Pattern
Qianlong Reign, Qing Dynasty 120

202 Sacrificial-red-glazed Mortar Jar
Qianlong Reign, Qing Dynasty 120

203 Blue-and-white Wine Vessels (Zun) with Elephant-trunk Handles
Qianlong Reign, Qing Dynasty 121

204 Blue-and-white Jar with Floral Pattern
Qianlong Reign, Qing Dynasty 122

205 Bean-green Glazed Jar with Animal-shaped Handles
Qianlong Reign, Qing Dynasty 122

206 Ruby Glazed Vase in the Shape of Awl Handle
Qianlong Reign, Qing Dynasty 123

207 Red Glazed Globular Vase
Qianlong Reign, Qing Dynasty 124

208 Bobbin-shaped Vase with the Design of Famille Verte Dragon
Chasing Pearls as an Imitation of Jiajing Reign Style
Qianlong Reign, Qing Dynasty 124

209 Famille-rose Glazed Small Bowl with the Design of Eight Buddhist Ritual Instruments
Jiaqing Reign, Qing Dynasty 125

210 Green Ground Glazed Writing-brush Washer with the Design of Famille-rose Glazed Baoxiang Flowers
Jiaqing Reign, Qing Dynasty 125

211 Blue-and-white Glazed Plate with the Design of Phoenix among Clouds
Jiaqing Reign, Qing Dynasty 126

212 Bean-green Ground Glazed Plate-shaped Mouth Vase with Elephant-trunk Handles
Jiaqing Reign, Qing Dynasty 127

213 Blue-and-white Glazed Beaker Vase as an Imitation of Chenghua Reign Period Style
Jiaqing Reign, Qing Dynasty 127

214 Blue-and-white Double Tubular Handled Vase with the Design of as Longevity as Song Qiao
Jiajing and Daoguang Reign, Qing Dynasty 128

215 Blue-and-white Glazed Bowl with the Design of Kui-phoenix Crossing Lotus
Daoguang Reign, Qing Dynasty 129

216 Doucai (Contrasting-colors) Bamboo Hat Shaped Bowl with the Eight Immortals' Ritual Instruments
Daoguang Reign, Qing Dynasty 130

217 Tea-dust Glazed Biqi-shaped (water chestnut shaped) Vase
Daoguang Reign, Qing Dynasty 131

218 Sacrificial-blue-glazed Bowl
Daoguang Reign, Qing Dynasty 132

219 Red Flambé Glazed Globular Vase
Daoguang Reign, Qing Dynasty 133

220 Blue-and-white Glazed Prunus Vase with the Design of Ice Crystal Structure
Daoguang Reign, Qing Dynasty 134

221 An Imitation of Ge Kiln Vase in the Kangxi Period Style with the Design of Rust-red Colored Dragon and Crane
Daoguang Reign, Qing Dynasty 134

222 Bobbin-shaped Vase with the Design of Famille Verte Phoenix and Peony
Daoguang Reign, Qing Dynasty 135

223 Bean-green Glazed Globular Vase with the Graffito Dragon Design as an Imitation of the Yongzheng Period Style
Daoguang Reign, Qing Dynasty 136

224 An Imitation Hat Stand of the Qianlong Period Style with the Design of Blue-and-white Glazed "Wealthy and Happiness" Flower-and-bird Pattern
Daoguang Reign, Qing Dynasty 136

225 Blue-and-white Pear-shaped Vase with the Design of Bamboo, Stone and Plantain
Tongzhi Reign, Qing Dynasty 137

226 Blue-and-white Pear-shaped Vase with the Design of Bamboo, Stone and Plantain
Tongzhi Reign, Qing Dynasty 138

227 Six-linked Vase with the Design of Ice Crystal Structure and Plum Blossoms Pattern with a Lotus Shaped Mouth
Tongzhi Reign, Qing Dynasty 138

228 Blue-and-white Glazed Vase in the Shape of Mallet
Tongzhi Reign, Qing Dynasty 139

229 An Imitation of the Kangxi Period Style Jar with the Design of Butterfly-touching-flower in Pastel Shade
Tongzhi Reign, Qing Dynasty 140

230 Famille-rose Glazed Hexagonal-sided Vessel with the Kaiguang Pattern as an Imitation of the Qianlong Period Style
Tongzhi Reign, Qing Dynasty 141

231 Assorted Bowl Painted in Black Color as an Imitation of Qianlong Period Style on a Yellow Ground Glazed
Tongzhi Reign, Qing Dynasty 141

232 Blue-and-white Glazed Plate with the Design of Dragons Chasing Pearls
Guangxu Reign, Qing Dynasty 142

233 White Ground Glazed Ornamental Vase with the Design of Hundred Butterflies
Guangxu Reign, Qing Dynasty 143

234 Famille-rose Glazed Ornamental Vase with the Design of Hundred Bats and Two Dragons Play with a Pearl Pattern
Guangxu Reign, Qing Dynasty 144

235 White Ground Glazed Bowl with the Design of Famille-rose Glazed Kui-phoenix Crossing Lotus
Guangxu Reign, Qing Dynasty 145

236 Yellow and Green Glazed Bowl with the Design of Veiled Dragon Patterns
Guangxu Reign , Qing Dynasty 145

237 Yellow Ground Glazed Gallbladder-shaped Vase with the Design of Tri-color Glazed Two Dragons Play with a Pearl
Guangxu Reign, Qing Dynasty 146

238 Yellow Ground Glazed Famille-rose Kettle with the Design of Kaiguang Frame and "Wanshou wujiang"
Guangxu Reign, Qing Dynasty 147

239 Blue-and-white Bowl with the Design of Eight Trigrams Kaiguang Pattern
Guangxu Reign, Qing Dynasty 148

240 Sacrificial-blue-glazed Ornamental Vase with the Design of Gold Outlines Elk and Landscape Pattern
Guangxu Reign, Qing Dynasty 149

241 Variable Glazed Garlic-head Shaped Vase
Guangxu Reign, Qing Dynasty 150

242 Ge Kiln Small Vase with the Design of Rust-red Colored Branches and Plum Blossoms
Guangxu Reign, Qing Dynasty 150

243 Black Color Ground Glazed Square Wooden-club Shaped Vase with the Design of Tri-color Glazed Plum Flowers, Bamboo, and Stones
Guangxu Reign, Qing Dynasty 150

244 Yellow Ground Glazed Stool with the Design of Famille-rose Glazed Happiness and Longevity
Guangxu Reign, Qing Dynasty 151

245 Green Ground Glazed Covered Jar with the Design of Tri-color Glazed Magpie Stepping on Plum Blossom
Guangxu Reign, Qing Dynasty 151

246 Famille-rose Glazed Bowl with the Eight Immortals' Ritual Instruments
Guangxu Reign, Qing Dynasty 151

247 Bean-green Glazed Long Straight Necked Vase Covering with White Flowers
Guangxu Reign, Qing Dynasty 152

248 Blue-and-white Glazed Jar with the Design of Ying-dragons Holding Lotus in Mouth as an Imitation of the Kangxi Period Style
Guangxu Reign, Qing Dynasty 153

249 Blue-and-white Glazed Bowl with the Design of Dragons Chasing Pearls as an Imitation of the Kangxi Period Style
Guangxu Reign, Qing Dynasty 153

250 Green Ground Glazed Bowl with the Design of Purple Colored Walking Dragons as an Imitation of the Kangxi Period Style
Guangxu Reign, Qing Dynasty 154

251 Sacrificial-blue-glazed Plate as an Imitation of the Qianlong Period Style
Guangxu Reign, Qing Dynasty 154

252 Light Blue-and-white Glazed Bowl with Bamboo Pattern as an Imitation of the Yongzheng Period Style
Guangxu Reign, Qing Dynasty 155

253 White Glazed Cup as an Imitation of the Yongzheng Period Style
Guangxu Reign, Qing Dynasty 155

254 Light Blue Glazed Square-shaped Vase as an Imitation of Yongzheng Period Style
Guangxu Reign, Qing Dynasty 156

255 White Ground Glazed Plate with the Design of Green Colored Dragons Chasing Pearls as an Imitation of the Qianlong Period Style
Guangxu Reign, Qing Dynasty 157

256 Blue-and-white Ground Glazed Vase with the Design of Red and Green Colored Two Dragons Play with a Pearl as an Imitation of the Qianlong Period Style
Guangxu Reign, Qing Dynasty 158

257 High Foot Bowl with Tianji Cover in the Design of Red Colored Ying-dragons as an Imitation of the Qianlong Period Style
Guangxu Reign, Qing Dynasty 159

258 Light Greenish-blue Glazed Vessel (Zun) with the Design of Chi-dragon Shaped Handles as an Imitation of the Qianlong Period Style
Guangxu Reign, Qing Dynasty 160

259 Famille-rose Glazed Snuff Bottle with the Design of Two Dragons Play with a Pearl as an Imitation of the Qianlong Period Style
Guangxu Reign, Qing Dynasty 160

260 Square Green Ground Glazed Brush Holder with Tri-color Glazed Relief Carved as an Imitation of the Qianlong Period Style
Guangxu Reign, Qing Dynasty 161

261 Biography of Waxberry
Shen Zhou, Ming Dynasty, Running Script 162

262 Landscape Painting of Nuanxi River
Zhang Fengxiang, Ming Dynasty 164

263 Ink Bamboo
Pan Dinglan, Qing Dynasty 165

264 Carp
Shen Zishan, Qing Dynasty 166

265 Tiger in the Morning
Gengshi, Qing Dynasty 167

266 Fine Brushwork Painting of Flowers and Birds
Yun Bing, Qing Dynasty 168

267 Bamboo in the Rock
Mochan, Guangxu Reign, Qing Dynasty 169

268 Plum Blossom Painting
Hu Jun, Qing Dynasty 170

269 Peony under the Pine Trees
Chen Banding, Modern 171

270 Plum Blossom and Mandarin Duck
He Xiangning (Marked), Modern 172

271 Lotus Painting
Yu Feichang, Modern 173

272 "Beidaihe" Running Script Seven Character Poem
Guo Moruo, Modern 174

273 Painting of Excellent People
Pu Xinyu, Modern 175

274 Five Oxen
Li Keran, Modern 176

275 Pigeon Painting
Wu Zuoren, Modern 177

Caption 231

1 石核 旧石器时代

Stone Cores
Period: Paleolithic Age

2 石磨盘、磨棒 新石器时代

Stone Saddle-quern, Frotton
Period: Neolithic Age

3 石镞 新石器时代

Stone Arrowhead
Period: Neolithic Age

4 石斧 新石器时代

Stone Axe
Period: Neolithic Age

5 石斧 新石器时代

Stone Axe
Period: Neolithic Age

6 五角石纺轮 新石器时代

Pentagram Stone Spinning Wheel
Period: Neolithic Age

7 尖状石器 新石器时代

Cuspidate Stone Tool
Period: Neolithic Age

8 环首翘尾小铜刀 商

Copper Knife with Ring Head and Warped Tail
Period: Shang Dynasty

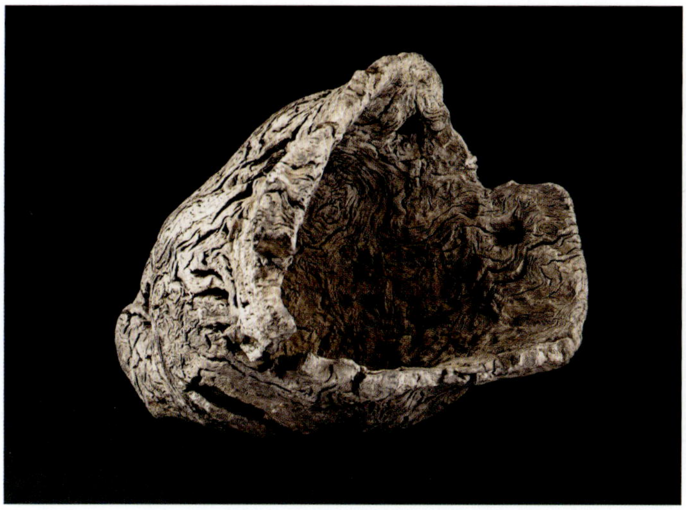

9 木桶（一对）商

A Pair of Wooden Barrels
Period: Shang Dynasty

10 木锤 商

Wooden Mallet
Period: Shang Dynasty

11 高领四鋬陶罐 商

High Neck Pottery Jar with Four Handles (Pan)
Period: Shang Dynasty

12 陶鬲 商周

Pottery Pot (Li)
Period: Shang and Zhou Dynasty

13 三足铜甗 西周

Tripod Copper Vessel (Yan)
Period: Western Zhou Dynasty

14 蟠虺纹青铜罍 春秋

Bronze Urn-shaped Vessel (Lei) with Coiling Snake Patterns
Period: Spring and Autumn Period

15 青铜啄斧 春秋

Bronze Hatchet
Period: Spring and Autumn Period

16 直内青铜戈 战国

Straight Bronze Dagger-axe (Ge)
Period: Warring States Period

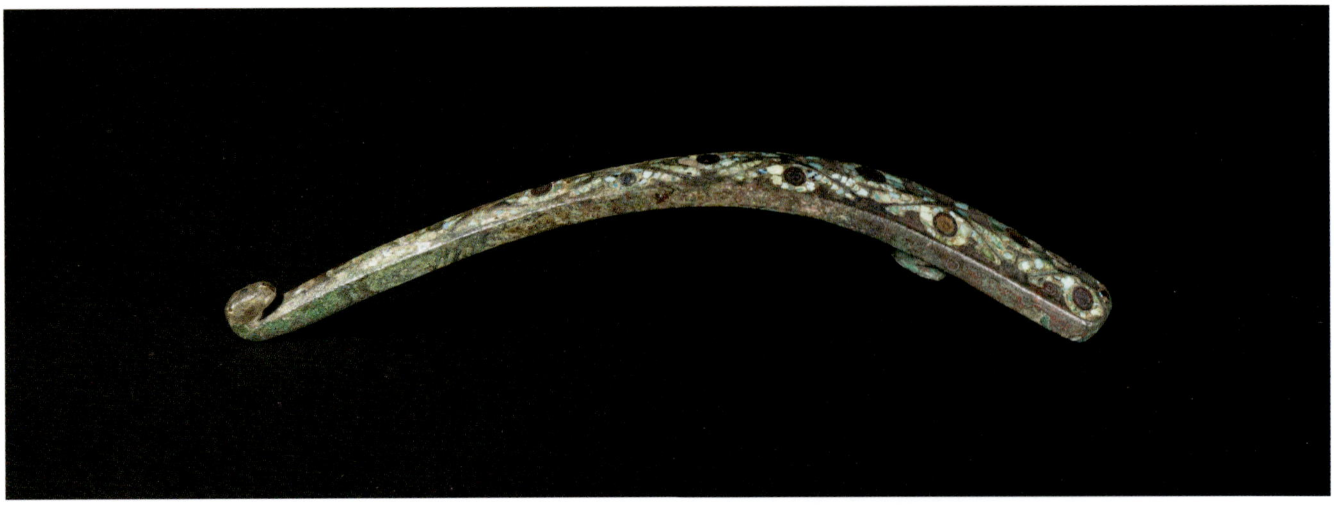

17 错金银镶嵌绿松石铜带钩 战国

Gold and Silver Inlaid Turquoise Copper Band Hook
Period: Warring States Period

18 球腹陶豆 战国

Pottery Food Container with Ball-shaped Belly
Period: Warring States Period

19 泥质灰陶子母口豆 战国

Clay Grey Pottery Food Container (Dou)
Period: Warring States Period

20 带盖陶豆 战国

Covered Pottery Food Container
Period: Warring States Period

外壁唇沿下“建阳”铭文
the two-word inscription “Jian Yang” is engraved below the exterior lip rim

21 陶鉴 秦
Pottery Basin (Jian)
Period: Qin Dynasty

22 夔纹大瓦当 秦

Eaves Tile with Kui-dragon Pattern
Period: Qin Dynasty

23 卷云夹贝纹大圆瓦当 秦

Round Eaves Tile with Scallop on Cirrus Cloud Pattern
Period: Qin Dynasty

24 鎏金铜蒜头壶 汉

Gilded Copper Garlic-shaped Pot
Period: Han Dynasty

25 铜壶 汉

Copper Pot
Period: Han Dynasty

26 铜钫 汉

Copper Square Pot (Fang)
Period:Han Dynasty

27 圆环耳兽足铜卣 汉

Ring-Handled Copper Ewer (You) with Hoof-shaped Feet

Period:Han Dynasty

28 铜匜 汉

Copper Gourd-shaped Ladle (Yi)

Period: Han Dynasty

29 四神铜温酒炉 汉

Copper Wine-warming Burner with Four Divine Beasts
Period: Han Dynasty

30 铜剑 汉

Copper Sword
Period: Han Dynasty

31 双胡铜戈 汉

Double Hu Dagger-axe (Ge)
Period: Han Dynasty

32 铜鎏金威烈将军印 汉

Copper Gilded Seal of General Weilie
Period: Han Dynasty

33 兽面铺首衔环铜壶 东汉

Copper Kettle with Animal Head Appliques Holding Rings
Period: Eastern Han Dynasty

兽面铺首衔环耳
animal head appliques holding ring handle

34 兽面铺首衔铁环铜簋 东汉

Copper Food Vessel (Gui) with Animal Head Appliques Holding Rings
Period: Eastern Han Dynasty

铺首耳
animal head appliques handle

内底部宝鼎山水纹图案
interior pattern of copper washbasin bottom

35 宝鼎山水纹铜洗 东汉

Copper Washbasin with Treasure Tripod (Ding) and Mountain and River Pattern
Period: Eastern Han Dynasty

内底部双鱼凤纹图案
interior bottom double fish and phoenix pattern of copper washbasin bottom

外底部双圈内三凸脊纹图案
exterior bottom pattern of copper washbasin bottom

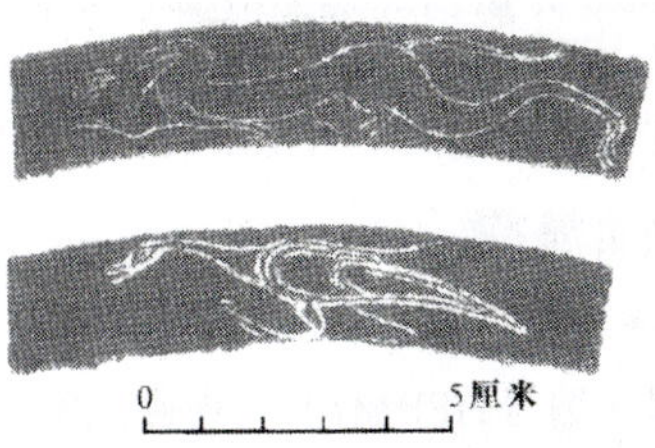

口沿龙凤图案
dragon and phoenix pattern on mouth edge

36 双鱼龙凤纹铜洗 东汉

Copper Washbasin with Double Fish Pattern and Dragon-phoenix Pattern
Period: Eastern Han Dynasty

内底部凤鸟登鼎纹图案
inner pattern of copper washbasin bottom

37 凤鸟登鼎纹铜洗 东汉

Copper Washbasin with Phoenix Climbing Tripod Pattern
Period: Eastern Han Dynasty

其中一足“大吉利君宜官”铭文
one foot is engraved with the inscription: “Good luck on everything”

38 大吉利铜鼎 东汉

Copper Tripod (Ding) of Good Luck
Period: Eastern Han Dynasty

侧面篆书“范”字
the character “Fan” in Seal Script on one side

39 军司马印铜印 东汉

Copper Seal of Minister of War in Ancient China
Period: Eastern Han Dynasty

40 三扁平足铁釜 辽金

Iron Cauldron (Fu) with Triple Flat Feet
Period: Liao and Jin Dynasty

41 六鋬铁釜 辽金

Six-handled (Pan) Iron Cauldron (Fu)
Period: Liao and Jin Dynasty

42 六鋬铁釜 辽金

Six-handled (Pan) Iron Cauldron (Fu)
Period: Liao and Jin Dynasty

43 双耳三足铁铛 辽金

Iron Tripod Cauldron with Two Handles
Period: Liao and Jin Dynasty

44 铁漏勺 辽金

Iron Strainer
Period: Liao and Jin Dynasty

45 铁犁铧 辽金

Iron Plowshare
Period: Liao and Jin Dynasty

46 铁马蹬 辽金

Iron Horse Pedal
Period: Liao and Jin Dynasty

47 铁门铃 辽金

Iron Ring Bell
Period: Liao and Jin Dynasty

48 铁鐎斗 辽金

Iron Ladle

Period: Liao and Jin Dynasty

49 镂空团龙铜饰件 辽金

Copper Round Hollow Ornaments with Encircling Dragons
Period: Liao and Jin Dynasty

50 三足铜釜 辽金

Copper Tripod Cauldron (Fu)

51 铜熨斗 辽金

Copper Iron
Period: Liao and Jin Dynasty

52 铜熨斗 金

Copper Iron
Period: Jin Dynasty

内底部阴刻宝相花
Baoxiang flowers pattern is incised carving on interior bottom

53 铜熨斗 辽金

Copper Iron
Period: Liao and Jin Dynasty

54 铜印 辽金

Copper Seal
Period: Liao and Jin Dynasty

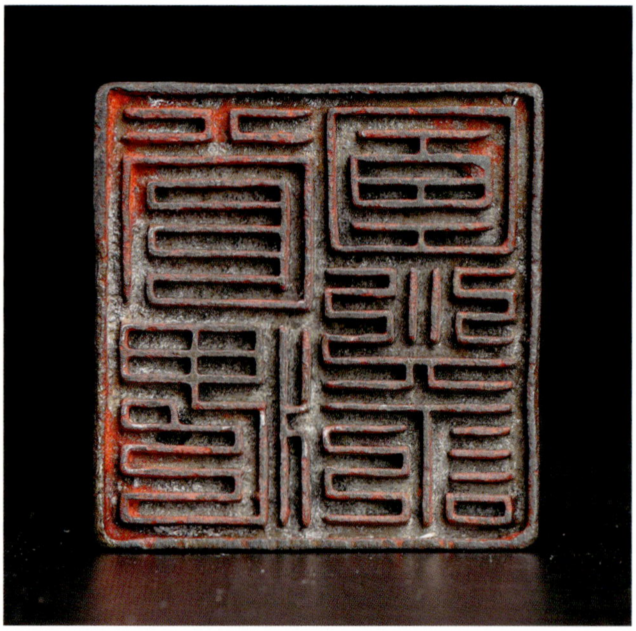

55 行军副统所铜印 金

Copper Seal of Vice Marching Control
Period: Jin Dynasty

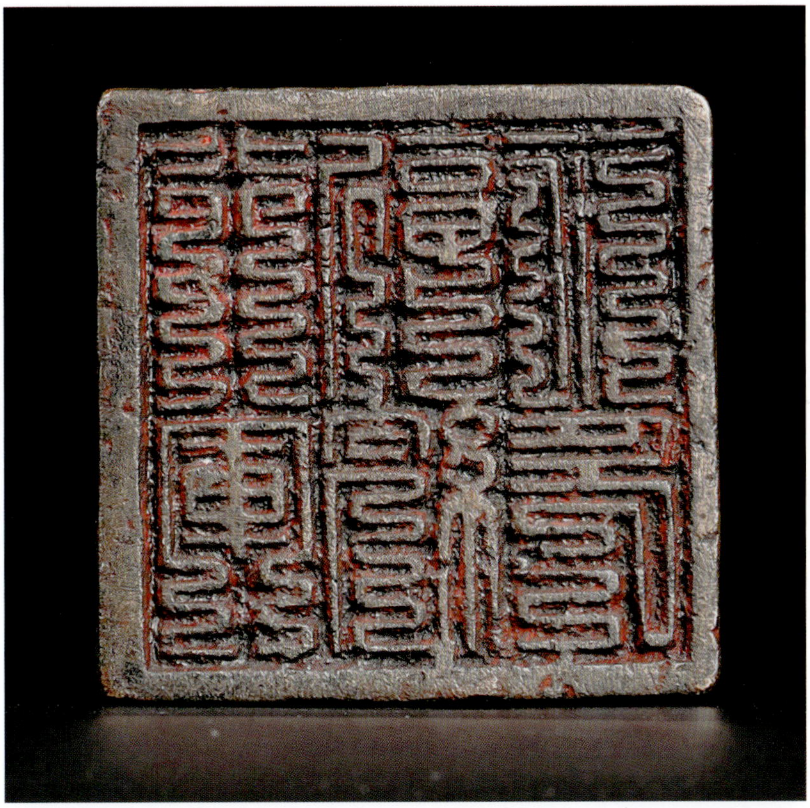

56 行军副统所印铜印 金

Copper Seal of Vice Marching Control
Period: Jin Dynasty

57 西京皇甫铜权 辽金

Copper Sliding Weight (Quan) with Xijing and Huangfu
Period: Liao and Jin Dynasty

58 南京皇甫铜权 辽金

Copper Sliding Weight (Quan) with Nanjing and Huangfu
Period: Liao and Jin Dynasty

59 象骨算筹 辽金

Elephant Bone Counting Rod
Period: Liao and Jin Dynasty

60 六錾铜釜 元

Six-handled (Pan) Copper Cauldron (Fu)
Period: Yuan Dynasty

61 京运铜子母铳 明・隆庆四年

Jingyun Copper Blunderbuss
Period: Forth Year of Longqing , Ming Dynasty

62 石炮 明

Stone Cannon
Period: Ming Dynasty

63 石炮 明

Stone Cannon
Period: Ming Dynasty

64 铜安边神炮 明·天启三年

Copper Anbian Divine Cannon
Period: Third Year of Tianqi, Ming Dynasty

65 三箍平尾铁炮 明

Three Hoop Flat Tail Iron Cannon
Period: Ming Dynasty

炮尾部 92 字铭文
92 character inscription is cast on the tail of the iron cannon

66 “崇祯十六年”大铁炮 明·崇祯十六年

Iron Cannon of “The Sixteenth Year of Chongzhen Period”
Period: Sixteenth Year of Chongzhen, Ming Dynasty

陶筒内的铁蒺藜
iron caltrops in the pottery barrel

67 陷马陶筒 明

Pottery Barrel for Trapping Horse
Period: Ming Dynasty

68 二龙戏珠纹石药斗 明

Two Dragons Play with a Pearl Pattern Stone Medicine Cup
Period: Ming Dynasty

69 明长城年号砖 明・万历十二年

The Great Wall Brick “Made by Yanhe Road in the Twelfth Year of Wanli”
Period: Twelfth Year of Wanli, Ming Dynasty

70 燕尾形铁榫 明

Iron Dovetail Tenon
Period: Ming Dynasty

71 三兽足铜火盆 明

Copper Fire-pan with Three Hoof-shaped Feet
Period: Ming Dynasty

底部铭文
the inscription of the box bottom

装佛像的函匣
the box of Buddha statues

72 张仓卧佛铜鎏金像 明

Gild-copper of Zhangcang Reclining Buddha
Period: Ming Dynasty

73 铜胎掐丝珐琅太平有象 清·乾隆

Elephant-shaped Cloisonne with Meaning of Peace and Ceremony
Period: Qianlong Reign, Qing Dynasty

74 铜胎掐丝珐琅镂空开光云龙纹天球瓶

清・乾隆

Cloisonne Hollowed-out Globular Vase with Kai-guang Cloud Dragon Pattern

Period: Qianlong Reign, Qing Dynasty

75 船形铜盒 清

Copper Box in the Shape of Ship

Period: Qing Dynasty

76 三足铜火盆 清

Copper Tripod Fire-pan
Period: Qing Dynasty

77 覆斗形铜印 清

Bucket Shaped Copper Seal
Period: Qing Dynasty

78 微刻牛角印 清

Micro Carving Ox Horn Seal
Period: Qing Dynasty

79 天汇缠枝花纹金簪 清

Golden Hairpin with Tianhui Interlocking Branches Pattern
Period: Qing Dynasty

80 五山纹铜镜 战国

Copper Mirror with Five Mountain Character Pattern
Period: Warring States Period

81 四神博局纹铜镜 汉

Copper Bo-ju Mirrors with Four Divine Beasts Designs
Period: Han Dynasty

82 鼍龙铜镜 唐

Copper Mirror with Chinese Alligator Pattern
Period: Tang Dynasty

83 真子飞霜铜镜 唐

Copper Mirror with "Zhenzi Feishuang" Pattern
Period: Tang Dynasty

84 四瑞兽葡萄纹铜镜 唐

Copper Mirror with Four Auspicious Animals and Grapes Pattern
Period: Tang dynasty

85 婴戏图直柄铜镜 辽金

Straight Handled Copper Mirror with
Children Playing Pattern
Period: Liao and Jin Dynasty

86 双鱼纹铜镜 辽金

Copper Mirror with Double Fishes Pattern
Period: Liao and Jin Dynasty

87 祥云双鹤铜镜 辽金

Copper Mirror with Two Cranes among
Auspicious Clouds Pattern
Period: Liao and Jin Dynasty

88 海马丹凤纹铜镜 辽金

Copper Mirror with Mythical Animal in the Ocean and Phoenix Pattern
Period: Liao and Jin Dynasty

89 百鸟朝凤纹铜镜 辽金

Copper Mirror with Hundred Birds Pay Homage to the Phoenix Pattern
Period: Liao and Jin Dynasty

90 二龙戏珠卷叶纹铜镜　金

Copper Mirror with Two Dragons Play with a Pearl and Curly Leaves Pattern
Period: Jin Dynasty

91 五子登科铜镜 明

Copper Mirror of "Wu Zi Deng Ke"
Period: Ming Dynasty

92 五子登科铜镜 明

Copper Mirror of "Wu Zi Deng Ke"
Period: Ming Dynasty

93 观音菩萨石造立像 唐

Stone Statue of Avalokitesvara (Guanyin Bodhisattva)
Period: Tang Dynasty

94 释迦牟尼佛铜立像 金

Copper Statue of Sakyamuni
Period: Jin Dynasty

95 普贤菩萨坐象鎏金彩绘铜像 明

Gild-copper and Colored Decoration Statue of Samantabhadra Sitting on Elephant
Period: Ming Dynasty

96 释迦牟尼佛鎏金彩绘铜坐像 明

Gild-copper and Colored Seated Statue of Sakyamuni
Period: Ming Dynasty

97 释迦牟尼佛铜坐像 明

Copper Seated Statue of Sakyamuni
Period: Ming Dynasty

98 阿难尊者铜立像 明

Copper Statue of Ananda
Period: Ming Dynasty

99 迦叶尊者泥金铜立像 明

Copper Statue of Maha Kasyapa Coated by Powdered Gold
Period: Ming Dynasty

101 释迦牟尼佛泥金铜坐像 明

Gold Coating Copper Seated Statue of Sakyamuni
Period: Ming Dynasty

100 释迦牟尼佛石造坐像 明

Stone Seated Statue of Sakyamuni
Period: Ming Dynasty

102 观音铜坐像 明

Copper Seated Statue of Avalokitesvara (Guanyin Bodhisattva)
Period: Ming Dynasty

103 释迦牟尼佛鎏金铜坐像 清

Gild-copper Seated Statue of Sakyamuni
Period: Qing Dynasty

104 释袈牟尼佛鎏金彩绘铜坐像 清

Gild-copper and Colored Seated Statue of Sakyamuni
Period: Qing Dynasty

105 尊胜佛母鎏金铜造像 清

Gild-copper Figure of Ushnishavijaya
Period: Qing Dynasty

106 绿度母鎏金铜坐像 清

Gild-copper Seated Statue of Green Tara Buddha
Period: Qing Dynasty

107 释迦牟尼佛鎏金铜坐像 清

Gild-copper Seated Statue of Sakyamuni
Period: Qing Dynasty

108 大势至菩萨舟形背光鎏金铜坐像 清

Gild-copper Seated Statue of Mahasthamaprapta with Boat-shaped Mandorla
Period: Qing Dynasty

109 送子观音石像 清

Stone Statue of Songzi Avalokitesvara
Period: Qing Dynasty

110 道士铜立像 清

Copper Statue of Taoist
Period: Qing Dynasty

111 白水晶道人坐像 清

White Crystal Sitting Statue of Taoist
Period: Qing Dynasty

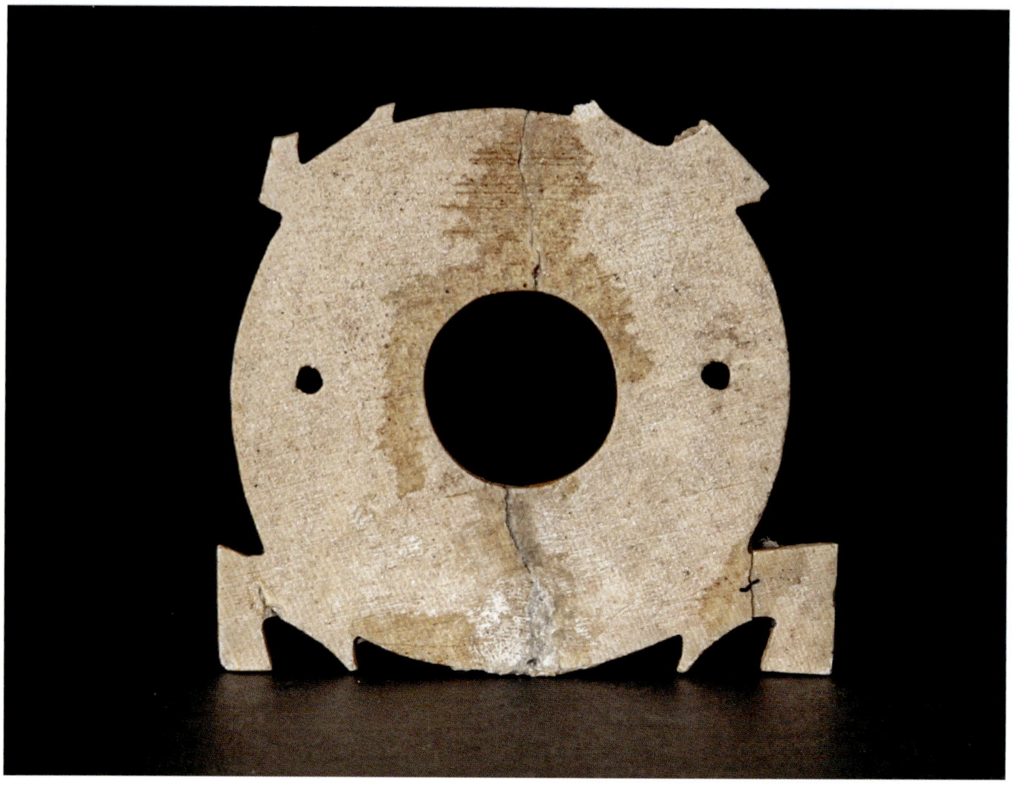

112 蟾形玉饰 战国

Toad-shaped Jade Ornament
Period: Warring States Period

113 龙形玉饰 战国

Dragon-shaped Jade Ornament
Period: Warring States Period

114 白玉龙纹绔尾带板 唐

White Jade Decoration Belt Plate with Dragon Tail Pattern
Period: Tang Dynasty

115 青玉苍龙教子带钩 明

Green Jade Belt Hook in the Shape of Dragon Head and a Small Dragon
Period: Ming Dynasty

116 青白玉苍龙教子带钩 明

Light Green Jade Belt Hook in the Shape of Dragon Head and a Small Dragon
Period: Ming Dynasty

117 白玉镂雕双獾佩 明

White Jade Hollow Double Badger Pendant
Period: Ming Dynasty

118 福寿白玉佩 清

White Jade Pendant of Happiness and Longevity
Period: Qing Dynasty

119 青玉浮雕梅花如意瓦 清

Green Jade Embossed Plum Blossom Ruyi Tile
Period: Qing Dynasty

120 青玉透雕重环转心佩 清

Green Jade Pendant Carved in Concentric
Circle Shape with a Rotating Hub
Period: Qing Dynasty

121 青白玉大吉双夔龙佩 清

Light Green Jade Pendant with Auspicious
Double Kui-dragon Design
Period: Qing Dynasty

122 白玉童子持莲抚狗坠 清

White Jade Pendant in the Shape of Child Holding Lotus and Petting Dog
Period: Qing Dynasty

123 翡翠苍龙教子带钩 清

Jadeite Belt Hook in the Shape of
Dragon Head and a Small Dragon
Period: Qing Dynasty

124 翡翠如意首带钩 清

Jadeite Belt Hook in the Shape of Ruyi
Period: Qing Dynasty

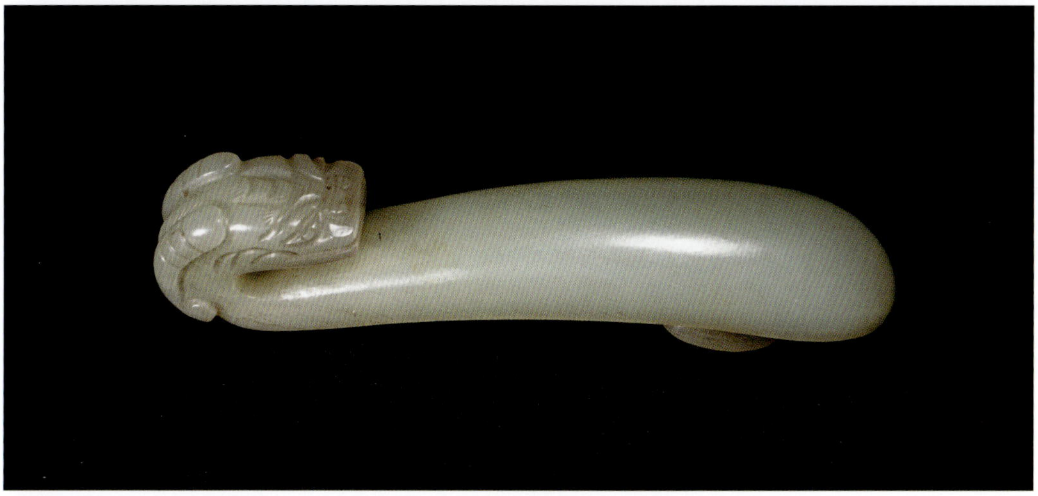

125 青白玉羊角龙首带钩 清

Light Green Jade Belt Hook in the Shape of Dragon Head and Ram's Horns
Period: Qing Dynasty

126 白玉透雕双喜佩 清

White Jade Hollow Double Happiness Pendant
Period: Qing Dynasty

127 白玉螭纹指环 清·乾隆

White Jade Chi-dragon Pattern Ring
Period: Qianlong Reign, Qing Dynasty

128 透雕瓜蝶纹玉佩 清

Jade Pendant with Hollow Melon and Butterfly Patterns
Period: Qing Dynasty

129 白玉莲蓬菱角坠 清

White Jade Lotus Seedpod and Water Chestnut Pendant
Period: Qing Dynasty

130 玛瑙兽头铺首耳鼻烟壶 清

Agate Snuff Bottle with Handles in Animal Head Applique Shaped
Period: Qing Dynasty

131 玛瑙鸟兽纹鼻烟壶 清

Agate Snuff Bottle with Bird and Beast Pattern
Period: Qing Dynasty

132 玛瑙素面鼻烟壶 清

Agate Snuff Bottle with Plain Surface
Period: Qing Dynasty

133 蚌螺钿人物字纹鼻烟壶 清

Mother-of-pearl Snuff Bottle with Portrait and Characters Pattern
Period: Qing Dynasty

134 缠丝玛瑙鼻烟壶 清

Sardonyx Snuff Bottle
Period: Qing Dynasty

135 白玉浮雕花卉纹鼻烟壶 清

White Jade Embossed Floral Snuff Bottle
Period: Qing Dynasty

136 珊瑚翡翠串珠项链 清

Coral Emerald Beaded Necklace
Period: Qing Dynasty

137 褐釉三足陶奁 东汉

Three-feet Pottery Dresser Set Box with Brown Glaze
Period: Eastern Han Dynasty

138 黄釉绿彩兽形三足罐 唐

Yellow Ground Glazed and Green Colored Jar with Three Animal-shaped Legs
Period: Tang Dynasty

139 龙泉窑青釉刻花大盘 宋

Cyan Glazed Plate with Incised Decoration of Longquan Kiln
Period: Song Dynasty

140 酱釉鸡腿瓶 辽金

Dark Brown Glazed Vase in the Shape of Chicken Leg
Period: Liao and Jin Dynasty

141 黑褐色鸾凤和鸣四系瓶 辽金

Four-handled Vase with the Design of Black Colored Phoenixes
Period: Liao and Jin Dynasty

142 云龙纹四系瓶 辽金

Four-handled Vase with the Design of Black Colored Dragon among Clouds
Period: Liao and Jin Dynasty

143 褐色卷茎大叶草四系瓶 辽金

Four-handled Vase with the Brown Colored and Large Leaf Pattern Curled Stems
Period: Liao and Jin Dynasty

144 褐色草叶纹四系瓶 辽金

Four-handled Vase with the Brown
Colored Grass and Leaf Pattern
Period: Liao and Jin Dynasty

145 褐色草叶纹四系瓶 金

Four-handled Vase with the Brown Colored
Grass and Leaf Pattern
Period: Jin Dynasty

146 青釉四系橄榄瓶 辽金

Four-handled Olive-shaped Vase with Yellowish Green Glaze
Period: Liao and Jin Dynasty

147 黑釉双系瓷樽 辽金

Two-handled Vessel (Zun) with Black Glazed
Period: Liao and Jin Dynasty

148 酱釉双系罐 辽金

Dark Brown Glazed Two-handled Jar
Period: Liao and Jin Dynasty

149 酱釉竖条纹双系罐 金

Dark Brown Glazed Two-handled Jar with Vertical Stripes
Period: Jin Dynasty

150 黑釉敞口双系罐 金

Two-handled Jar with Black Glazed
Period: Jin Dynasty

151 钧釉双系罐 金

Two-handled Jar of Jun Kiln
Period: Jin Dynasty

152 白釉广圈足大碗 辽

Wide Round Foot Large Bowl with White Glaze
Period: Liao Dynasty

153 白釉深腹碗 辽

Deep Belly Bowl with White Glaze
Period: Liao Dynasty

154 白釉深腹小碗 辽

Deep Belly Small Bowl with White Glaze
Period: Liao Dynasty

155 磁州窑双弦纹碗 辽金

Double Circle Pattern Bowl of Cizhou Kiln
Period: Liao and Jin Dynasty

156 黑白釉瓷碗 辽金

Black and White Glazed Bowl
Period: Liao and Jin Dynasty

157 磁州窑白釉大碗 宋

White Glazed Large Bowl of Cizhou Kiln
Period: Song Dynasty

158 定窑模印荷塘鱼跃盘 宋

Ding Kiln Mold Printing Plate with Lotus Pond Fish Jumping

159 定窑模印莲花盘 辽金

Ding Kiln Mold Printing Plate with Lotus

160 定窑模印莲花碗 辽金

Ding Kiln Mold Printing Plate with Lotus

161 白釉圈足盘 辽

Round Foot Plate with White Glaze
Period: Liao Dynasty

162 黑釉大瓷坛 辽金

Black Glazed Porcelain Jar
Period: Liao and Jin Dynasty

163 黑釉葫芦瓶 辽金

Black Glazed Gourd-shaped Vase
Period: Liao and Jin Dynasty

164 三彩刻画花卉碗 辽

Tri-color Bowl with Engraved Floral Pattern
Period: Liao Dynasty

165 绿釉香炉 辽金

Green Glazed Censer
Period: Liao and Jin Dynasty

166 钧釉天蓝瓷碟 宋

Azure Glazed Dish of Jun Kiln
Period: Song Dynasty

167 钧窑天蓝釉红斑碗 元

Azure Glazed Bowl with Red Colored Patch of Jun Kiln
Period: Yuan Dynasty

168 钧窑天蓝釉深腹碗 元

Azure Glazed Bowl with Deep Belly of Jun Kiln
Period: Yuan Dynasty

169 钧窑天蓝釉浅腹盘 元

Azure Glazed Dish with Shallow Belly of Jun Kiln
Period: Yuan Dynasty

170 钧窑天青釉直腹杯 元

Azure Glazed Cup with Straight Belly of Jun Kiln
Period: Yuan Dynasty

171 钧窑天蓝釉直腹杯 元

Azure Glazed Cup with Straight Belly of Jun Kiln
Period: Yuan Dynasty

172 白釉雕塑二甲传胪尊 明 · 成化款

White Glazed Sculpture Vessel (Zun) of Two Crabs Delivering Reed
Period: Chenghua Reign, Ming Dynasty

173 青花龙凤纹小缸 明・成化款

Blue-and-white Glazed Small Mortar Jar with the Design of Dragon and Phoenix
Period: Chenghua Reign, Ming Dynasty

174 青釉刻花碗 明

Cyan Glazed Bowl with Incised Floral Pattern
Period: Ming Dynasty

175 青釉回纹大碗 明

Cyan Glazed Bowl with Hui Pattern
Period: Ming Dynasty

176 青白釉高足碗 明

Azure Glazed Bowl with High Foot
Period: Ming Dynasty

177 白釉高足碗 明

White Glazed High Foot Bowl
Period: Ming Dynasty

178 五彩凤凰牡丹纹小罐 明

Small Porcelain Jar with the Design of Polychrome Phoenix and Peony Pattern
Period: Ming Dynasty

179 珐华彩鹭鸶莲池纹罐 明

Fahua Color Jar with Lotus Pond and Egret Design
Period: Ming Dynasty

180 青花缠枝莲纹罐 明・崇祯

Blue-and-white Glazed Jar with the Design of Interlocking Branches of Lotus
Period: Chongzhen Reign, Ming Dynasty

181 青花人物罐 明・崇祯

Blue-and-white Glazed Jar with the Design of Figures
Period: Chongzhen Reign, Ming Dynasty

182 青花山水纹大盘 清・康熙款

Blue-and-white Glazed Plate with the Design of Landscape Pattern
Period: Kangxi Reign, Qing Dynasty

183 黄釉绿彩桃树鸟纹碗 清·康熙款

Yellow Glazed Bowl with Green Colored Peach Trees and Birds Patterns
Period: Kangxi Reign, Qing Dynasty

184 青花地黄彩二龙赶珠纹碗 清·康熙款

Bowl with the Design of Two Yellow-colored Dragons Chasing a Pearl on Blue-and-white Ground Glaze
Period: Kangxi Reign, Qing Dynasty

185 孔雀蓝釉鸽子 清・康熙

Peacock-blue Glazed Pigeon
Period: Kangxi Reign, Qing Dynasty

186 霁红釉花觚 清・康熙

Sacrificial-red-glazed Beaker Vase
Period: Kangxi Reign, Qing Dynasty

187 青花百蝠纹盘 清·雍正款

Blue-and-white Dish with the Design of Hundred Bats
Period: Yongzheng Reign, Qing Dynasty

188 霁兰釉小盘 清·雍正款

Sacrificial-blue-glazed Plate
Period: Yongzheng Reign, Qing Dynasty

189 粉青釉四方八卦琮式瓶 清·雍正款

Light Greenish-blue Glazed Cong-shaped Vase with the Design of the Eight Diagrams
Period: Yongzheng Reign, Qing Dynasty

190 粉彩花蝶纹笔筒 清・雍正款

Famille-rose Glazed Brush Holder with the Design of Flower and Butterfly
Period: Yongzheng Reign, Qing Dynasty

191 青花小筒子瓶 清・雍正

Blue-and-white Glazed Bobbin-shaped Vase
Period: Yongzheng Reign, Qing Dynasty

192 粉彩凤尾花觚 清・雍正

Famille-rose Beaker Vase with the Design of Phoenix-tail
Period: Yongzheng Reign, Qing Dynasty

193 粉彩凤尾花觚 清・雍正

Famille-rose Beaker Vase with the Design of Phoenix-tail
Period: Yongzheng Reign, Qing Dynasty

194 青花冰梅盖罐 清・雍正

Blue-and-white Glazed Covered Jar with Plum Pattern
Period: Yongzheng Reign, Qing Dynasty

195 青花狮子穿花将军罐 清・雍正

Blue-and-white Glazed General Jar with the Design of Lions Playing among Flowers
Period: Yongzheng Reign, Qing Dynasty

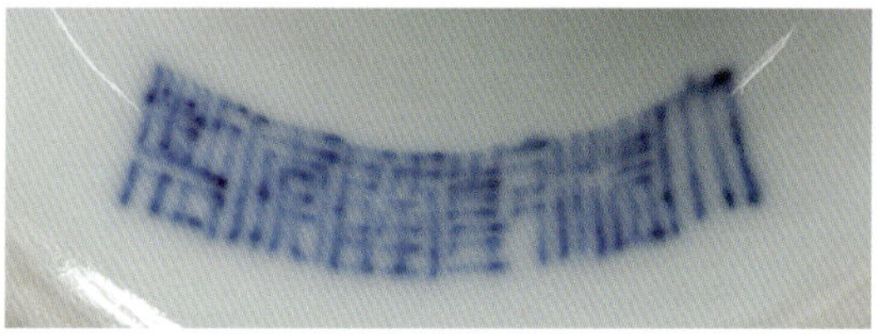

196 青花梵文高足碗 清・乾隆款

Blue-and-white Glazed High-footed Bowl with the Design of Sanskrit Inscriptions
Period: Qianlong Reign, Qing Dynasty

197 青花三果碗 清·乾隆款

Blue-and-white Glazed Bowl with Three Fruits Pattern
Period: Qianlong Reign, Qing Dynasty

198 青花矾红彩宝相花小碗 清·乾隆款

Blue-and-white and Alum Red-colored Glaze Small Bowl with Baoxiang Flowers Pattern
Period: Qianlong Reign, Qing Dynasty

199 青花留白海水红彩龙纹盘 清・乾隆款

Blue-and-white Glazed Dish with the Design of Red Dragon Crossing the Ocean in Blank
Period: Qianlong Reign, Qing Dynasty

200 黄地绿彩龙纹菊瓣口盘 清·乾隆款

Yellow Ground Glaze Chrysanthemum Petal-shaped Dish with the Design of Green-colored Dragon
Period: Qianlong Reign, Qing Dynasty

201 斗彩团花缠枝莲纹小缸 清・乾隆款

Doucai (Contrasting-colors) Jar with Flowers and Interlocking Lotus Pattern
Period: Qianlong Reign, Qing Dynasty

202 霁红罐 清・乾隆款

Sacrificial-red-glazed Mortar Jar
Period: Qianlong Reign, Qing Dynasty

203 青花象鼻耳樽 清·乾隆款

Blue-and-white Wine Vessels (Zun) with Elephant-trunk Handles
Period: Qianlong Reign, Qing Dynasty

204 青花花卉罐　清·乾隆

Blue-and-white Jar with Floral Pattern
Period: Qianlong Reign, Qing Dynasty

205 豆青釉红斑兽耳罐　清·乾隆

Bean-green Glazed Jar with Animal-shaped Handles
Period: Qianlong Reign, Qing Dynasty

206 窑变釉宝石红锥把瓶 清·乾隆

Ruby Glazed Vase in the Shape of Awl Handle
Period: Qianlong Reign, Qing Dynasty

207 红釉天球瓶 清・乾隆

Red Glazed Globular Vase
Period: Qianlong Reign, Qing Dynasty

208 仿嘉靖款五彩游龙戏珠筒子瓶 清・乾隆

Bobbin-shaped Vase with the Design of Famille Verte Dragon Chasing Pearls as an Imitation of Jiajing Reign Style
Period: Qianlong Reign, Qing Dynasty

209 粉彩八宝小碗 清・嘉庆款

Famille-rose Glazed Small Bowl with the Design of Eight Buddhist Ritual Instruments
Period: Jiaqing Reign, Qing Dynasty

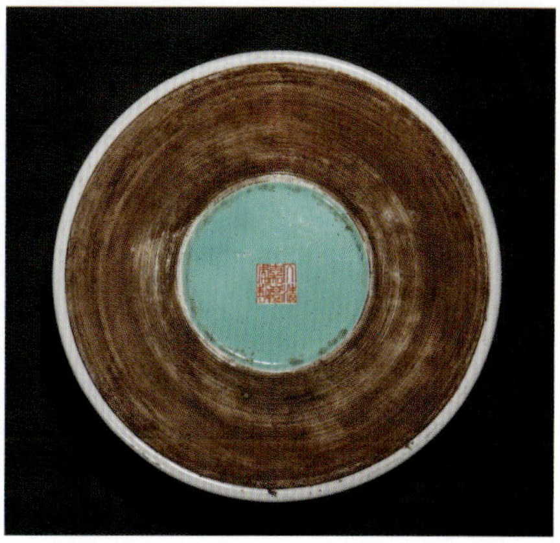

210 绿地粉彩宝相花直壁洗 清・嘉庆款

Green Ground Glazed Writing-brush Washer with the Design of Famille-rose Glazed Baoxiang Flowers
Period: Jiaqing Reign, Qing Dynasty

211 青花鸾凤云纹盘 清·嘉庆款

Blue-and-white Glazed Plate with the Design of Phoenix among Clouds
Period: Jiaqing Reign, Qing Dynasty

212 豆青青花象耳洗口瓶 清・嘉庆

Bean-green Ground Glazed Plate-shaped Mouth Vase with Elephant-trunk Handles
Period: Jiaqing Reign, Qing Dynasty

213 仿成化款青花花觚 清・嘉庆

Blue-and-white Glazed Beaker Vase as an Imitation of Chenghua Reign Period Style
Period: Jiaqing Reign, Qing Dynasty

214 青花加白松乔之寿贯耳瓶　清・嘉道

Blue-and-white Double Tubular Handled Vase with the Design of as Longevity as Song Qiao
Period: Jiajing and Daoguang Reign, Qing Dynasty

215 青花夔凤穿莲纹碗 清·道光款

Blue-and-white Glazed Bowl with the Design of Kui-phoenix Crossing Lotus
Period: Daoguang Reign, Qing Dynasty

216 斗彩暗八仙束腰碗 清・道光款

Doucai (Contrasting-Colors) Bamboo Hat Shaped Bowl with the Eight Immortals' Ritual Instruments
Period: Daoguang Reign, Qing Dynasty

217 茶叶末釉荸荠瓶 清・道光款

Tea-dust Glazed Biqi-shaped (water chestnut shaped) Vase
Period: Daoguang Reign, Qing Dynasty

218 霁蓝釉碗 清·道光款

Sacrificial-blue-glazed Bowl
Period: Daoguang Reign, Qing Dynasty

219 窑变红釉天球瓶 清·道光

Red Flambé Glazed Globular Vase
Period: Daoguang Reign, Qing Dynasty

220 青花冰梅瓶 清·道光

Blue-and-white Glazed Prunus Vase with the Design of Ice Crystal Structure
Period: Daoguang Reign, Qing Dynasty

221 仿康熙款哥窑铁锈花龙鹤纹瓶 清·道光

An Imitation of Ge Kiln Vase in Kangxi Period Style with the Design of Rust-red Colored Dragon and Crane
Period: Daoguang Reign, Qing Dynasty

222 五彩凤凰牡丹象腿瓶 清・道光

Bobbin-shaped Vase with the Design of Famille Verte Phoenix and Peony
Period: Daoguang Reign, Qing Dynasty

223 仿雍正款豆青釉剔花龙纹天球瓶 清・道光

Bean-green Glazed Globular Vase with the Graffito Dragon Design as an Imitation of the Yongzheng Period Style
Period: Daoguang Reign, Qing Dynasty

224 仿乾隆款青花富贵白头花鸟纹帽筒 清・道光

An Imitation Hat Stand of the Qianlong Period Style with the Design of Blue-and-white Glazed "Wealthy and Happiness" Flower-and-bird Pattern
Period: Daoguang Reign, Qing Dynasty

225 青花竹石芭蕉纹玉壶春瓶 清·同治款

Blue-and-white Pear-shaped Vase with the Design of Bamboo, Stone and Plantain
Period: Tongzhi Reign, Qing Dynasty

226 青花竹石芭蕉纹玉壶春瓶 清·同治款

Blue-and-white Pear-shaped Vase with the Design of Bamboo, Stone and Plantain
Period: Tongzhi Reign, Qing Dynasty

227 冰梅莲花口六连瓶 清·同治

Six-linked Vase with the Design of Ice Crystal Structure and Plum Blossoms Pattern with a Lotus Shaped Mouth
Period: Tongzhi Reign, Qing Dynasty

228 青花纸槌瓶 清・同治

Blue-and-white Glazed Vase in the Shape of Mallet
Period: Tongzhi Reign, Qing Dynasty

229 仿康熙款淡描红彩蝴蝶探花罐 清·同治

An Imitation of the Kangxi Period Style Jar with the Design of Butterfly-touching-flower in Pastel Shade
Period: Tongzhi Reign, Qing Dynasty

230 仿乾隆款粉彩开光六棱小瓶　清・同治

Famille-rose Glazed Hexagonal-sided Vessel with the Kaiguang Pattern as an Imitation of the Qianlong Period Style
Period: Tongzhi Reign, Qing Dynasty

231 仿乾隆款黄地墨彩什锦碗　清・同治

Assorted Bowl Painted in Black Color as an Imitation of the Qianlong Period Style on a Yellow Ground Glazed
Period: Tongzhi Reign, Qing Dynasty

232 青花云龙赶珠纹盘 清・光绪款

Blue-and-white Glazed Plate with the Design of Dragons Chasing Pearls
Period: Guangxu Reign, Qing Dynasty

233 白地粉彩百蝶纹赏瓶 清·光绪款

White Ground Glazed Ornamental Vase with the Design of Hundred Butterflies
Period: Guangxu Reign, Qing Dynasty

234 粉彩百蝠二龙戏珠纹赏瓶 清・光绪款

Famille-rose Glazed Ornamental Vase with the Design of Hundred Bats and Two Dragons Play with a Pearl Pattern
Period: Guangxu Reign, Qing Dynasty

235 白地粉彩夔凤穿莲纹碗 清·光绪款

White Ground Glazed Bowl with the Design of Famille-rose Glazed Kui-phoenix Crossing Lotus
Period: Guangxu Reign, Qing Dynasty

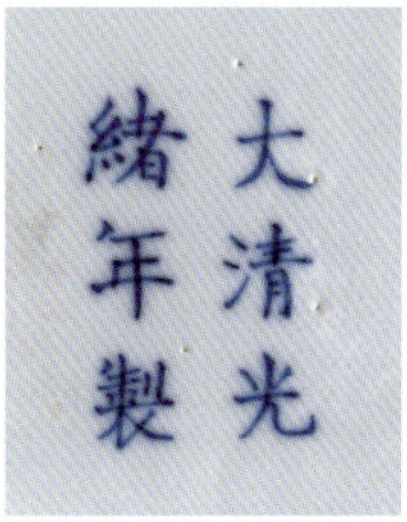

236 黄绿釉暗龙纹碗 清·光绪款

Yellow and Green Glazed Bowl with the Design of Veiled Dragon Patterns
Period: Guangxu Reign , Qing Dynasty

237 黄地三彩二龙戏珠纹胆式瓶 清·光绪款

Yellow Ground Glazed Gallbladder-shaped Vase with the Design of Tri-color Glazed Two Dragons Play with a Pearl
Period: Guangxu Reign, Qing Dynasty

238 黄地粉彩开光“万寿无疆”壶 清·光绪款

Yellow Ground Glazed Famille-rose Kettle with the Design of Kaiguang Frame and "Wanshou wujiang"
Period: Guangxu Reign, Qing Dynasty

239 青花开光八卦碗 清·光绪款

Blue-and-white Bowl with the Design of Eight Trigrams Kaiguang Pattern
Period: Guangxu Reign, Qing Dynasty

240 宝石蓝釉描金麋鹿山水纹赏瓶 清·光绪

Sacrificial-blue-glazed Ornamental Vase with the Design of Gold Outlines Elk and Landscape Pattern
Period: Guangxu Reign, Qing Dynasty

241 窑变釉蒜头口瓶 清・光绪

Variable Glazed Garlic-head Shaped Vase
Period: Guangxu Reign, Qing Dynasty

242 哥瓷铁锈花干枝梅小瓶 清・光绪

Ge Kiln Small Vase with the Design of Rust-red Colored Branches and Plum Blossoms
Period: Guangxu Reign, Qing Dynasty

243 墨地三彩梅竹石纹方瓶 清・光绪

Black Color Ground Glazed Square Wooden-club Shaped Vase with the Design of Tri-color Glazed Plum Flowers, Bamboo, and Stones
Period: Guangxu Reign, Qing Dynasty

244 黄地粉彩万福万寿纹绣墩 清・光绪

Yellow Ground Glazed Stool with the Design of Famille-rose Glazed Happiness and Longevity
Period: Guangxu Reign, Qing Dynasty

245 绿地三彩喜鹊登梅盖罐 清・光绪

Green Ground Glazed Covered Jar with the Design of Tri-color Glazed Magpie Stepping on Plum Blossom
Period: Guangxu Reign, Qing Dynasty

246 粉彩暗八仙碗 清・光绪

Famille-rose Glazed Bowl with the Eight Immortals' Ritual Instruments
Period: Guangxu Reign, Qing Dynasty

247 豆青釉堆白花卉长颈瓶 清・光绪

Bean-green Glazed Long Straight Necked Vase Covering with White Flowers
Period: Guangxu Reign, Qing Dynasty

248 仿康熙款青花应龙衔莲纹罐 清・光绪

Blue-and-white Glazed Jar with the Design of Ying-dragons Holding Lotus in Mouth as an Imitation of the Kangxi Period Style
Period: Guangxu Reign, Qing Dynasty

249 仿康熙款青花云龙赶珠纹碗 清・光绪

Blue-and-white Glazed Bowl with the Design of Dragons Chasing Pearls as an Imitation of the Kangxi Period Style
Period: Guangxu Reign, Qing Dynasty

250 仿康熙款绿釉地紫彩蛟龙赶珠纹碗 清・光绪

Green Ground Glazed Bowl with the Design of Purple Colored Walking Dragons as an Imitation of Kangxi Period Style
Period: Guangxu Reign, Qing Dynasty

251 仿康熙款霁蓝釉瓷盘 清・光绪

Sacrificial-blue-glazed Plate as an Imitation of the Qianlong Period Style
Period: Guangxu Reign, Qing Dynasty

252 仿雍正款淡描青花竹纹碗 清・光绪

Light Blue-and-white Glazed Bowl with Bamboo Pattern as an Imitation of the Yongzheng Period Style
Period: Guangxu Reign, Qing Dynasty

253 仿雍正款白釉杯 清・光绪

White Glazed Cup as an Imitation of the Yongzheng Period Style
Period: Guangxu Reign, Qing Dynasty

254 仿雍正款淡蓝釉四方瓶 清・光绪

Light Blue Glazed Square-shaped Vase as an Imitation of the Yongzheng Period Style
Period: Guangxu Reign, Qing Dynasty

255 仿乾隆款白釉绿彩赶珠纹龙盘 清・光绪

White Ground Glazed Plate with the Design of Green Colored Dragons Chasing Pearls as an Imitation of the Qianlong Period Style

Period: Guangxu Reign, Qing Dynasty

256 仿乾隆款青花地红绿彩二龙戏珠纹赏瓶 清・光绪

Blue-and-white Ground Glazed Vase with the Design of Red and Green Colored Two Dragons Play with a Pearl as an Imitation of the Qianlong Period Style
Period: Guangxu Reign, Qing Dynasty

257 仿乾隆款红彩应龙纹天鸡高足盖碗 清·光绪

High Foot Bowl with Tianji Cover in the Design of Red Colored Ying-dragons as an Imitation of the Qianlong Period Style
Period: Guangxu Reign, Qing Dynasty

258 仿乾隆款粉青釉螭龙耳鹿头樽 清・光绪

Light Greenish-blue Glazed Vessel (Zun) with the Design of Chi-dragon Shaped Handles as an Imitation of the Qianlong Period Style
Period: Guangxu Reign, Qing Dynasty

259 仿乾隆款粉彩二龙戏珠纹鼻烟壶 清・光绪

Famille-rose Glazed Snuff Bottle with the Design of Two Dragons Play with a Pearl as an Imitation of the Qianlong Period Style
Period: Guangxu Reign, Qing Dynasty

260 仿乾隆款绿地凸雕三彩四方笔筒 清·光绪

Square Green Ground Glazed Brush Holder with Tri-color Glazed Relief Carved as an Imitation of the Qianlong Period Style
Period: Guangxu Reign, Qing Dynasty

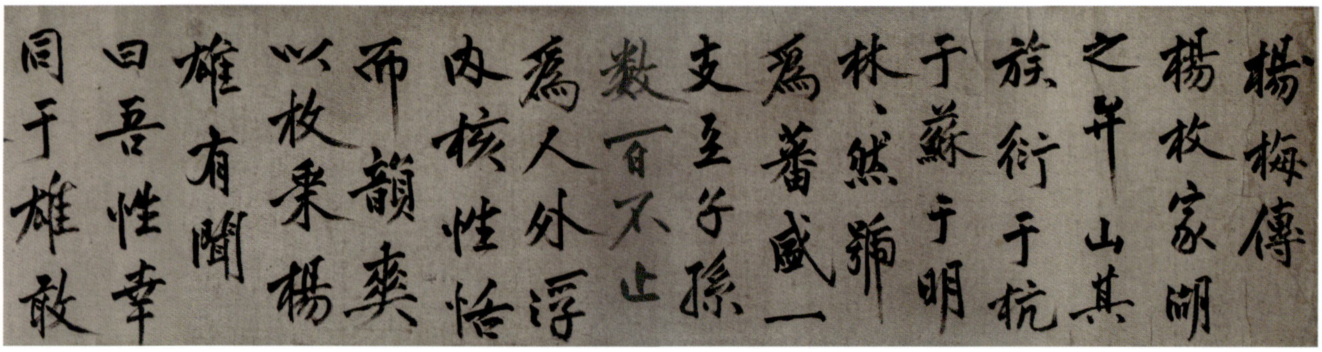
楊梅傳
楊枚家胡
之干山其
族衍于杭
于蘇于明
林、然獅
爲蕃盛一
支至子孫
數百不止
爲人外浮
内核性恬
而韻爽
以枚柔楊
雄有聞
曰吾性幸
同于雄敢

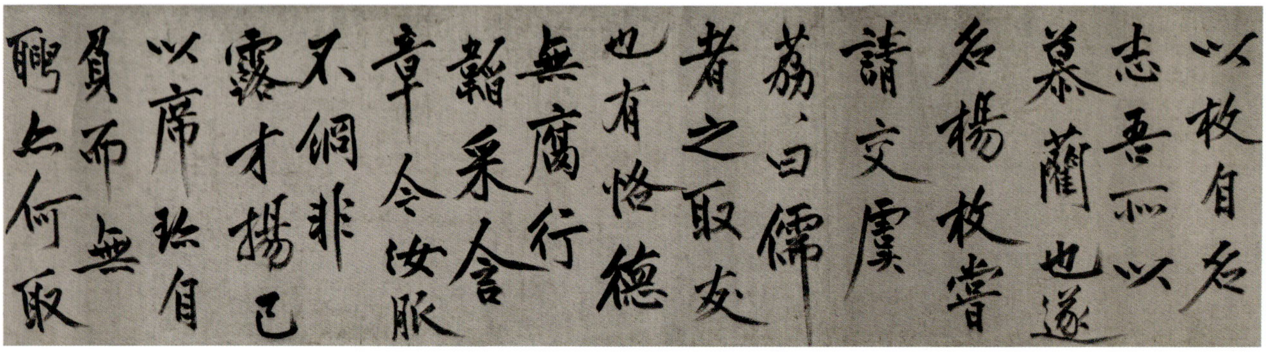
以枚自名
志吾而以
慕藺也遂
名楊枚嘗
請交虞
荔、曰儒
者之取交
也有恬德
無腐行
豁采含
章令汝服
不侗非
露才揚已
以席然自
負而無
聘亦何取

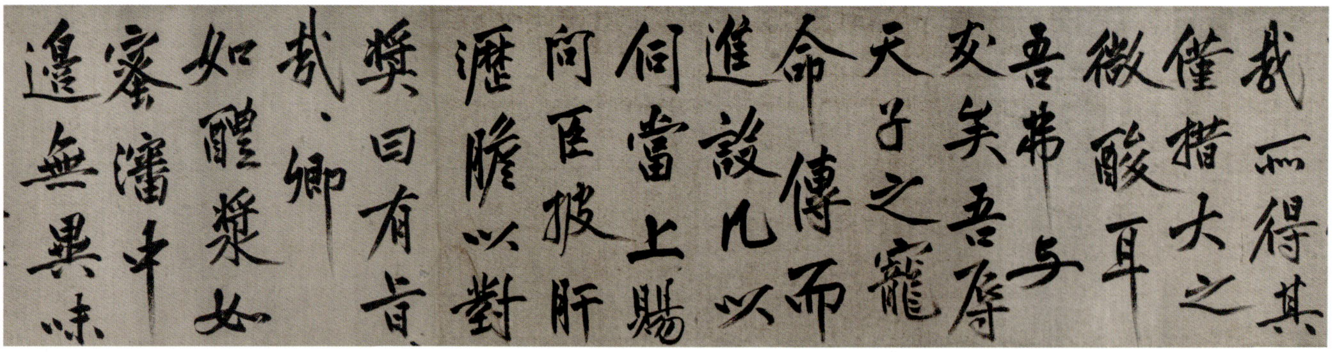
哉而得其
僅措大之
微酸耳
吾弗与
交矣吾辱
天子之寵
命傳而
進設几以
伺當上賜
向臣披肝
瀝膽以對
奬曰有旨
哉、卿
如醍漿女
蜜瀋中
邊無異味

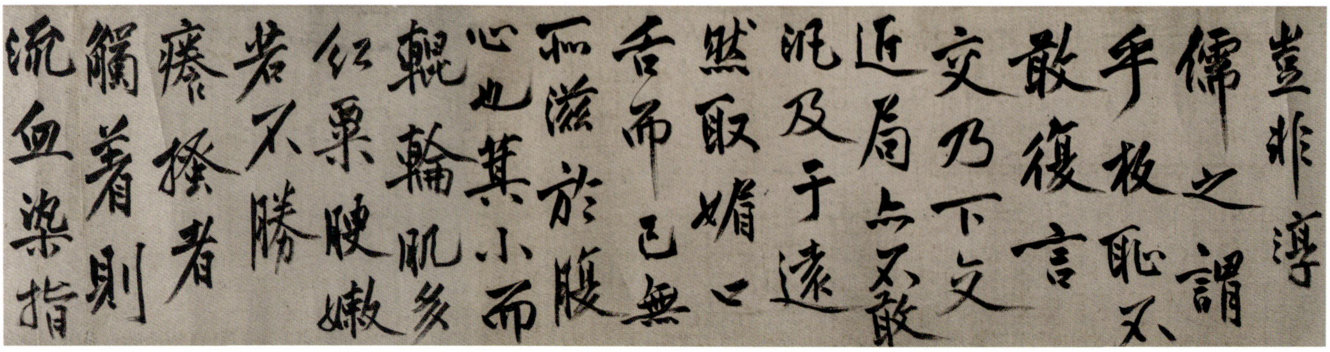
豈非淳
儒之謂
手枚恥不
敢復言
交乃下文
近局亦不敢
泥及于遠
然取媚亡
香而已無
而滋於腹
心也其小而
輾輪肌多
紅栗腴嫩
若不勝
療搔者
觸着則
流血染指

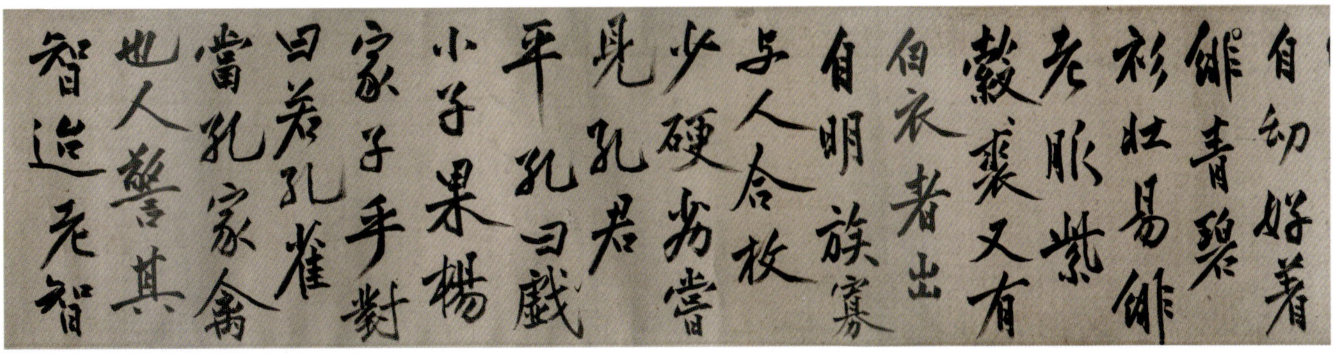

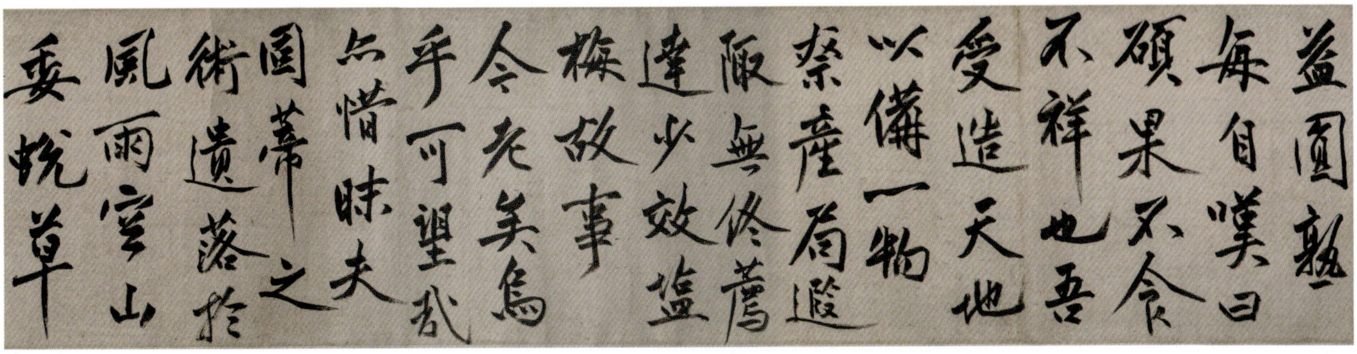

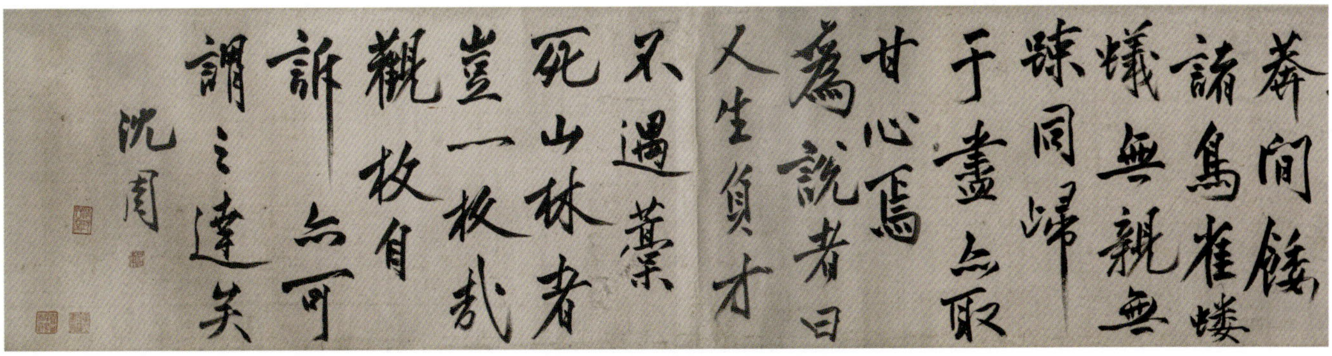

261 杨梅传 明 沈周

Biography of Waxberry
Shen Zhou, Ming Dynasty, Running Script

262 渜溪山水图 明 张凤翔

Landscape Painting of Nuanxi River
Zhang Fengxiang, Ming Dynasty

263 墨竹图 清 潘定澜

Ink Bamboo
Pan Dinglan, Qing Dynasty

264 鲤鱼图 清 宋紫山

Carp
Shen Zishan, Qing Dynasty

265 晨虎图 清 耕石

Tiger in the Morning
Gengshi, Qing Dynasty

266 工笔花鸟图 清 恽冰

Fine Brushwork Painting of Flowers and Birds
Yun Bing, Qing Dynasty

267 竹石图 清·光绪 墨禅

Bamboo in the Rock
Mochan, Guangxu Reign, Qing Dynasty

268 梅花图 清 胡峻

Plum Blossom Painting
Hu Jun, Qing Dynasty

269 松下牡丹图 现代 陈半丁

Peony under the Pine Trees
Chen Banding, Modern

270 梅花鸳鸯图 现代 何香凝（款）

Plum Blossom and Mandarin Duck
He Xiangning (Marked), Modern

271 荷花图 现代 于非厂

Lotus Painting
Yu Feichang, Modern

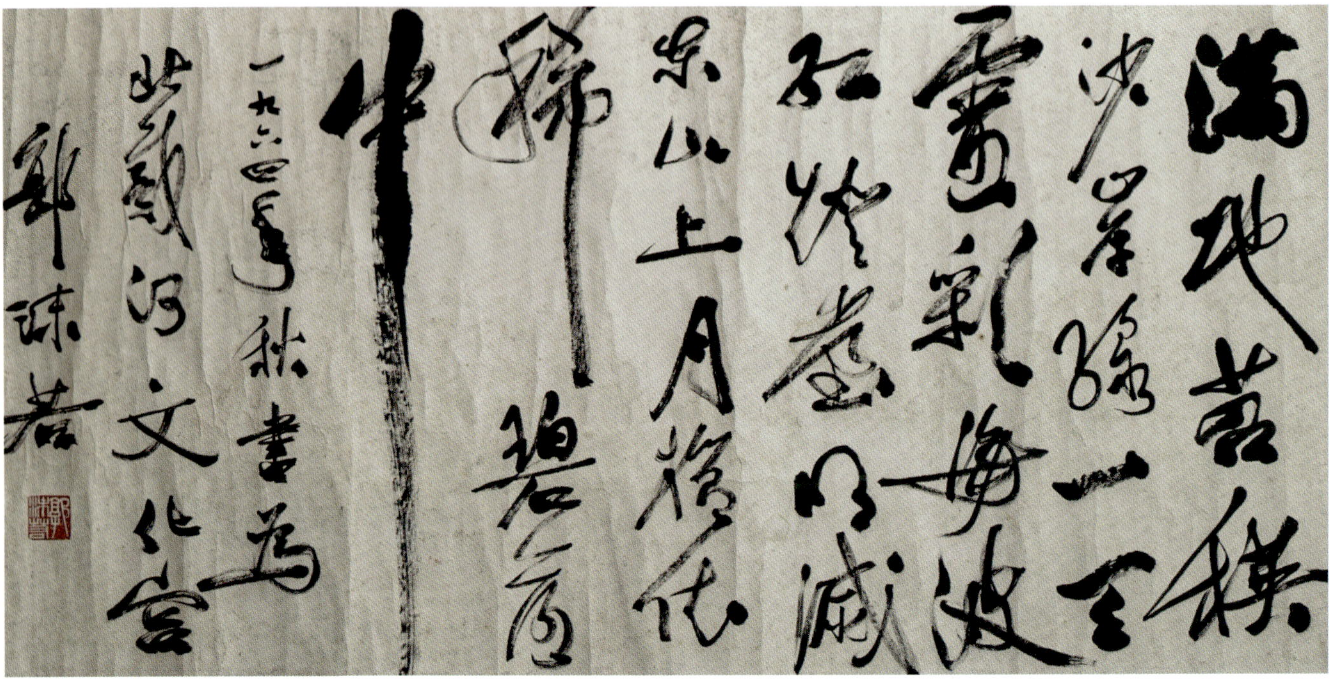

272《北戴河》行书七言诗 现代 郭沫若

"Beidaihe" Running Script Seven Character Poem
Guo Moruo, Modern

273 高士图 现代 溥心

Painting of Excellent People
Pu Xinyu, Modern

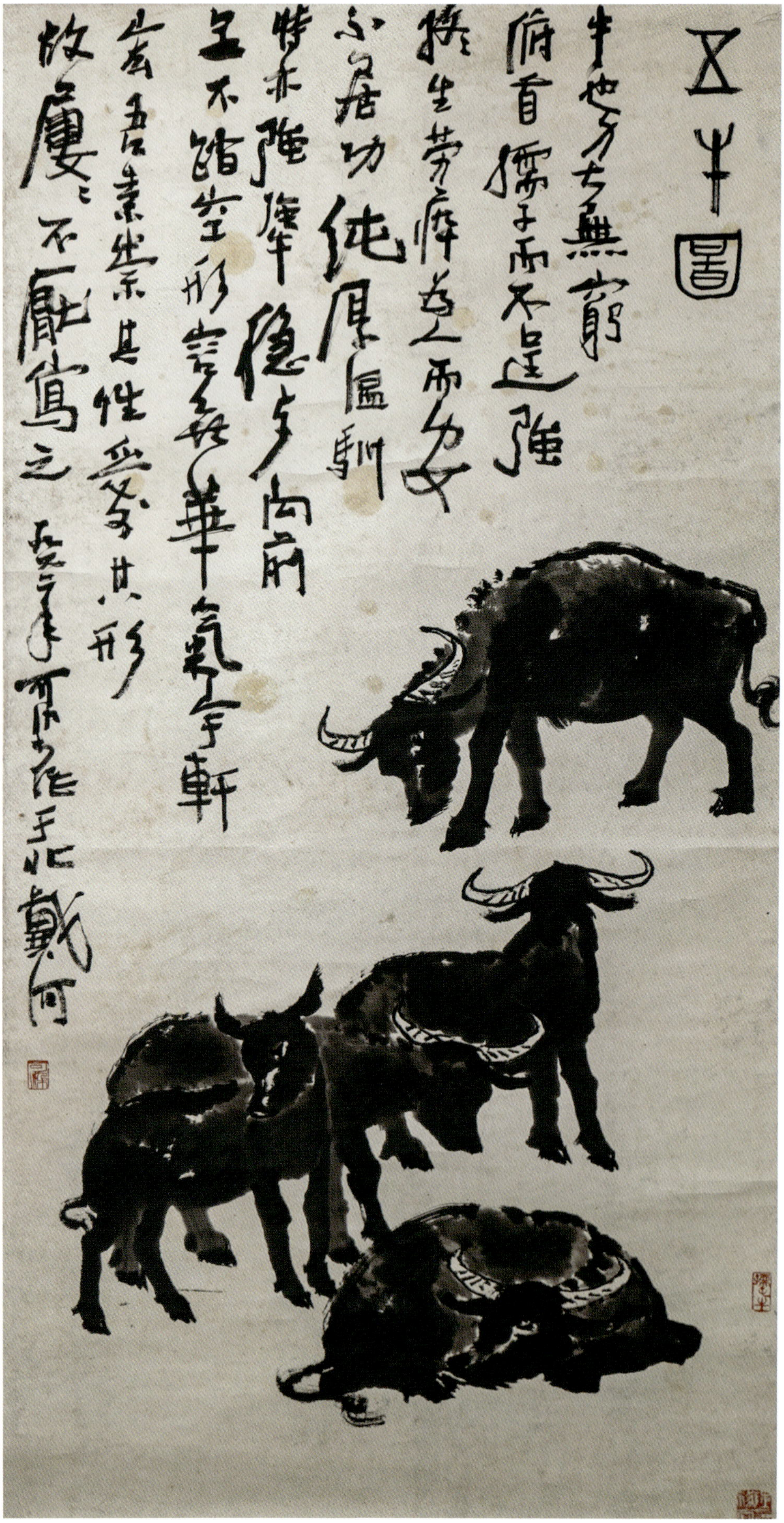

274 五牛图 现代 李可染

Five Oxen
Li Keran, Modern

275 鸽子图 现代 吴作人

Pigeon Painting
Wu Zuoren, Modern

图版说明

❶ 石核 旧石器时代（约 1 万年前）

长 8.2 厘米，宽 5.8 厘米。

抚宁区文物保护中心藏。

燧石质。柱体硕大，上端略尖，下端较平。两端可见打击点、小疤、碎屑疤及工作着力台面，柱体可见打击剥离石叶片时形成的大面积条状疤痕。抚宁区大所庄出土。

❷ 石磨盘、磨棒 新石器时代（约 1 万—4000 年前）

磨盘长 43 厘米，宽 27.5 厘米。磨棒长 26 厘米，直径 7 厘米。

抚宁区文物保护中心藏。

花岗岩质。石磨盘呈长方形，因使用时间较久，盘面磨损严重，呈一端薄一端厚，薄端处厚 10 厘米；中部磨损凹陷深，最薄处厚 2 厘米。石磨棒呈圆柱体。这组研磨器是新石器时代研磨谷物的典型工具。抚宁区郝各庄出土。

❸ 石镞 新石器时代（约 1 万—4000 年前）

高 3.8 厘米，厚 1.6 厘米。

抚宁区文物保护中心藏。

赭色燧石质。呈等腰三角形。底边微凹，形成两尖角尾翼。三边薄，呈刃状，由三个角向中间渐厚，呈脊状。通体呈现打制修整的大小疤痕。抚宁区骊城遗址出土。

❹ 石斧 新石器时代（约 1 万—4000 年前）

长 14.9 厘米，刃宽 4.7 厘米，厚 1.5 厘米。

抚宁区文物保护中心藏。

呈长方形，扁平状。通体磨制而成，表面精细光滑，造型规整。一端双面琢磨形成斜弧面开刃，另一端为椭圆状截面。古代用于砍砸等的石质工具。抚宁区魏庄出土。

❺ 石斧 新石器时代（约 1 万—4000 年前）

长 17 厘米，宽 6.5 厘米，厚 2 厘米。

青龙满族自治县文物保护所藏。

呈长方形。一端磨制成双面弧刃。古代用于砍砸等的石质工具。

❻ 五角石纺轮 新石器时代（约 1 万—4000 年前）

直径 9 厘米，厚 3.5 厘米。

抚宁区文物保护中心藏。

花岗岩质。呈不规则五角星形，中心有直径为 3.8 厘米的对钻圆孔。抚宁区大新寨镇出土。

7 尖状石器 新石器时代（约 1 万—4000 年前）

长 33 厘米，最大直径 3.3 厘米。

抚宁区文物保护中心藏。

呈不规则圆柱状。两头渐细尖，向中部渐粗。尖部有因使用而破损的痕迹。抚宁区马家峪征集。

8 环首翘尾小铜刀 商（公元前 1600—前 1046 年）

长 26.7 厘米，宽 4 厘米，刀环直径约 3.5 厘米。

青龙满族自治县文物保护所藏。

椭圆形环首，短柄长刃，刃与柄之间有一小尖状格。薄刃，厚弯脊，刀尖微翘。

9 木桶（一对） 商（公元前 1600—前 1046 年）

高 18 厘米，口径约 22 厘米。高 21.5 厘米，口径约 18 厘米。

卢龙县文物保护管理所藏。

木质桶形器，不规则，两侧凿有小孔为系。卢龙县李黄岭出土。

10 木锤 商（公元前 1600—前 1046 年）

长 12.7 厘米，宽 6.6 厘米。

卢龙县文物保护管理所藏。

木制锤形器，不规则，中间凿有一长方孔，用于安柄。卢龙县李黄岭出土。

11 高领四鋬陶罐 商（公元前 1600—前 1046 年）

高 27 厘米，口径 13.5 厘米，底径 11 厘米。

卢龙县文物保护管理所藏。

泥质夹砂灰陶。撇口，圆唇，高领，溜肩，鼓腹，平底。腹部周施四个柱状鋬。卢龙县李黄岭出土。

12 陶鬲 商周（公元前 1600—前 256 年）

高 17.6 厘米，口径 14 厘米，腹径 13.6 厘米。

卢龙县文物保护管理所藏。

泥质夹砂灰陶。撇口，圆唇，束颈，微鼓腹，乳袋形三足。

13 三足铜甗 西周（公元前 1046—前 771 年）

高 12 厘米，口径 13 厘米，腹径 14.2 厘米。

秦皇岛市文物保护中心藏。

由上甑下鬲两部分组成，素面。甑为广口，折沿，折肩，斜腹，榫口圈足，可插入鬲口，底部为条形箅孔，肩两侧各施有蟠龙立柱耳。鬲为子母直口、矮直颈、袋形腹、三兽蹄形足，肩两侧各施有一圆环耳。

⑭ 蟠虺纹青铜罍 春秋（公元前 770—前 476 年）

通高 8 厘米，腹径 20.5 厘米。

秦皇岛市文物保护中心藏。

由罍体、盖两部分组成，通体饰蟠虺纹。器广口，平折沿，束颈、溜肩、折腹，平底。盖弧顶呈盔状，顶设短柄圆钮，盖折沿边周设等距离四个小兽头扣，用于盖与罍口咬合。

⑮ 青铜啄斧 春秋（公元前 770—前 476 年）

通长 18 厘米，厚 2.6 厘米，宽 3 厘米。

山海关文物保管所藏。

由援、銎、斧铸成一体，器身两面各起一条通体脊棱。援部似匕首，上、下刃渐收成鹤嘴状锐锋；銎部厚出器身，内孔椭圆形，用于安柄；斧部短于援，似斧头，起到平衡作用的同时增加了啄斧的砍劈功能。啄斧为骑兵所用冷兵器，可啄、可推、可钩、可砍，挥击啄砍，肃杀逼人。

⑯ 直内青铜戈 战国（公元前 475—前 221 年）

援长 12.5 厘米，内长 7 厘米，阑长 11.3 厘米。

青龙满族自治县文物保护所藏。

援起脊，双刃上平下弧，单胡齐尾，阑部有三个长方形穿，直内中部有长方形单穿。长柲兵器，可用于钩、啄、椹。

⑰ 错金银镶嵌绿松石铜带钩 战国（公元前 475—前 221 年）

通长 21.4 厘米，宽 2.6 厘米。

山海关长城博物馆藏。

呈弧状，正面为琵琶形。自钩首部向尾部由窄渐宽。正面饰错金银棱形几何纹和圆点，其间镶嵌不规则绿松石。背部有椭圆形钮。

⑱ 球腹陶豆 战国（公元前 475—前 221 年）

通高 27 厘米，口径 5.5 厘米，盖高 2.5 厘米，足径 11.8 厘米。

抚宁区文物保护中心藏。

泥质夹砂灰陶。带盖，子母口。盖呈蘑菇头状。豆为直口，束颈，丰肩，圆鼓腹，持柄细长下展外撇，形成喇叭状高圈足。抚宁区郝各庄征集。

⑲ 泥质灰陶子母口豆 战国（公元前 475—前 221 年）

高 24.4 厘米，口径 16 厘米，足径 13.3 厘米。

卢龙县文物保护管理所藏。

泥质夹砂灰陶。子母口，弧腹，高直柄下外撇，柄饰多道凸旋纹，扁平圈足。

⑳ 带盖陶豆 战国（公元前 475—前 221 年）

通高 27.5 厘米，盖高 6.8 厘米，口径 15.2 厘米，足径 12.8 厘米。

抚宁区文物保护中心藏。

泥质灰褐色陶。带盖，子母口。盖为浅覆盘形，顶设一个圆纽。豆为浅钵形，持柄细长下展外撇，形成喇叭形高圈足。抚宁区部各庄征集。

21 陶鉴 秦（公元前221—前206年）

高64.8厘米，口外径120.6厘米，腹径120.1厘米。

秦皇岛市文物保护中心藏。

泥质灰陶，广直口，方唇外侈，直壁微弧，平底微凹。腹部周施3个环形錾。唇部饰米字纹和弦纹，腹部附加两道箍状凸起加强带，上饰菱格纹。外壁唇沿下刻“建阳”二字。秦行宫遗址出土。

22 夔纹大瓦当 秦（公元前221—前206年）

当面直径52厘米，高37厘米，厚2.5厘米。

秦皇岛市文物保护中心藏。

泥质灰陶。当面呈大半圆形，边轮廓凸出。当面饰两条高浮雕对称夔纹，当面连接筒瓦身。北戴河秦行宫遗址出土。

23 卷云夹贝纹大圆瓦当 秦（公元前221—前206年）

当面直径42厘米，厚2.5厘米，瓦筒残长21.6厘米。

秦皇岛市文物保护中心藏。

泥质灰陶。当面呈圆形，当心圆鼓周饰凸弦纹，用双线界隔将当面分成对称四区，每区各饰两朵卷云纹，两云纹间贴塑一“贝”形装饰，极具地域古建筑文化装饰特点。北戴河秦行宫遗址采集。

24 鎏金铜蒜头壶 汉（公元前206—220年）

高36.5厘米，口径3厘米，腹径22.5厘米，足径12.5厘米。

秦皇岛市文物保护中心藏。

通体鎏金，小直口，口周围凸起呈倒蒜头状，细长颈，溜肩，圆腹略扁，高圈足微撇。

25 铜壶 汉（公元前206—220年）

高37厘米，口径16厘米，足径18.8厘米。

秦皇岛市文物保护中心藏。

直口微敞，束颈，溜肩，圆鼓腹，圈足微撇。口沿、肩、腹、下腹各施一周凸起宽带，上腹两侧各施兽面铺首衔环耳。

26 铜钫 汉（公元前206—220年）

高37.5厘米，口边长11厘米，底边长13厘米。

秦皇岛市文物保护中心藏。

方形，素面。直口，方唇，弧颈，溜肩，四面鼓腹，高方足微撇。上腹部两侧各施兽面铺首衔环耳。口沿外施一周凸起宽带箍口。

27 圆环耳兽足铜卣 汉（公元前 206—220 年）

通高 17.5 厘米，口径 8.1 厘米，腹径 15.2 厘米。

山海关长城博物馆藏。

卣分上下两部分，用子母口咬合，素面。盖为一杯形器，可单独使用。撇口，深腹，平弧顶，上设有三个环形鋬钮。下部为球状腹，敛口。肩部两侧有圆环耳，器底部承三个兽蹄形足。

28 铜匜 汉（公元前 206—220 年）

高 11.8 厘米，口径 30.5 厘米。

抚宁区文物保护中心藏。

撇口，薄唇，深腹，平底，假圈足。口沿一侧向上伸出弧形把柄，柄端下勾。内口沿、上腹各饰两周弦纹。古代舀水器。

29 四神铜温酒炉 汉（公元前 206—220 年）

通高 11.5 厘米，宽 9.2 厘米，长 14 厘米。

秦皇岛市文物保护中心藏。

由耳杯、炭炉、承盘组成。耳杯为椭圆形口，斜壁，平弧底，两侧有折沿状长耳。炭炉上身为椭圆形，四壁镂雕朱雀、玄武、青龙、白虎四神像，两侧沿口各立有两个小支护柱。下身为长方形，四角施凸起包角，一端有扁平曲折长柄，炉底有条形箅孔。炉下有四个背手力士足承托炉体。承盘呈长方形，四周上翘，敞口，委角，平底。

30 铜剑 汉（公元前 206—220 年）

通长 47.7 厘米，宽 4.3 厘米，剑身长 39 厘米，剑柄长 8.7 厘米。

秦皇岛市文物保护中心藏。

剑身前端略窄，凸起剑脊与两刃保持平距，至锋处尖削。剑从渐薄，两锷刃利。剑柄圆杆有两箍，平头剑首，剑格略凸起。

31 双胡铜戈 汉（公元前 206—220 年）

援长 18.3 厘米，阑长 16.3 厘米。

青龙满族自治县文物保护所藏。

长援短胡，援双刃间起脊，双胡溜尾，两胡间起凸脊。阑中部宽脊两侧有两个长方形穿，内残缺。长柲兵器，可用于钩、啄、摧。

32 铜鎏金威烈将军印 汉（公元前 206—220 年）

通高 2.3 厘米，重 53.1 克。印面长 2.3 厘米，宽 2.3 厘米。

青龙满族自治县文物保护所藏。

铜质鎏金，立兽钮。印面阴刻篆书“威烈将军印”二行五字。

33 兽面铺首衔环铜壶 东汉（公元 25—220 年）

高 46.8 厘米，口径 16.5 厘米，最大腹径 34 厘米，圈足高 8.7 厘米。

抚宁区文物保护中心藏。

直口，方唇，长颈微束，圆鼓腹，八角形高圈足。肩部两侧施兽面铺首衔环耳，在腹上、中、下部各饰一组三弦纹宽带凸腹箍。口外沿施宽带箍口。抚宁区安庄村出土。

34 兽面铺首衔铁环铜簋 东汉（公元 25—220 年）

高 15 厘米，口径 25.6 厘米，圈足径 16.8 厘米。

抚宁区文物保护中心藏。

广口微撇，圆唇，弧壁，深腹略鼓，平弧底，高圈足外撇。腹中部施两周凸弦纹腹箍，并在两侧弦纹下各施有一兽面铺首衔铁环耳。足端饰凸弦纹一周。抚宁区安庄村出土。

35 宝鼎山水纹铜洗 东汉（公元 25—220 年）

高 7.5 厘米，口径 33 厘米，足径 28 厘米。

抚宁区文物保护中心藏。

广口微敛，宽折沿外撇，浅腹直壁，平弧底，假圈足。腹壁两侧各施有兽面铺首耳，内底面微凹，弦纹圈内饰硕大宝鼎纹，辅以山水纹。抚宁区安庄村出土。

36 双鱼龙凤纹铜洗 东汉（公元 25—220 年）

高 6.1 厘米，口径 39.5 厘米，足径 32 厘米。

抚宁区文物保护中心藏。

广口，平折沿，直壁浅斜腹，平弧底，矮圈足。两侧沿下各施一个头朝下的兽面小穿耳。内底饰菱格纹，菱格的一对角各饰一条鱼，菱格内饰一凤。外底饰双圈凸弦纹，内圈中心饰均分三凸脊纹。口沿上对称线刻二龙及二凤。抚宁区安庄村出土。

37 凤鸟登鼎纹铜洗 东汉（公元 25—220 年）

高 9.5 厘米，口径 38.2 厘米。

抚宁区文物保护中心藏。

广口微敛，宽折沿外撇，浅腹直壁，平弧底，矮圈足。腹壁两侧各施有一兽面铺首耳。内底面微凹，弦纹圈内饰一只凤鸟展翼立于宝鼎之上。外底边缘有凸弦纹三周。抚宁区安庄村出土。

38 大吉利铜鼎 东汉（公元 25—220 年）

通高 19.5 厘米，口径 15.3 厘米，腹径 20 厘米。

抚宁区文物保护中心藏。

子口内敛，鼓腹，圜底，三蹄形足微外撇。上腹两侧近沿处竖立硕大圆环形附耳，高出口沿。腹中部偏上环施一周高出脊扁平挡火。器一足刻“大吉利君宜官”六字铭文。抚宁区安庄村出土。

39 军司马印铜印 东汉（公元 25—220 年）

通高 1.65 厘米，边长 2.2 厘米，厚 0.7 厘米。

抚宁区文物保护中心藏。

桥形钮。印面方形，阴刻篆书“军司马印”二行四字，字体工整，苍劲浑厚。印一侧阴刻篆书“范”字。

40 三扁平足铁釜 辽金（公元 907—1234 年）

通高 30 厘米，口径 25 厘米。

青龙满族自治县文物保护所藏。

广口，外折弧沿，圆唇。沿口上对称施两个立环耳。束颈圆鼓腹，弧底，底部承三个高大扁平足。炊具。青龙满族自治县大狮子沟村征集。

41 六鋬铁釜 辽金（公元 907—1234 年）

高 43 厘米，口径 65 厘米。

抚宁区文物保护中心藏。

直口，方唇，矮立颈，鼓腹，弧底。肩部饰有若干凸弦纹，腹周施六个扁平鋬手。底有铸脐。

42 六鋬铁釜 辽金（公元 907—1234 年）

高 54 厘米，口径 68 厘米，壁厚 3 厘米。

青龙满族自治县文物保护所藏。

广口，方唇，内折平沿，鼓腹，圆弧底。口沿外壁饰有若干凹弦纹；上腹周边铸有六个扁平鋬手。炊具，俗称“行军锅”。青龙满族自治县吉利峪村征集。

43 双耳三足铁铛 辽金（公元 907—1234 年）

通高 24 厘米，口径 40.2 厘米，壁厚 1.7 厘米，足高 13.8 厘米。

青龙满族自治县文物保护所藏。

敞口，方唇外侈，斜壁，浅腹，平底。口沿立环形双耳，底部承瓦状三足。炊具。青龙满族自治县小石盘村出土。

44 铁漏勺 辽金（公元 907—1234 年）

勺口径 17 厘米，柄长 20 厘米。

青龙满族自治县文物保护所藏。

勺身布满细密的孔洞，用于漏水。长柄连带长豁口銎。炊具。青龙满族自治县小石盘村出土。

45 铁犁铧 辽金（公元 907—1234 年）

长 21 厘米，宽 21 厘米。

青龙满族自治县文物保护所藏。

呈等腰三角形。正面隆起，背面平直，底端呈月牙形銎。正面隆脊上开一小三角形榫孔。犁地用生产工具。青龙满族自治县双山子镇出土。

46 铁马蹬 辽金（公元 907—1234 年）

高 20 厘米，踏板长 17.5 厘米。

青龙满族自治县文物保护所藏。

梯形，上边梁有椭圆形长穿，下底边为扁平踏板。两侧边为圆柱梁。青龙满族自治县小石盘村出土。

47 铁门铃 辽金（公元 907—1234 年）

高 14.7 厘米，铃口径 10.7 厘米。

青龙满族自治县文物保护所藏。

呈柱体。中空，平顶，顶施半环系。青龙满族自治县小石盘村出土。

48 铁鐎斗 辽金（公元 907—1234 年）

高 9.5 厘米，口径 21 厘米。流高 5.5 厘米，流长 6.5 厘米，流宽 8 厘米。

青龙满族自治县文物保护所藏。

敞口，斜立沿，深斗折腰，平底。侧有长方形流，斗两侧壁折腰处铸有扁平錾。青龙满族自治县大汇河村征集。

49 镂空团龙铜饰件 辽金（公元 907—1234 年）

圆直径 6.1 厘米，厚 0.35 厘米，穿长 1.95 厘米。

卢龙县文物保护管理所藏。

呈圆形。圆外缘施五个凸出长方形穿，圆内透雕一对首尾相逐团龙纹。马车饰件。

50 三足铜釜 辽金（公元 907—1234 年）

通高 33 厘米，直径 25 厘米，足高 15 厘米。

青龙满族自治县文物保护所藏。

有盖。广口，直腹微鼓，平底微弧，三高足，腹中部施一周高出脊扁平挡火，用作錾。錾、口间壁面饰有若干细密凹凸弦纹。高足呈内平、外鼓、半圆柱状，面施多道竖凸脊。盖作斗笠状，顶上有一帽形钮。青龙满族自治县牧马村征集。

51 铜熨斗 辽金（公元 907—1234 年）

高 8 厘米，口径 20 厘米，底径 16 厘米。

青龙满族自治县文物保护所藏。

呈圆形。侧面铸有上翘的短持柄。敞口，方唇外侈，弧腹，平底略鼓。柄部与口沿相接处铸有花冠形护手。

52 铜熨斗 金（公元 1115—1234 年）

高 9.2 厘米，口径 20 厘米，底径 16 厘米。

昌黎县文物研究保护所藏。

呈圆形。侧面铸有上翘的长柄。敞口，方唇外侈，直壁，平底略鼓。斗内壁沿饰两周弦纹。外壁沿饰一道凸弦纹。柄部与沿口相接处铸有冠形护手，护手内侧面饰凸脊卷云纹。

53 铜熨斗 辽金（公元 907—1234 年）

高 5.7 厘米，口径 18 厘米，底径 15.5 厘米。

青龙满族自治县文物保护所藏。

呈圆形。侧面铸有翘首空心短柄。广口，方唇，沿微外撇，直壁，平底略鼓。柄部与口沿相接处铸有冠形护手，护手内侧面饰凸起的缠枝纹。斗内底阴刻宝相花。

54 铜印 辽金（公元 907—1234 年）

通高 3 厘米，印面直径 3.1 厘米。

青龙满族自治县文物保护所藏。

坐狮钮，印面呈圆形，阳文。

55 行军副统所铜印 金（公元 1115—1234 年）

通高 5.8 厘米。印面：长 5.4 厘米，宽 5.4 厘米。

青龙满族自治县文物保护所藏。

长方形立柱钮，顶刻“十”字标识。印面呈正方形，边框内为二、三字排列阳刻九叠篆书“行军副统所”五字。此为金代军队中高级将领持印。青龙满族自治县大汇河村出土。

56 行军副统所印铜印 金（公元 1115—1234 年）

通高 5.5 厘米，重 120 克。印面：长 6.6 厘米，宽 6.6 厘米。

青龙满族自治县文物保护所藏。

长方形立柱钮，顶刻“十”字标识。印面呈正方形，阳刻九叠篆书“行军副统所印”三行六字。此为金代军队中高级将领持印。青龙满族自治县干树沟村出土。

57 西京皇甫铜权 辽金（公元 907—1234 年）

高 9 厘米，足径 4.5 厘米，重 400 克。

青龙满族自治县文物保护所藏。

合范铸造。由钮、身、座三部分组成。扁钮呈倒梯形，中有穿孔。身丰肩，鼓腹下渐收敛。腹与底座连接处呈两层倒梯形。底座呈三层台阶状。权前后腹部分别铸有阴文楷书“西京”“皇甫”。

58 南京皇甫铜权 辽金（公元 907—1234 年）

高 8 厘米，宽 3.8 厘米，重 220 克。

青龙满族自治县文物保护所藏。

合范铸造。呈扁六棱柱体。由钮、身、座三部分组成。扁钮近方形，中有圆穿孔。身平肩，六面直腹下微宽。腹与底座连接处起凸脊。底座呈六边形。权前后腹部分别铸有阴文楷书“南京”“皇甫”。

59 象骨算筹 辽金（公元 907—1234 年）

长 12 厘米，宽 0.18 厘米，厚 0.19 厘米。

青龙满族自治县文物保护所藏。

骨质，多根，长短和粗细大体一致的方棍。古代用于记数运算。青龙满族自治县张杖子村出土。

60 六鋬铜釜 元（公元 1206—1368 年）

高 7 厘米，口径 28.8 厘米。

昌黎县文物研究保护所藏。

广口，内折平沿，深腹，弧壁，圆底，有圆脐。上腹外附六个扁平鋬手，鋬手间连有凸起铸线。

61 京运铜子母铳 明·隆庆四年（公元 1570 年）

母铳长 64 厘米，内口径 2 厘米。子铳长 15.1 厘米，最大直径 5 厘米。

抚宁区文物保护中心藏。

由母铳和子铳两部分构成，与西式佛朗机工作原理相似。母铳分前膛、子铳室（后室）和尾銎三部分。前膛为长管状，用于发射弹丸；子铳室位于母铳后部，管壁上部开一长 11.8 厘米、宽 4 厘米的下凹修口，形成弹膛，用于填装子铳。修口尾端两侧壁各开有一个长 4.6 厘米、宽 1 厘米的长方形锁板孔，用于锁定子铳；銎位于母铳后尾，中空，内径 3 厘米，口大里小，用于安装手持柄，銎左侧有一个 2 厘米宽的横系。整个铳身铸有七道凸起管箍。母铳管壁上阴刻“胜字一千一百四十八号隆庆四年京运鉒匠徐荣小匠郝英”铭文。子铳，多枚，由子铳口、药室、尾冠构成，形制均一致，短体鼓腹，尾冠呈半圆形，用于装入母铳后锁位。通体铸三道凸起管箍，身上铸两个小提梁耳，尾部有点火孔。子铳管壁上阴刻“胜字二千六百八十二号”等铭文，均是“胜字”款“号”。这组子母铳，铭文清晰，工艺精湛，对研究兵器史具有特别珍贵的研究价值。抚宁区城子峪村出土。

62 石炮 明（公元 1368—1644 年）

长 94 厘米，外径 50 厘米，内口径 15 厘米。

抚宁区文物保护中心藏。

砂岩质，呈柱状。炮身后部凿有前浅、后深的长方形石槽，引火孔位于石槽前端下部，与炮膛相通。炮尾上端凿有一系孔。

63 石炮 明（公元 1368—1644 年）

长 97.8 厘米，外径 44.5 厘米。

山海关长城博物馆藏。

白砂岩雕凿而成，外形呈不规则圆柱体。炮口和炮膛底内径均为 11.5 厘米，炮膛深 52 厘米，炮膛中部最大内径为 17.2 厘米。炮身后部凿有前浅、后深的长方形石槽，引火孔位于石槽前端下部，与炮膛相通。炮尾上端凿有一系孔。

64 铜安边神炮 明·天启三年（公元 1623 年）

长 49.5 厘米，炮口外径 12.2 厘米，炮口内径 4.3 厘米，重 38.75 千克。

山海关长城博物馆藏。

由炮身、药室、炮尾三部分组成。炮身呈圆柱体，身上铸有四道凸起管箍，口部铸有一道护口箍。药室呈隆起灯笼罩状，最大内径为 14.3 厘米，上铸凸起长方形火门，中间开直径为 0.4 厘米的引火孔通向膛内，引火孔距炮口39厘米。炮尾铸单箍，与药室箍之间由右向左阴刻五行楷书“天启癸亥年造安边神炮”十字铭文。

65 三箍平尾铁炮 明（公元1368—1644年）

长89.5厘米，外口径17厘米，内口径8厘米，尾径21厘米。

卢龙县文物保护管理所藏。

分为炮筒、药室、炮尾三部分。炮口加厚唇，炮身外壁铸有三道凸脊管箍，药室与炮尾之间呈亚腰形，腰中设有引信孔。平齐炮尾。

66 “崇祯十六年”大铁炮 明·崇祯十六年（公元1643年）

长281.2厘米，炮口外径33.7厘米，炮口内径10.5厘米。

山海关长城博物馆藏。

炮分两次铸造而成，前段粗，后段细，造型十分特殊。先锻造熟铁炮管，再用生铁浇铸，包裹加厚前段炮管。炮中部铸有圆柱形双耳，炮口至炮耳长140厘米，其间铸四道宽窄不同的隆起宽带箍。最大外径处为43.5厘米；炮耳处最细，外径为28厘米。炮耳至炮尾由细渐粗，炮尾部最大外径为37.5厘米，其间铸两道隆起管箍，并铸有92字铭文。引火孔直径为0.6厘米，距炮口230厘米。炮尾自尾箍起层层收敛如覆笠状，末端铸有圆尾珠。

67 陷马陶筒 明（公元1368—1644年）

高23.5厘米，外径18厘米。

卢龙县文物保护管理所藏。

泥质灰陶，筒状兵器，陷骑之具。埋入地下深尺许，内置铁蒺藜，虚棚顶，待敌进入，遇马踏，陷马蹄，铁蒺藜自刺蹄踝。卢龙县刘家营乡刘家口关东侧出土。

68 二龙戏珠纹石药斗 明（公元1368—1644年）

高10.5厘米，口径16.5厘米，厚2.2厘米。

青龙满族自治县文物保护所藏。

呈圆墩状，直口平沿，厚壁，深腹，平弧底。外一侧有流嘴口。周身饰高浮雕二龙戏珠图案。捣搅容器。

69 明长城年号砖 明·万历十二年（公元1584年）

长37.6厘米，宽18厘米，高9.5厘米。

山海关长城博物馆藏。

呈长方体，侧面模印长方形阴线框及文字，框内竖向模印楷书“万历拾贰年燕河路造”九字。明长城年号文字砖有十余种，这是其中一种。

70 燕尾形铁榫 明（公元1368—1644年）

长20厘米，最宽处11厘米，高6厘米。

山海关长城博物馆藏。

形状如燕尾，两头宽中间窄。连接锁扣，用于建筑构件相接处。

71 三兽足铜火盆 明（公元 1368—1644 年）

高 17 厘米，口径 48 厘米，底径 34 厘米。

昌黎县文物研究保护所藏。

敞口，平折沿，沿缘微向上折翘。浅腹，直壁，平底。底部承三个兽面蹄形足。呈瓦状，宽体内空，兽面瞠目龇牙。

72 张仓卧佛铜鎏金像 明（公元 1368—1644 年）

长 12 厘米，宽 5.8 厘米，高 4 厘米，重 650 克。

昌黎县文物研究保护所藏。

佛像呈右侧卧身状，头枕方形花顶枕。头饰螺发，高肉髻顶宝珠，高鼻大耳，弯眉慈目，面颊丰腴，神态自若。右手依托枕头支垫于头下，左手持一串黑色念珠，搭于腰间，入寂安卧于长方形床榻之上。上身袒露，下身覆盖僧被，露跣足。僧被面为金黄色，衬里为朱红色。造型写实传神，做工精致。昌黎县源影寺塔出土。

张仓卧佛床榻长 12 厘米，宽 5.8 厘米，厚 0.6 厘米。背面阴刻有楷书记事铭文："大明嘉靖二十六年春季月昌黎县之北水洊寺住持长老净释发心造张仓卧佛壹尊铜匠高聪" 38 个字。

水洊寺，今昌黎县水岩寺，在明朝嘉靖二十六年（1547 年）时曾名"水洊寺"。

卧佛函匣长 18.5 厘米，宽 7.5 厘米，高 7.2 厘米。银质，素面光滑，局部略有氧化。匣盖为推拉式，盖板两端有花叶形镶边，一端安有锁扣。函匣内垫有棉絮，除了安放张仓卧佛外，还存放有"熙宁重宝""建炎通宝""元丰通宝""元祐通宝"铜钱。

73 铜胎掐丝珐琅太平有象 清·乾隆（公元 1736—1795 年）

通高 61.1 厘米，长 56 厘米，宽 35.6 厘米。

北戴河文物保管所藏。

分卧象、须弥座两部分。上部为卧象，四肢伏地，卧姿回首，大扇耳，长獠牙，上卷鼻。象身施宽带龙套，背上搭一锦袱，上放鞍鞯，绶带宝瓶置于鞍上。象身、锦袱、鞍鞯、宝瓶均以纤细的掐丝珐琅进行装饰，象身施宝石红色珐琅釉；锦袱和宝瓶均以浅蓝色珐琅釉为地，饰蝙蝠、缠枝莲等吉祥纹样；鞍鞯以玄采珐琅釉为地，饰缠枝莲纹。下部为束腰委角仰俯莲须弥台座，台座帷幔形足，台顶周立鎏金栏柱及镂空围栏板。仰俯莲与围栏柱鎏金，其余部分均施珐琅釉，饰掐丝珐琅花卉纹。此器为一对，体形硕大，做工精巧细致，纹饰繁缛而不乱，色彩艳丽而不俗，气度雍容华贵，应为宫廷御用珐琅器之精品。

74 铜胎掐丝珐琅镂空开光云龙纹天球瓶 清·乾隆（公元 1736—1795 年）

高 34 厘米，口径 9 厘米，底径 10.5 厘米。

昌黎县文物研究保护所藏。

铜胎。撇口，圆唇外侈，细颈，溜肩，圆鼓腹，圈足外撇。以玄采为地，饰珐琅彩花纹，掐丝精细，填彩饱满，穷态极妍。颈、肩以垂花如意云头纹、缠枝宝相花卉纹、蕉叶纹、勾连花如意云头纹为饰。腹为主题纹饰区，以缠枝花卉纹衬托四面高浮雕圆形开光，每个开光内饰镂空浮雕团龙纹，开光之间均用纵向排列不同色的三朵宝相花相隔。下腹饰嵌珠仰莲一周。圈足饰四组缠枝花卉，施环箍足带。最为精巧别致、独具匠心的设计是腹、颈部可转动，转动时透过圆形开光看团龙似在祥云间飞舞盘旋。四面圆形开光均采用镀金工艺，更显得璀璨夺目，富丽华贵。

75 船形铜盒 清（公元 1616—1911 年）

长 12.8 厘米，宽 6.2 厘米，高 7.8 厘米。

卢龙县文物保护管理所藏。

呈杯状。上部为船状，一头宽，一头窄，有顶盖。顶盖边缘饰有一周齿形纹，中间有横轴连接两侧，一边固定，一边为活动盖。下部为喇叭口形底座，施三层外展折台阶。永平府教堂用器。

76 三足铜火盆 清（公元 1616—1911 年）

通高 18.4 厘米，口径 34 厘米。

抚宁区文物保护中心藏。

直口，外折平沿，周缘上翘，深直腹，平底。三空心兽蹄形足铆于腹壁上。

77 覆斗形铜印 清（公元 1616—1911 年）

高 4.8 厘米，长 6.8 厘米，宽 4.9 厘米。上顶：长 5.6 厘米，宽 3.9 厘米。

青龙满族自治县文物保护所藏。

印面刻诸葛亮《出师表》。

78 微刻牛角印 清（公元 1616—1911 年）

高 3.7 厘米。下底：长 5.7 厘米，宽 3.7 厘米。上顶：长 4.4 厘米，宽 3.1 厘米。

青龙满族自治县文物保护所藏。

印面微刻文字。

79 天汇缠枝花纹金簪 清（公元 1616—1911 年）

长 13 厘米，宽 1.5 厘米，厚 0.1 厘米，重 31 克。

昌黎县文物研究保护所藏。

扁平身，蘑菇形帽。身攒刻萱草、缠枝莲花卉纹。头一端攒刻圆形双喜字纹。

80 五山纹铜镜 战国（公元前 475—前 221 年）

直径 22 厘米，缘厚 0.5 厘米。

抚宁区文物保护中心藏。

圆形，三弦纹桥形钮，圆钮座，素缘。镜背饰两圈凹面弦纹环带，一圈绕钮座而饰，一圈绕镜缘而饰。两圈环带间为主题纹饰区，由纤细密布羽状纹、垂丝海棠花朵纹、五个倾斜的“山”字纹叠合而成。五个倾斜的“山”字，中笔画很长，倾斜度较大，均等分布，整体绕钮作左旋排列，其间分布垂丝海棠花朵。

81 四神博局纹铜镜 汉（公元前 206—220 年）

直径 18 厘米。

秦皇岛市文物保护中心藏。

圆形，圆钮，方钮座。钮座内饰柿蒂纹，向外与出脊弦纹方框之间环列十二枚乳钉纹，间饰十二地支铭。方框外周饰八枚大乳钉纹及博局纹，将内区分为四方八极，分别配置四象神兽，即左青龙、右白虎、前朱雀、后玄武，并辅以凤鸟、独角兽、禽鸟、蟾蜍等纹饰。各方空间填以规矩丁字纹、曲尺纹、V 字形纹。外区饰一周多字铭文，其外再饰短斜线和锯齿纹各一周。镜缘饰连锁云气纹。此类镜铭文中记有“博局”二字，故得名。

82 鼍龙铜镜 唐（公元 618—907 年）

直径 13.6 厘米，厚 0.6 厘米。

昌黎县文物研究保护所藏。

圆形，圆钮，圆钮座，素缘。镜背内区饰四条鼍龙纹，或躬身匍匐游水，或曲颈怒目圆睁，或蜷身回首探望，或低头摆尾潜行，神态各异，妙趣横生。外区分别饰篦纹、锯齿纹、水波纹及隔开纹饰用的一粗二细凹弦纹。

83 真子飞霜铜镜 唐（公元 618—907 年 ）

直径 15.6 厘米，厚 0.5 厘米。

山海关文物保管所藏。

呈六出葵瓣形，龟钮，荷叶座，素缘。镜背纹饰分为四组，分布在龟纽的上、下、左、右，内容为唐镜中多见的民间故事，纹饰配置为：竹林配贤士抚琴，仙树配凤凰展翅，云山配丹凤朝阳，怪石配莲塘荷叶。纹饰制作精细，画境传神。特别是用龟伏在荷叶上组钮，颇有意趣，独具匠心。同类唐镜中有的带铭文“真子飞霜”四字，故得名。

84 四瑞兽葡萄纹铜镜 唐（公元 618—907 年）

直径 11.4 厘米，厚 0.9 厘米。

青龙满族自治县文物保护所藏。

圆形，伏兽钮。镜背凸起的一周高脊弦纹将主题纹饰分为内外两区。内区饰四只瑞兽环绕伏兽钮攀缘嬉戏，其间点缀缠绕的叶蔓和饱满的葡萄纹。外区环饰姿态各异的雀鸟在葡萄叶蔓和果实间穿梭，其间还有蜜蜂、蜻蜓、蝴蝶在飞舞。镜缘环饰一周重瓣花纹。伏兽昂首前视，瑞兽圆润俏皮，镜纹刻画纤毫毕现，生动有趣。

85 婴戏图直柄铜镜 辽金（公元 907—1234 年）

直径 9 厘米，厚 0.4 厘米，柄长 8.1 厘米。

青龙满族自治县文物保护所藏。

圆形，素缘，有直柄。镜背右侧为一棵树，树枝横生，上面挂满灯笼。树下三个顽童嬉戏，或举双手跳跃，或展双臂欢呼，其中一个匍匐在地，伸手欲点燃面前的大爆竹。左侧一位扛着案几的大人向孩子这边走来，抬起左腿，恐被爆竹炸到。虽然画面线条简练，但人物神情动态刻画精妙入微。娇憨天真、淘气致雅的顽童加上满树的灯笼，呈现出欢快浓郁的节日氛围，给予人祥和、愉悦的感受，更有祈福求安的意境。

86 双鱼纹铜镜 辽金（公元 907—1234 年）

直径 10.5 厘米，厚 0.6 厘米。

青龙满族自治县文物保护所藏。

圆形，圆钮，素缘。镜背饰两条鱼环绕镜钮，在湍急的水流中，它们折身摆尾、逐游嬉戏。

87 祥云双鹤铜镜 辽金（公元 907—1234 年）

直径 9.4 厘米，厚 0.5 厘米。

青龙满族自治县文物保护所藏。

圆形，圆钮，素缘。在三朵祥云下，两只鹤相互追逐，自由飞翔。

88 海马丹凤纹铜镜 辽金（公元 907—1234 年）

直径 13 厘米，厚 0.4 厘米。

青龙满族自治县文物保护所藏。

圆形，圆钮，素缘。钮下部水波惊沸，海马踏浪回首仰望；钮上部丹凤展翅向下俯瞰，两侧点缀神树。丹凤与海马遥相呼应，象征着祥瑞与和谐。

89 百鸟朝凤纹铜镜 辽金（公元 907—1234 年）

直径 9.4 厘米，厚 0.5 厘米，柄长 8.2 厘米。

青龙满族自治县文物保护所藏。

圆形，素缘，有柄。镜背用一周凸脊线分成内外两区。内区为一只站立的凤凰引首回望，间以花草纹装饰。外区百鸟围绕着内区站立的凤凰穿梭在花枝中，形成百鸟朝凤之势。柄把上下带有花边护手。“百鸟朝凤”是民俗文化喜用的题材。

90 二龙戏珠卷叶纹铜镜 金（公元 1115—1234 年）

直径 18.5 厘米，厚 0.8 厘米。

青龙满族自治县文物保护所藏。

圆形，圆钮，素缘。镜背主题纹饰为二龙戏珠：两条首尾相逐的龙，曲颈昂首，张嘴、飞鬃，前肢均作一按一舞状，以钮为珠嬉戏。一条龙弓身弩背，四肢粗壮有力，后爪一只蹬地、一只后伸，后伸的那一只被尾缠绕。另一条龙相对较弱小，身体较直，身躯扭转，后肢伸直盘尾。二龙张牙舞爪，互相追逐，动感十足。近缘处饰有一周卷叶纹。

91 五子登科铜镜 明（公元 1368—1644 年）

直径 17.3 厘米，厚 0.7 厘米。

青龙满族自治县文物保护所藏。

圆形，圆平顶钮。钮上、下、左、右各铸有一个凸起菱花纹框，框内楷书“五子登科”四字，其外缘饰高低双脊圈带。

⑨② 五子登科铜镜 明（公元1368—1644年）

直径24.7厘米，厚0.7厘米。内圈直径7.5厘米。

山海关文物保管所藏

圆形，圆平扣形钮，素宽边缘。钮顶面上铸有“湖州薛近河自造”三行七字小楷书铭文。钮四周铸有“五子登科”四字隶书铭文，每个字外围饰菱纹框。寓多子多福、福荫子孙、吉祥喜庆之意。

⑨③ 观音菩萨石造立像 唐（公元618—907年）

通高58厘米，宽17.5厘米，厚14厘米。须弥座高11厘米。

山海关文物保管所藏。

此像顶戴化佛宝冠，头微侧，宽额丰颐，眼睑低垂，神情肃穆慈祥，褒衣博带，法相庄严。颈戴项圈，腕戴串镯，胸前及衣裙上饰挂连珠璎珞。右手托插花净瓶于胸前，左手挽衣带于身侧。双脚跣足并立于卷云纹束腰莲花须弥座上，披帛展带，飘带垂搭于宝座两侧。造型端庄大气，线条简练流畅。

⑨④ 释迦牟尼佛铜立像 金（公元1115—1234年）

通高11厘米，宽2.6厘米，重100克。

昌黎县文物研究保护所藏。

此像头饰螺发，顶现硕大肉髻，肉髻正面嵌髻珠，大耳垂肩。面颊丰腴，双目低垂，神态宁静慈和，身形瘦高匀称，曲双臂结印于腹前。上身着广袖圆领通肩大襟长袍。由胸前大襟梯次向下的四组弧形衣襞形成福田格。由小臂弯垂落的广袖似瀑布般倾泻而下，线条简练畅快。下身着裳裙，跣足站立在亚腰长方形须弥座上。

⑨⑤ 普贤菩萨坐象鎏金彩绘铜像 明（公元1368—1644年）

通高35.5厘米，宽28.3厘米。

山海关长城博物馆收藏。

此像头戴化佛宝冠，身着菩萨装，高绾双髻，面部丰腴，弯眉慈目。长发，发带遮掩双耳，耳铛垂搭于肩。丰肩束腰，披帛展带。颈挂戴串珠项链，胸前及身上披挂满璎珞。右臂曲肘上举于胸前，手掌向外结施无畏印；左臂曲肘于腹前，手掌向上结与愿印。腰围蓝裙，下着长裤，坐于六牙白象背上。跣双足，右脚踩在莲花踏上，左腿斜搭于象背。白象跪卧在椭圆形单层莲台上。这尊造像鎏金饰彩绘，做工精湛，保存基本完好，十分难得。

⑨⑥ 释迦牟尼佛鎏金彩绘铜坐像 明（公元1368—1644年）

通高41.5厘米，宽28厘米，厚20.5厘米。须弥座高10厘米。

山海关文物保管所藏。

此像高隆肉髻，蓝色螺发，头顶宝珠。双目微闭，下颌微收，大耳垂肩，广肩束腰，神态恬静，表情殊胜庄严，呈现沉静肃穆之态。上身着袒露右肩袈裟，右肩头敷搭袈裟边角，下身着裙，衣质写实。结跏趺坐在束腰仰俯莲花须弥座上，施禅定印。造型比例匀称，线条生动流畅，体现了明代佛造像的风格。

⑨⑦ 释迦牟尼佛铜坐像 明（公元1368—1644年）

高16.8厘米，宽13.2厘米。

青龙满族自治县文物保护所藏。

此像头饰螺发，顶现宝珠，大耳齐垂，法相端庄。身着袒胸式袈裟，呈半露右肩头，分开衣襟双垂状，结跏趺坐，双手置于小腹前结禅定印。整体线条简练粗犷，自然流畅。

98 阿难尊者铜立像 明（公元 1368—1644 年）

通高 28.7 厘米，宽 11.3 厘米，厚 9.9 厘米 。

山海关文物保管所藏。

此像面阔额圆，双目低视，大耳齐垂，身披广袖袈裟，双手合掌站立在束莲须弥座之上。造型洗练传神，工艺巧妙，刻画出阿难端庄、聪慧的形象，给人一种静穆美。阿难为释迦牟尼佛十大弟子中最小的一个，又叫多闻第一。

99 迦叶尊者泥金铜立像 明（公元 1368—1644 年）

通高 18.7 厘米，宽 7.6 厘米。

青龙满族自治县文物保护所藏。

此像面相方圆，脸颊丰腴，双目微闭，戴头箍、嵌髻珠，大耳齐垂，神态慈和，微含笑意。内着僧坎，薄衣贴体，下着长裙，外披袒露右肩木棉袈裟。双手抱拳于胸前，跣足立于俯莲须弥座上，行谦逊之法，独领“拈花一笑”之意。披挂的博带顺肩、臂飘落而下，一侧垂落于莲台。风格写实，富有较强的艺术感染力。大迦叶是释迦牟尼佛的十大弟子之一。

100 释迦牟尼佛石造坐像 明（公元 1368—1644 年）

高 116 厘米，宽 65 厘米，厚 41 厘米。

抚宁区文物保护中心藏。

此像由花岗岩雕凿而成。头顶螺发，容貌饱满，双目微闭，大耳齐垂。身着通肩式大衣，集衣襞于左臂，右肩衍搭襞角。胸前衣领对称下垂后结缔，腰结花带。下身着裙。左手置于腹前施禅定印，右手覆腿结触地印，结跏趺坐。线条简洁明快，造型肃穆端庄。

101 释迦牟尼佛泥金铜坐像 明（公元 1368—1644 年）

高 10 厘米，重 314 克。

抚宁区文物保护中心藏。

此像通体泥金，头饰螺发高肉髻，大耳垂肩。脸形方圆，慈目低垂，神态庄肃。身着圆领袒胸百襞薄衣，衣襞呈弧形次第下垂，下身着裙。双手置于小腹前施禅定印，结跏趺坐。纹饰简练粗犷，圆垂宽领线条流畅醒目。

102 观音铜坐像 明（公元 1368—1644 年）

通高 15.8 厘米。

青龙满族自治县文物保护所藏。

此像面容方圆，头戴化佛宝冠，髻顶饰宝珠，双耳坠宝相花圆耳珰，胸前饰挂璎珞。上身着菩萨装，下身着长裙。左手托净瓶置于腹前，右曲臂手扶净瓶，结跏趺坐在仰莲宝座之上。衣服领口錾刻精美纹饰。

103 释迦牟尼佛鎏金铜坐像 清（公元 1616—1911 年）

通高 33.5 厘米，厚 14 厘米，宽 21 厘米。

山海关文物保管所藏。

此像头饰螺发，顶有高肉髻，顶宝珠。双目微闭，大耳齐垂，脖颈上饰一组项圈。上身着袒露右肩袈裟，右肩头敷搭袈裟边角，下身着裙。结跏趺坐在宽大束腰仰俯莲须弥座上，左手置腹前结禅定印，右手扶膝指地结触地印。表面鎏金，但已基本脱落。整体线条饱满流畅，神态端庄自若。

104 释袈牟尼佛鎏金彩绘铜坐像 清（公元 1616—1911 年）

高 24.5 厘米，宽 16 厘米，厚 10.2 厘米。

山海关文物保管所藏。

此像头饰蓝色螺发，长圆髻，面正方圆，双目微闭，大耳垂肩，神态庄严肃穆。身披袈裟，袒露上胸，结跏趺坐，施禅定印。造像头部比例较大，且微前倾，构成向前俯视之态。无须弥座。

105 尊胜佛母鎏金铜造像 清（公元 1616—1911 年）

通高 17.5 厘米，宽 11.4 厘米，厚 8 厘米。须弥座高 3.2 厘米。

山海关文物保管所藏。

尊胜佛母主化相为三面八臂，三面为一正面、两侧面，皆顶戴五叶花冠宝珠，双耳坠宝相花耳珰，面容表情威严慈祥。八臂均曲肘结手印，主臂双手当胸，左手竖食指立掌在上，右手虚掐指横掌在下，施无畏印。其余六臂分别伸向身体两侧。左侧：第一只手上扬，呈托举状；第二只手掐指，掌心向外；第三只手放于腿上，掌心向上。右侧：第一只手曲食指掌心向上，呈托举状；第二只手掐中指，掌心向外；第三只手倚腿结与愿印。各手臂高低错落，姿态纷呈，甚是精美。

佛母身着华丽精美的制衣，佩戴璎珞钏环，博带绕臂，灵动飘逸，在硕大的束腰仰俯莲花须弥座上结跏趺坐。身形优雅，造型精致。此造像为藏传佛教身形，与无量寿佛和白度母佛共同组成“长寿三尊”。

106 绿度母鎏金铜坐像 清（公元 1616—1911 年）

通高 10.5 厘米，宽 8.5 厘米，厚 8.5 厘米。

昌黎县文物研究保护所藏。

绿度母为观世音菩萨的化现之身，面相如年轻女子，头戴五叶花冠，高发髻，顶饰葫芦形宝珠。修眉长目，宽额丰颊，清秀肃穆。双耳戴圆耳珰，齐垂肩。颈饰项圈、璎珞，臂、腕、踝分别饰臂钏、手镯、脚镯。上身袒露，着束腰天衣绸裙。头略向右偏，腰肢稍左倾，细腰丰肩，曼妙优雅。右手施与愿印，左手施三宝严印，并持有柳叶枝条搭其手臂伸展出肩头。跣足，左腿屈坐，右腿向外舒展，端坐于瑞兽当康驮着的莲花月轮之上。当康呈四肢伏地，昂头挺胸状。此像风格写实，神情温婉自然，体态典雅端庄。

107 释迦牟尼佛鎏金铜坐像 清（公元 1616—1911 年）

通高 13.2 厘米，底座宽 8.6 厘米。

抚宁区文物保护中心藏。

此像头饰螺发，高肉髻，顶宝珠，大耳齐垂。脸形方正，神态庄肃。身着袒右肩袈裟，下身着裙。左手置于腹前结禅定印，右手搭于腿上结触地印，结跏趺端坐于双层束腰莲花宝座上。

108 大势至菩萨舟形背光鎏金铜坐像 清（公元 1616—1911 年）

通高 12.3 厘米，重 206 克。

抚宁区文物保护中心藏。

此像头戴花冠，束发高髻，顶莲花宝珠，双圆耳珰垂肩。面容清秀，双目俯视，慈和宁静。两手叠掌于腹前，结禅定印托插花宝瓶。颈饰项圈，璎珞垂挂于胸前，臂、腕处戴手镯、臂钏。帔帛披于双肩，缠绕双臂翻转而下，尾端由身两侧向上飘展。下身着长裙，大腿上横搭五彩绫罗垂于两侧台面，小腿正面各展一俯莲叶形博带。善跏趺坐于束腰仰俯莲宝座上。宝座上下沿分别饰一周连珠纹。身后有围绕主像凸起的精美浮雕舟形背光，背光内缘饰两周凸弦纹，中间夹连珠纹，其外缘饰卷叶纹。造型优雅华丽，工艺精湛。

109 送子观音石像 清（公元 1616—1911 年）

通高 47.8 厘米，宽 15 厘米，厚 14.8 厘米。

山海关长城博物馆藏。

此像顶戴莲花宝冠，发髻高挽，两耳齐垂，脸颊丰腴，慈眉善目，面带微笑。颈部及胸前挂璎珞。身着长衫，下着长裙，跣双足。身坐于由方形台座升起的双层莲台之上，右腿曲膝下踏小莲台，右手揽左腿搭在右腿之上，左手撑于莲台上。莲台下伏一只凶猛神兽金毛犼，扭颈向前挺进。

110 道士铜立像 清（公元 1616—1911 年）

通高 39.5 厘米，底座长 14 厘米，底座宽 11.2 厘米。

青龙满族自治县文物保护所藏。

道士束高发髻，戴莲花冠。开脸方正，弯眉醒目，两眼平视，面带微笑，大耳齐垂，三绺飘飘长髯。上着对襟袍服，广袖衬摆；下着长裙，露靴履。双手叠掌持物，举于胸前，站立在方斗形台座上。袖口及袍面攒刻精美花卉、卷云纹。

111 白水晶道人坐像 清（公元 1616—1911 年）

通高 11.8 厘米，宽 7 厘米。底座宽 6.1 厘米。

山海关文物保管所藏。

晶莹剔透，整体为立雕。道人束发髻，戴冠巾，着宽坦道服。方形脸颊，细长眉毛，双目微睁，嘴微闭，三绺长髯垂于胸前，神态谦和。左手扶山石，右手秉拂尘搭于臂弯，交叉双腿坐于危峭石岩上。

112 蟾形玉饰 战国（公元前 475—前 221 年）

长 6.7 厘米，宽 6.3 厘米，厚 0.3 厘米。

抚宁区文物保护中心藏。

以质软玉石为材料切割、镂空而成，呈土黄色，杂以紫、褐斑点。未经打磨，表面切割线痕犹存。蟾造型抽象，呈圆形体，四个方向出腿。中间为圆形穿孔，两侧对称施有一小穿孔，用于固定。抚宁区邴各庄出土。

113 龙形玉饰 战国（公元前475—前221年）

长9.8厘米，宽7厘米，厚0.2厘米。

抚宁区文物保护中心藏。

以质软玉石为材料切割、镂空而成，呈土黄色，杂以紫、褐斑点。未经打磨，表面切割线痕犹存。龙造型抽象，曲身回首。两侧对称施有一小穿孔，用于固定。抚宁区郝各庄出土。

114 白玉龙纹绔尾带板 唐（公元618—907年）

长12.44厘米，宽3.41厘米，厚0.95厘米。

山海关文物保管所藏。

玉质细润，呈长条状，一端为方角，一端呈圆弧状。正面用简练的线条浮雕一条回首绔尾苍龙。背面为素面，周边施有用于缝缀的对钻小孔十个。

115 青玉苍龙教子带钩 明（公元1368—1644年）

长13.5厘米，宽2.6厘米，高3厘米。

卢龙县文物保护管理所藏。

青玉镂雕而成，玉质带有棉絮。呈长条状，扁平腹，圆形钮。钩首立雕龙头，角、鼻、口、耳、眼一应俱全。腹面上镂雕一条小龙，目视大龙头。

116 青白玉苍龙教子带钩 明（公元1368—1644年）

长12.62厘米，宽2.88厘米，高2.95厘米。

山海关文物保管所藏。

青白玉镂雕而成，质闪棉絮。呈琵琶形，扁平宽腹，圆形纽。钩首立雕龙头，角、鼻、口、耳、眼俱全。腹面上镂雕一条昂首小苍龙，曲线优美，身躯灵动，首、尾、四肢动感十足，目视大龙头。雕工精细。

117 白玉镂雕双獾佩 明（公元1368—1644年）

长4.13厘米，宽3.41厘米，厚1.24厘米。

山海关文物保管所藏。

玉质细腻莹润，镂空立雕而成。造型对称布局，刻画了一上一下两个顽皮的獾子，它们四足互握，嬉戏打闹，惟妙惟肖。民俗中取其谐音“合欢”之意。

118 福寿白玉佩 清（公元1616—1911年）

长7.3厘米，宽4.9厘米，厚0.5厘米。

卢龙县文物保护管理所藏。

玉质洁白无瑕。佩首部浮雕品字形分布的三朵卷云纹，中间有一小孔为系。佩身部呈长方形，委角，外边缘剔刻出脊框线。中部线刻长方形双线框，内浮雕篆刻“福寿”二字。内外框之间，上两委角处向内分别饰单枝斜出缠枝卷叶纹；下底边向上饰两枝斜出缠枝卷叶纹。佩尾部浮雕对称四朵结索卷云纹。造型秀丽典雅，稳重大气。

119 青玉浮雕梅花如意瓦 清（公元 1616—1911 年）

长 8.9 厘米，宽 7.5 厘米，厚 1.76 厘米。

卢龙县文物保护管理所藏。

如意配饰。瓦形，一面凹，一面凸。凸面上浮雕干枝梅，梅树枝干劲展轻舒，盘虬交错。辅以洞石、翠竹入景，令人赏心悦目。

120 青玉透雕重环转心佩 清（公元 1616—1911 年）

直径 5.9 厘米，厚 0.4 厘米。

卢龙县文物保护管理所藏。

青玉透雕，呈重环圆形。由外环、内环、中毂组成。内外环之间透雕并用八条辐条链接。外环呈花瓣缘，两面线刻勾云纹；内环两面线刻回形纹。中毂微鼓，嵌在凹口里，可转动，透雕四出禾苗状纹饰。

121 青白玉大吉双夔龙佩 清（公元 1616—1911 年）

长 5.8 厘米，宽 4 厘米，厚 0.55 厘米。

卢龙县文物保护管理所藏。

白玉闪青，呈长方形。两条对称透雕拏空立夔龙，头顶祥云，龙之间透雕篆书“大吉”二字。琢磨精巧，曲线优美。

122 白玉童子持莲抚狗坠 清（公元 1616—1911 年）

高 3.92 厘米，宽 3.8 厘米，厚 1.98 厘米。

山海关文物保管所藏。

造型为一头发挽成两髻、扭头蹲伏的顽童，其左手持一大莲叶，莲叶遮盖在背上；右手抚摸小狗，小狗回头仰望。雕工细腻、流畅，造型生动、有趣。

123 翡翠苍龙教子带钩 清（公元 1616—1911 年）

长 8.8 厘米，宽 1.9 厘米，厚 2.55 厘米。

山海关文物保管所藏。

翡翠巧色，造型扁平，宽腹，圆形纽。钩首施龙头，腹面上俯卧一镂雕小龙，目视龙首。龙头和小龙为红巧色，余为青灰色闪绿。

124 翡翠如意首带钩 清（公元 1616—1911 年）

长 7.16 厘米，宽 1.7 厘米 ，厚 2.34 厘米。

山海关文物保管所藏。

翡翠巧色，呈琵琶形，扁鼓腹，圆形纽。钩首为如意形，腹面上浮雕一青蛙伏在荷叶上。如意头和青蛙均呈红色，其余为青灰色。

125 青白玉羊角龙首带钩 清（公元 1616—1911 年）

长 11.9 厘米，宽 2.59 厘米，厚 2.9 厘米。

山海关文物保管所藏。

玉质温润光滑。钩体呈琵琶形，圆鼓腹，圆形纽。钩首施羊角龙头，全身为素面。

126 白玉透雕双喜佩 清（公元 1616—1911 年）

高 5.7 厘米，宽 4.13 厘米，厚 0.54 厘米。

山海关文物保管所藏。

玉质细腻莹润。呈长方形，扁体。全身透雕一对喜字，上端有一穿孔为系。“囍”是中国民间传统吉祥图案，寓意喜庆与祝福，成双成对。

127 白玉螭纹指环 清·乾隆（公元 1736—1795 年）

高 2 厘米，外径 3.36 厘米，内径 1.96 厘米。

山海关文物保管所藏。

白玉泛青，局部有皮。指环周身浮雕螭纹，螭身曲突，呈盘卧状，首尾相接。

128 透雕瓜蝶纹玉佩 清（公元 1616—1911 年）

直径 5.4 厘米，厚 0.6 厘米，重 40 克。

昌黎县文物研究保护所藏。

玉质白润，呈圆形，透雕。上半部饰瓜与藤蔓纹，下半部为一只展翅蝴蝶。用双刀阴刻线条勾勒蝶、瓜、叶身上的细部纹脉。纹饰表现出浓郁的田园气息，寓意多子多福、福运绵长。

129 白玉莲蓬菱角坠 清（公元 1616—1911 年）

长 5.5 厘米，宽 4.1 厘米，厚 2.2 厘米。

昌黎县文物研究保护所藏。

玉质白润。形如莲蓬，花托穴内嵌合圆鼓的莲子，周边饰菱角。寓意圆满和美、佳偶天成、子孙满堂。

130 玛瑙兽头铺首耳鼻烟壶 清（公元 1616—1911 年）

通高 6.2 厘米，口径 2 厘米，足长径 3.2 厘米。

昌黎县文物研究保护所藏。

呈扁圆状。质硬脆，面细润，有光泽。镶铜口，直颈，溜肩，扁腹，椭圆形矮平足。佩一只镶嵌银底边红料圆帽盖，肩两侧浮雕硕大兽头铺首耳。通体色泽浓郁，层次丰富，色映成趣。天然绿色缠丝曲蟮玛瑙纹理相互交织，似涧瀑般流淌，跌宕击石，空谷回声。

131 玛瑙鸟兽纹鼻烟壶 清（公元 1616—1911 年）

通高 6.6 厘米，口径 2.1 厘米，足长径 3 厘米。

昌黎县文物研究保护所藏。

呈扁圆状。质纯，坚硬而脆，细润半透明，通体天然米黄色。镶铜花边口，直颈，溜肩，扁腹，椭圆形矮平足。佩一只镶嵌银底边红料圆帽盖，肩两侧浮雕硕大兽头铺首耳，正面左上方线刻一只站立在巨岩上的雄鹰俯视大地，右下角刻山崖小溪。

132 玛瑙素面鼻烟壶 清（公元 1616—1911 年）

高 7.9 厘米，口径 2.4 厘米，足长径 3.6 厘米。

昌黎县文物研究保护所藏。

呈扁圆状。质坚，硬而脆，色洁净，细润半透明。小口，直颈，溜肩，扁腹，椭圆形矮平足。肩两侧浮雕硕大兽头铺首耳，身素面，有不规则天然纹理隐现。通体呈现黄棕色，色相较单一，色彩温暖恬静，给人一种富足、快乐、幸福的感觉。

133 蚌螺钿人物字纹鼻烟壶 清（公元 1616—1911 年）

高 5 厘米，口径 1.3 厘米，足径 1.3 厘米。

昌黎县文物研究保护所藏。

呈扁圆状。蚌螺钿有环状纹，闪蛤蜊光。小直口，直颈，丰肩，扁腹下渐收，矮平足。两面沿着壶缘一周饰刻双阴线开光。一面开光内饰浮雕穿蟒袍、挎蟒带人物；另一面开光内阴刻“落花流影是文章侈书”行书诗文。

134 缠丝玛瑙鼻烟壶 清（公元 1616—1911 年）

高 5 厘米，腹宽 3.62 厘米，厚 2.76 厘米。

山海关文物保管所藏。

周身为天然螺形纹理，多种颜色线带相间缠绕。小口平沿，直颈，溜肩、鼓腹下收，圆平底。巧色素雅，纹样瑰丽。

135 白玉浮雕花卉纹鼻烟壶 清（公元 1616—1911 年）

高 6 厘米， 宽 5.54 厘米，厚 2 厘米。

山海关文物保管所藏。

呈扁圆状。玉质细润，浅浮雕工艺。小直口，平沿，唇外侈，束颈，溜肩，扁平体圆腹。壶身刻梅花竹石图案，侧面有回形纹饰。纹饰清新，恬静凝神。

136 珊瑚翡翠串珠项链 清（公元 1616—1911 年）

通长 52 厘米。

山海关文物保管所藏。

由大小相同的 108 粒珊瑚珠和 3 个定位翠珠、1 个三通翠件、3 个刻有花纹的叶片翠坠缀合而成。

137 褐釉三足陶奁 东汉（公元 25—220 年）

高 24 厘米，口径 14.5 厘米，底径 15 厘米。

昌黎县文物研究保护所藏。

泥质夹砂釉陶，胎质粗松，内外皆施酱褐釉。直口毛边，圆筒形腹，腹部有三组凹弦纹。平底，下承三个憨态可掬的熊形兽足。

138 黄釉绿彩兽形三足罐 唐（公元 618—907 年）

高 14.45 厘米，口径 14.3 厘米，腹径 20.5 厘米。

山海关文物保管所藏。

撇沿，圆唇外侈，矮颈，鼓腹，弧底，兽形三足。胎质疏松，色灰白，整罐表面施加一层白色化妆土，半施浅黄釉，口、肩及腹饰垂流状绿彩，色块分布自然错落，参差不齐。口沿、三足局部残缺。

139 龙泉窑青釉刻花大盘 宋（公元 960—1279 年）

高 5 厘米，口径 26.5 厘米。

青龙满族自治县文物保护所藏。

敞口，斜弧壁，广圈足。胎体坚厚，质细腻。通体施豆青釉，釉面肥厚润泽，玻化程度高。盘内底刻一周弦纹框，内刻花卉纹。

140 酱釉鸡腿瓶 辽金（公元 907—1234 年）

高 37 厘米，口径 5.5 厘米。

青龙满族自治县文物保护所藏。

撇口，侈唇，束颈，溜肩，腹部修长渐下收，形似鸡腿状，小圈足。胎厚质坚，施酱褐色釉，肩部刮釉一圈露胎，腹密布凸旋纹，底内凹，足墙平切。青龙满族自治县朱石岭村征集。

141 黑褐色鸾凤和鸣四系瓶 辽金（公元 907—1234 年）

高 38 厘米，口径 7.7 厘米，足径 12 厘米。

青龙满族自治县文物保护所藏。

撇口，侈唇，矮颈，溜肩，鼓腹渐收，圈足。胎质较硬，上部施牙白釉，下腹至足施黑釉。肩颈间施四系绶带耳。腹部划画主题纹，饰黑褐色鸾凤和鸣写意画。肩部辅饰四朵萱草纹，肩腹之间用两组三条弦线为隔带。修足不规整，底内凹。纹饰抽象写意，一鸾一凤相互追逐，应和鸣叫。寓意夫妻和谐、家和万事兴。青龙满族自治县陆杖子村出土。

142 云龙纹四系瓶 辽金（公元 907—1234 年）

高 32 厘米，口径 4.7 厘米，足径 10.5 厘米。

青龙满族自治县文物保护所藏。

撇口，侈唇，束颈，溜肩，鼓腹渐下收，广圈足。肩颈间施四系绶带耳。中腹区白釉上饰黑褐色写意云龙纹。肩部辅以多道酱褐色弦纹。下腹施酱褐色釉至足。青龙满族自治县青龙第一实验小学出土。

143 褐色卷茎大叶草四系瓶 辽金（公元 907—1234 年）

高 26 厘米，口径 5.9 厘米，足径 9.8 厘米。

青龙满族自治县文物保护所藏。

撇口，侈唇，矮颈，溜肩，鼓腹下坠，圈足。颈、上腹施灰白釉，下腹至足施黑釉。肩颈间施四系绶带耳。肩部、下腹部各饰以两道酱褐色弦纹锁边隔带，内绘褐色写意卷茎大叶草纹饰。足平削，底内凹。旧藏。

144 褐色草叶纹四系瓶 辽金（公元 907—1234 年）

高 30 厘米，口径 5 厘米，底径 9.5 厘米。

昌黎县文物研究保护所藏。

撇口，侈唇，矮颈，溜肩，橄榄腹，圈足。上部施白釉，下部施褐色釉。主题纹绘在腹上部，为褐色写意草叶纹，用上部一组水波纹线和下部酱褐色宽带纹进行装饰。颈施四系扁平绶带耳。

145 褐色草叶纹四系瓶 金（公元 1115—1234 年）

高 26 厘米，口径 4.3 厘米，腹径 14 厘米，足径 8.3 厘米。

山海关长城博物馆藏。

撇口，侈唇，细颈，溜肩，橄榄腹，圈足壮厚。上半部施白釉，下半部施酱褐色釉。肩与颈衔接处施四系绶带耳。肩部饰有两道酱褐色弦纹，之下白釉区绘简练的酱褐色草叶纹。

146 青釉四系橄榄瓶 辽金（公元 907—1234 年）

高 40 厘米，口径 8.2 厘米，足径 9 厘米。

青龙满族自治县文物保护所藏。

呈橄榄形。直口，圆唇，立颈，溜肩，鼓腹下渐收至足，小圈足微外撇。胎质较细密坚实，呈棕色。肩颈施青釉，腹、足不施釉。肩施四个蟠龙衔环耳，耳之间刻楷书“魏家得士”四字。

147 黑釉双系瓷樽 辽金（公元 907—1234 年）

高 10 厘米，口径 4.5 厘米，足径 5.8 厘米。

青龙满族自治县文物保护所藏。

直口，平唇，矮颈，溜肩，下垂腹，广圈足，肩施一对大绶带扁耳。胎质较粗坚硬，半施黑釉，下腹、足未施釉。

148 酱釉双系罐 辽金（公元 907—1234 年）

高 14.7 厘米，口径 17.4 厘米，底径 8 厘米，腹围 63 厘米。

青龙满族自治县文物保护所藏。

直口，圆唇，矮立颈，弱肩，腹微鼓收至底，圈足。胎质细腻较松软，身半施酱釉，下腹及足不施釉。颈肩之间施一对扁宽系耳，器表隐现深浅不一的凹弦纹。青龙满族自治县拉马沟村征集。

149 酱釉竖条纹双系罐 金（公元 1115—1234 年）

高 31 厘米，口径 21 厘米，足径 12 厘米。

昌黎县文物研究保护所藏。

直口，侈唇，粗颈略束，溜肩，圆鼓腹下渐收，圈足。胎质细润坚硬，白灰色。通体半施酱褐色釉，下腹部、足施透明釉。颈肩间施宽大扁平绶带二系耳，基本与口持平。腹部密集饰竖状凸棱条纹，似柳条低垂，俗称“柳条罐”。

150 黑釉敞口双系罐 金（公元 1115—1234 年）

高 10.3 厘米，口径 12.4 厘米，底径 7.1 厘米。

昌黎县文物研究保护所藏。

直口，方唇，矮立颈，弱肩，圆腹下收，圈足。胎质坚实覆化妆土，半施黑釉，上满下露胎，釉面莹润光亮。肩颈间施二系扁平绶带耳，基本与口持平。通体隐现旋纹。

151 钧釉双系罐 金（公元 1115—1234 年）

高 14.3 厘米，口径 12 厘米，腹径 18.1 厘米，足径 9 厘米。

山海关长城博物馆藏。

子母口，矮颈，圆腹下收，圈足不施釉。肩施扁绶带双耳。通体施蛋青色釉，有不规则的红色窑变色块。残缺。

152 白釉广圈足大碗 辽（公元 907—1125 年）

高 5.5 厘米，口径 19.5 厘米，足径 7.7 厘米。

昌黎县文物研究保护所藏。

芒口毛边，深腹，弧壁，广圈足。胎质粗松，施白釉色微泛灰。器表面有明显的修胎旋痕，外壁刻画一周锁口弦纹。

153 白釉深腹碗 辽（公元 907—1125 年）

高 4 厘米，口径 8 厘米，足径 3.3 厘米。

昌黎县文物研究保护所藏。

敞口，薄唇，深腹，弧壁，圈足。胎体较厚重坚致，施白釉，白中微闪灰。器表面有明显的修胎痕。

154 白釉深腹小碗 辽（公元 907—1125 年）

高 4.2 厘米，口径 6.8 厘米，足径 2.2 厘米。

昌黎县文物研究保护所藏。

敞口，薄唇，深腹，直壁微弧，小圈足。胎体较薄，施白釉，白中闪灰。

155 磁州窑双弦纹碗 辽金（公元 907—1234 年）

高 8.4 厘米，口径 20.5 厘米，足径 8.4 厘米。

青龙满族自治县文物保护所藏。

敞口，圆唇，斜壁深腹，圈足。胎质粗松，半施白釉，微闪黄，下腹、足不施釉。内壁饰两周褐色弦纹，外壁现修胎痕。青龙满族自治县拉马沟村征集。

156 黑白釉瓷碗 辽金（公元 907—1234 年）

高 7.4 厘米，口径 19.8 厘米，足径 7.1 厘米。

青龙满族自治县文物保护所藏。

敞口，圆唇，深腹斜壁，圈足。素面，口施黄褐色釉，内壁施白色釉，外壁施黑褐色釉。青龙满族自治县曾杖子村征集。

157 磁州窑白釉大碗 宋（公元960—1279年）

高7.1厘米，口径20.9厘米，足径5.8厘米。

青龙满族自治县文物保护所藏。

敞口，圆唇，斜弧腹，圈足。胎质粗松，半施釉，釉色白中微闪黄。青龙满族自治县小石盘村出土。

158 定窑模印荷塘鱼跃盘 宋（公元960—1279年）

高2厘米，口径11.6厘米，足径5.5厘米。

青龙满族自治县文物保护所藏。

芒口，浅斜腹，广圈足。胎质松弛，通体施白釉，釉中闪牙黄。外壁素面有砂眼，内壁模印一周菊瓣纹，底心模印四出菱花框开光，内饰荷塘鱼跃纹，框外饰一周卷叶纹。青龙满族自治县土门子村出土。

159 定窑模印莲花盘 辽金（公元907—1234年）

高3.2厘米，口径18.5厘米，足径5.7厘米。

青龙满族自治县文物保护所藏。

芒口，斜腹，圈足。通体施白釉，微闪黄，口沿黏附褐色水锈，外壁素面。内壁模印折枝花卉纹。青龙满族自治县小石盘村出土。

160 定窑模印莲花碗 辽金（公元907—1234年）

高5.1厘米，口径18.9厘米，足径5.7厘米。

青龙满族自治县文物保护所藏。

芒口，深腹斜壁，圈足。通体施白釉，微闪灰，口沿黏附褐色水锈，外壁素面。内壁模印折枝花卉纹。青龙满族自治县小石盘村出土。

161 白釉圈足盘 辽（公元907—1125年）

高3.2厘米，口径13.9厘米，底径4.7厘米，重100克。

昌黎县文物研究保护所藏。

芒口，浅腹，斜弧壁，小圈足。胎质粗松，通体施白釉，釉层稍厚，釉色泛黄。外壁隐现制作时修胎旋纹，足微敛，平切。

162 黑釉大瓷坛 辽金（公元907—1234年）

高46.2厘米，口径32.3厘米，腹围161厘米，底径20.5厘米。

青龙满族自治县文物保护所藏。

撇沿口，侈唇，矮颈，溜肩，鼓腹渐下收，小平底。通体施黑釉，釉质肥厚均匀，釉色稳重深邃，下腹饰密集旋纹。

163 黑釉葫芦瓶 辽金（公元 907—1234 年）

高 31 厘米，口径 2.8 厘米，足径 9.6 厘米。

青龙满族自治县文物保护所藏。

呈葫芦形。小直口，束腰，上腹小，下腹较大，圈足。胎质粗松，器表隐现旋痕，施黑釉至下腹，足未施釉。

164 三彩刻画花卉碗 辽（公元 907—1125 年）

高 5 厘米，口径 13.5 厘米，足径 5.8 厘米。

青龙满族自治县文物保护所藏。

直口，斜壁深腹，圈足。盘心刻花卉纹。粗胎夹细砂，呈棕红色，施化妆土半施釉，绿色釉为主，黄色釉为辅，交互云散，形成色斑。下腹、足部不施釉。青龙满族自治县拉马沟村出土。

165 绿釉香炉 辽金（公元 907—1234 年）

高 6.9 厘米，口径 8.3 厘米，足高 1 厘米。

青龙满族自治县文物保护所藏。

直口，折沿，圆唇外侈，粗直颈，圆鼓腹，弧底，捏制三个乳钉足。胎质坚实，施化妆土，半施绿釉，釉薄而云散，微闪黄色。下腹及足不施釉。

166 钧釉天蓝瓷碟 宋（公元 960—1279 年）

高 2.7 厘米，口径 12.9 厘米，足径 4 厘米。

青龙满族自治县文物保护所藏。

撇沿口，圆唇，斜壁浅弧腹，小圈足。胎质坚硬，施天蓝色釉，泛浅灰。器表有惊釉，闪现不规则的微红色斑。青龙满族自治县小石盘村出土。

167 钧窑天蓝釉红斑碗 元（公元 1206—1368 年）

高 8.5 厘米，口径 18.7 厘米，底径 7.3 厘米。

青龙满族自治县文物保护所藏。

直口，圆唇，深腹斜壁，圈足。胎质细密较硬，施天蓝色釉。器表有惊釉细纹及窑变淡红色斑块。鸡心底。

168 钧窑天蓝釉深腹碗 元（公元 1206—1368 年）

高 9.5 厘米，口径 22.7 厘米，足径 6.5 厘米。

昌黎县文物研究保护所藏。

敞口，圆唇，深腹，斜弧壁，圈足微外撇。胎质细润坚硬，施天蓝釉泛浅灰色，局部泛淡红色斑。口施酱褐色釉。腹与足相交处有积釉。

169 钧窑天蓝釉浅腹盘 元（公元 1206—1368 年）

高 2.5 厘米，口径 14.3 厘米，足径 5.8 厘米。

昌黎县文物研究保护所藏。

直口，圆唇，浅腹，斜壁。胎质细腻坚硬，呈白灰色，施天青釉，口施酱褐色釉。腹与足相交处有积釉。圈足不施釉，规整微侈。

170 钧窑天青釉直腹杯 元（公元 1206—1368 年）

高 5 厘米，口径 10.6 厘米，足径 5.6 厘米。

昌黎县文物研究保护所藏。

口微敛，圆唇，深腹，直壁微弧，下腹斜收，圈足外侈。胎质细腻坚硬，呈白灰色，施天青釉。器表有细密惊釉开片。腹与足部相交处有积釉。圈足不施釉。

171 钧窑天蓝釉直腹杯 元（公元 1206—1368 年）

高 4.6 厘米，口径 7.9 厘米，足径 4.4 厘米。

昌黎县文物研究保护所藏。

口微敛，圆唇，深腹，直壁，圈足。胎质坚硬，施天蓝釉，釉色莹亮。器表有细密惊釉开片，局部有淌釉积痕。足粘连匣残体。

172 白釉雕塑二甲传胪尊 明·成化款（公元 1465—1487 年）

高 22.25 厘米，口径 11.55 厘米，足径 11.45 厘米。

北戴河文物保管所藏。

波浪形器口，短立颈，溜肩，下垂腹，广圈足，通体高浮雕塑，满饰珍珠纹底。胎体坚实厚重，施透明白釉，釉质肥厚，现惊釉开片。口沿内外对称装饰一大一小两周锁口乳钉纹。腹一侧雕塑一对大螃蟹，辅以飞蓬草纹点缀。另一侧饰莲叶、飞蓬草纹。足规整，底有凹方印，阴刻楷书“成化年造”二行四字款。螃蟹形态憨态可掬、栩栩如生，情趣盎然。两只螃蟹钳芦苇，谐音“二甲传胪（芦）”，寓意金榜题名。

此尊为一对，形制大体一致，只是在纹饰位置上有所区别。

173 青花龙凤纹小缸 明·成化款（公元 1465—1487 年）

高 13.08 厘米，口径 18.65 厘米，足径 12.03 厘米。

山海关文物保管所藏。

子母口，深直腹，平底，广圈足，器型周正。施白釉青花，内光素，内口斜削刮釉。外壁两侧分绘云龙、飞凤纹饰，弦纹锁边。底部饰双栏圈，内署青花楷书“大明成化年制”三行六字款。龙姿遒劲，气势如虹；凤姿飘逸，振翅翱翔。龙、凤追逐穿行在云间，形成龙飞凤舞之势，呈现一派祥瑞气象。

174 青釉刻花碗 明（公元 1368—1644 年）

高 11 厘米，口径 19.5 厘米，腹径 6.6 厘米。

卢龙县文物保护管理所藏。

撇沿口，圆唇，深腹，弧壁，圈足。胎质紧致，内外施青釉，釉质肥厚，见惊釉。外壁暗刻简易花纹及双竖分区线。

175 青釉回纹大碗 明（公元 1368—1644 年）

高 11 厘米，口径 19.5 厘米，足径 6 厘米。

卢龙县文物保护管理所藏。

直口，圆唇，深腹，弧壁，小立圈足，底心微凸。胎质细腻致密，内外施青釉，通体有惊釉。口沿外隐约可见暗刻一周锁口回纹。

176 青白釉高足碗 明（公元 1368—1644 年）

高 8 厘米，口径 14.6 厘米，底径 5.5 厘米。

昌黎县文物研究保护所藏。

撇沿口，圆唇，深腹，斜壁微弧下收，高圈足微外撇。胎质致密，施青釉，不均匀。器表有明显的不规则旋修痕及棕眼。

177 白釉高足碗 明（公元 1368—1644 年）

高 8 厘米，口径 14.6 厘米，底径 5.5 厘米。

昌黎县文物研究保护所藏。

撇沿口，薄唇，深腹，壁微弧下平收，高圈足外撇。胎质细腻致密，施白釉，局部走釉，釉色白中微闪黄。腹面有淌釉，似泪痕。器表有明显的不规则旋修胎痕。

178 五彩凤凰牡丹纹小罐 明（公元 1368—1644 年）

高 9.1 厘米，口径 4.9 厘米，腹径 9 厘米，足径 6.2 厘米。

山海关长城博物馆藏。

直口，短颈，溜肩，鼓腹下收，圈足。饰五彩，用多组青花弦纹线分区。腹部绘主题纹饰凤凰牡丹纹，颈部饰变形蕉叶纹，肩部饰五彩祥云纹，下腹饰变形蕉叶纹。

179 珐华彩鹭鸶莲池纹罐 明（公元 1368—1644 年）

高 42.5 厘米，口径 23.8 厘米，足径 22.7 厘米。

秦皇岛市文物保护中心藏。

微撇口，侈唇，立颈，丰肩，鼓腹渐收至底，广圈足，平砂底。胎质较致密，呈糯白色。内壁施绿釉，器表通体以蓝釉为地，辅以堆花立粉技法做出的纹饰。即先入窑烧成涩胎，而后再填以黄、浅绿等釉彩，二次入窑烧成。颈周饰多朵双色祥云纹，肩次第饰褐红色如意垂云带、绿色素面宽带和黄绿彩璎珞纹，腹部主题堆塑鹭鸶莲池纹饰，近底部饰一周澎浪水岸。纹饰以莲塘景象最引人入胜，多只鹭鸶或飞翔或戏水，辅以盛开莲花，春色满园。器型端庄，珐华彩色调素雅醒目，立体感强，为难得的佳品。

180 青花缠枝莲纹罐 明·崇祯（公元 1628—1644 年）

高 17.8 厘米，口径 7.1 厘米，足径 10.15 厘米。

北戴河文物保管所藏。

直口，唇微侈，矮颈略束，丰肩，微鼓腹下敛，广圈足。胎质致密坚硬，体厚重。唇口施酱黄釉，肩饰折枝莲花卉纹，腹饰缠枝莲花卉纹，下腹饰蔓草纹，之间用弦纹线相隔。圆脊足，足墙宽厚。器底饰青花兔纹图记款。画面疏朗通透，青花勾勒平涂，色调深沉，纯正。

181 青花人物罐 明·崇祯（公元1628—1644年）

高17.95厘米，口径7.05厘米，足径9.85厘米。

北戴河文物保管所藏。

直口，唇微侈，矮颈略束，丰肩，微鼓腹下敛，广圈足，足墙宽厚。胎质致密坚硬，体厚重。唇口施酱黄釉，肩饰开光花卉及鱼鳞纹，腹饰人物、亭台、花草纹，下腹饰蔓草纹，之间用弦纹线相隔。器底饰青花三横纹。青花呈深蓝色，实笔点画，有晕散，色调灰暗。

182 青花山水纹大盘 清·康熙款（公元1662—1722年）

高11.8厘米，口径55.4厘米，足径31.4厘米。

北戴河文物保管所藏。

敞口，圆唇，展弧壁，广圈足。胎质致密，洁白坚硬，釉面莹润清亮。外壁饰三组折枝花卉纹，内壁满饰山水人物画。近景溪涧交错，绿树成荫，两只瑞鹿在水岸自由嬉戏；平远处崇山峻岭，峰峦叠嶂，两人在山间小路上荷长杆交语而行。内口用蔓草花卉纹带锁口。底栏圈内署青花楷书“大清康熙年制”三行六字款。画面构图饱满，层次丰富，青花分水明快，发色浓郁纯正。内容极富乡间山野情趣，恬静山水跃然眼前。此盘为康熙朝景德镇官窑生产的宫廷陈设用器。

183 黄釉绿彩桃树鸟纹碗 清·康熙款（公元1662—1722年）

高6.35厘米，口径12.35厘米，足径5.15厘米。

北戴河文物保管所藏。

敞口，圆唇，深腹，斜壁弧收，圈足微内敛。胎质细润坚致，外施黄釉地绿彩，内黄釉素面。外壁面暗刻两组图案纹饰，饰绿彩桃树、洞石、花鸟等，口沿下饰一周弦纹锁口。器底施黄釉饰赭色双栏圈，内署赭色楷书“大清康熙年制”二行六字款。黄地釉娇黄鲜净，釉面莹亮光润，绿彩青翠略有晕散。所饰纹饰均先在素胎上细致刻画、勾形后再施透明釉素烧，然后再施彩釉进行二次入窑焙烧。在沿袭明代黄釉瓷工艺的基础上，施以刻画饰彩等工艺，一改之前黄色釉单调的面貌，形成黄釉瓷发展史上的又一个高峰。

184 青花地黄彩二龙赶珠纹碗 清·康熙款（公元1662—1722年）

高6.45厘米，口径13.35厘米，足径6厘米。

北戴河文物保管所藏。

撇口沿，薄唇，深腹，弧壁微鼓，圈足微内敛。胎质致密洁白，釉面光亮润泽。内壁素白釉。外壁施青花地黄彩，青花地留白处勾绘图案，焙烧后在留白处填低温黄釉彩，二次入窑烧制而成。外口沿饰一周青花弦纹锁口。腹部饰两条犄角游龙，躬身曲颈，昂首摆尾，各自逐一个火珠，穿梭在火焰形云纹中。近足处饰三层仰莲纹。足饰小俯莲纹及两道弦纹。器底白釉地大双栏圈，内署青花楷书“大清康熙年制”二行六字款。

185 孔雀蓝釉鸽子 清 · 康熙（公元 1662—1722 年）

高 17.1 厘米，长 20.4 厘米，宽 9 厘米。

北戴河文物保管所藏。

鸽子挺身引颈侧首回望，站立在山石形底座之上，合拢双翼，紧闭尖喙，圆目炯炯，呈警觉状，塑形生动。胎质致密灰白，通体施孔雀蓝低温单色釉，呈绚蓝色彩，光鲜耀眼。底座正面、两侧面各有两个小孔用于悬挂安装。

186 霁红釉花觚 清 · 康熙（公元 1662—1722 年）

高 27.5 厘米，口径 15.15 厘米，足径 10.35 厘米。

北戴河文物保管所藏。

口沿外撇，形成大出沿，圆唇，筒形长腹，腰身施有一周凸起宽带。胎质白细坚硬，胎体厚重。器内施白釉，外表施霁红釉，发色不均，局部色灰暗。近足处外侈并积有厚釉。二层台式圈足，足墙平滑无釉。

187 青花百蝠纹盘 清 · 雍正款（公元 1723—1735 年）

高 4.1 厘米，口径 20.9 厘米，足径 13 厘米。

北戴河文物保管所藏。

敞口，圆唇，浅腹，斜壁微弧，广圈足。胎质硬洁，釉面青亮，体润莹彻，青花发色纯净淡雅。盘心饰五只蝙蝠连成团蝠图案，内壁饰不同姿态的十二只蝙蝠图案，两组图案之间和口部用双弦纹线相隔锁边。外壁饰八只蝙蝠，上下用双弦纹线锁边。泥鳅脊足，外墙饰回纹。底饰双栏圈，内署青花楷书“大清雍正年制”二行六字款。因“蝠”与“福”谐音，故俗称“百福”盘。图案清晰疏朗，画面隽秀、灵动。

188 霁兰釉小盘 清 · 雍正款（公元 1723—1735 年）

高 4.16 厘米，直径 15.7 厘米， 足径 9.9 厘米。

山海关文物保管所藏。

敞口，圆唇，斜弧腹、广圈足。外壁通体施霁蓝釉，内壁施青白釉。底施青白釉饰双栏圈，内署青花楷书“大清雍正年制”三行六字款。

189 粉青釉四方八卦琮式瓶 清 · 雍正款（公元 1723—1735 年）

高 30.06 厘米，口径 9.3 厘米，足径 11.45 厘米。

北戴河文物保管所藏。

直口，圆唇外侈，矮颈略外展，平肩，方形长腹，腹四面外壁模印凸起的八卦图案纹。胎质坚致洁白，通体施粉青釉，肥厚莹润，凸脊处走釉出白。圈足宽壮，底署青花楷书“大清雍正年制”三行六字款。瓶口与足径大小相当，其身形“内圆外方”，如古玉琮，故名琮式瓶。古朴典雅，神秘莫测。

190 粉彩花蝶纹笔筒 清 · 雍正款（公元 1723—1735 年）

高 12 厘米，口径 7.2 厘米，底径 6.7 厘米。

青龙满族自治县文物保护所藏。

呈圆柱状，直口，方唇，二层台式矮足。胎质洁白坚致，修胎规整。用红、绿、黄、蓝、紫等色在白釉底上施粉彩技法绘制花卉。器底双栏圈内署青花楷书“大清雍正年制”二行六字款。

191 青花小筒子瓶 清·雍正（公元 1723—1735 年）

高 19.95 厘米，口径 4.65 厘米，底径 5.1 厘米。

北戴河文物保管所藏。

撇口沿，圆唇，束颈，溜肩，直筒腹，平底。胎质坚硬，施白釉青花。腹部饰花好月圆图案，颈部辅以两组兰草纹。

192 粉彩凤尾花觚 清·雍正（公元 1723—1735 年）

高 44.8 厘米，口径 21.4 厘米，足径 14.05 厘米。

北戴河文物保管所藏。

口沿外撇，外展度较大，长颈，肩隆起，腹微鼓下收敛后又外撇至足，二层台式矮圈足。胎质致密洁白，施白釉，莹润光泽。器身绘一株高大花树，过肩至颈部，辅以花鸟、草虫、蝴蝶、洞石。颈腹之间有绿彩弦纹带装饰。口径大于腹、底径。器底饰青花双栏圈，无款。

193 粉彩凤尾花觚 清·雍正（公元 1723—1735 年）

高 44.8 厘米，口径 21 厘米，足径 14.2 厘米。

北戴河文物保管所藏。

口沿外撇，外展度较大，长颈，肩隆起，腹微鼓下收敛后又外撇至足，二层台式矮圈足。胎质致密洁白，施青白釉，莹润光泽。器身绘一株高大花树，过肩至颈部，两鸟栖息在枝干上，辅以草虫、洞石。颈部饰一头衔鹿。颈腹之间有松石绿地褐彩花带纹装饰。口径大于腹、底径。器底饰青花双栏圈，无款。

194 青花冰梅盖罐 清·雍正（公元 1723—1735 年）

通高 24.9 厘米，口径 8.45 厘米，足径 12.85 厘米。

北戴河文物保管所藏。

子母口，有盖，丰肩，鼓腹，圈足。施青花釉，留白处勾画梅花，青花隐现碎冰晶状图案。盖呈直壁圆弧顶形，饰折枝梅。肩饰有一圈几何纹带，腹部饰有四枝折枝梅花，底部饰有双栏圈。

195 青花狮子穿花将军罐 清·雍正（公元 1723—1735 年）

通高 33 厘米，口径 15.1 厘米，足径 15 厘米。

卢龙县文物保护管理所藏。

子母口，有盖，矮颈，溜肩，鼓腹下渐收至底，平砂底微凹。胎坚硬厚重，釉色白中闪青，通体饰青花纹，色泽浓艳。盖子凹顶，立柱帽钮，饰行龙赶珠纹。腹部饰双狮穿行在缠枝牡丹花海中，颈部辅饰变形海水江崖纹，近足处饰暗八仙图案，间衬火云纹。三组纹饰间用弦纹带分隔。纹饰清晰流畅，威猛的狮子与妖娆的牡丹形成鲜明对照，有驱邪去灾、富贵吉祥之寓意。

196 青花梵文高足碗 清·乾隆款（公元 1736—1795 年）

高 13.75 厘米，口径 14.75 厘米，足径 7.4 厘米。

北戴河文物保管所藏。

撇口沿，薄唇，深腹，弧壁，下腹折收，平底，高柄圈足外撇。胎质细白坚致，釉面光润亮洁，青花色泽纯净，略有晕散。碗口内沿饰双弦纹，碗心弦纹框内绘莲花。外壁腹部饰八朵宝相缠枝莲花衬托梵文，口沿、腹底双弦纹锁边。柄足上部施一周凸脊宽带，带面上饰四组金刚花卉纹，宽带下部饰瓔珞纹，双弦纹锁足底边。圈足内壁从右至左署青花篆书“大清乾隆年制”六字横款。此器多用于宗教礼仪当中，造型雅致，画面布局饱满精巧，温润莹白的釉面映衬出宝相莲花的绰约多姿。

197 青花三果碗 清·乾隆款（公元 1736—1795 年）

高 5.05 厘米，口径 12.05 厘米，足径 4.55 厘米。

北戴河文物保管所藏。

敞口，圆唇，深腹，斜壁敛腹，圈足。胎质细润洁白，釉色肥腴坚致、纯正淡雅。内、外口沿用波浪锦带纹锁边。碗心双弦纹圈内绘三果纹。外壁腹部饰寿桃、西瓜、石榴三组折枝瓜果纹。近足处饰变形莲瓣纹。外足墙饰双弦纹。器底署青花篆书“大清乾隆年制”三行六字款。用瓜果为饰，寓意多子、多福、多寿，表达人们对美好生活的愿景。

198 青花矾红彩宝相花小碗 清·乾隆款（公元 1736—1795 年）

高 4.35 厘米，口径 8.28 厘米，足径 3.4 厘米。

北戴河文物保管所藏。

敞口，圆唇，深腹，斜壁敛腹，圈足。胎质细腻坚致，体轻薄，施白釉，紧亮润泽，饰青花加矾红彩。碗内白素，外口沿青花双弦纹锁边，腹部周饰四朵对称青花加矾红彩宝相花朵纹。器底署青花篆书“大清乾隆年制”三行六字款。纹饰疏朗洗练，色彩绮丽典雅，红色花朵与青花叶蔓相映相衬，交相辉映。

199 青花留白海水红彩龙纹盘 清·乾隆款（公元 1736—1795 年）

高 4.15 厘米，口径 17.65 厘米，足径 10.75 厘米。

北戴河文物保管所藏。

撇口，圆唇，浅腹，斜壁微弧，广圈足微内敛。胎质细腻坚致，釉质紧亮润泽，微闪青，饰青花地留白海水加矾红彩。内口沿饰青花双弦纹，壁素白，盘心青花弦纹开光内饰一条红彩蛟龙，衬以青花留白海水纹。外沿口青花锦带纹锁边，外壁饰九条姿态各异的红彩小蛟龙，衬以青花留白海水纹及上下留白弦纹框。器底署青花篆书“大清乾隆年制”三行六字款。红彩致密浓艳，青花深沉稳重，白色海浪衬托红彩蛟龙，呈现群龙腾跃、九龙闹海之势，令人赏心悦目。

200 黄地绿彩龙纹菊瓣口盘 清·乾隆款（公元 1736—1795 年）

高 2.8 厘米，口径 13.2 厘米，足径 7.45 厘米。

北戴河文物保管所藏。

花瓣形口，撇沿，浅腹，斜壁微弧，广圈足。胎质细润坚致，釉质匀净、莹亮。里外均暗刻纹饰，施黄地绿彩，即先在素胎上细致刻画龙首、身、爪、鳞、折枝花等纹饰，施透明釉素烧，然后再按图施彩釉并二次入窑焙烧而成。沿口饰褐色线锁口。内、外壁各饰两条绿彩奔龙衔折枝花赶珠纹。

盘心弦纹圈内饰一只正面绿立龙衔折枝花戏珠纹。器底施白釉，内署青花篆书“大清乾隆年制”三行六字款。黄釉娇黄鲜净，绿彩青葱翠绿，略有晕散，暗刻纹饰呈现深浅变化，增强了画面立体感。

201 斗彩团花缠枝莲纹小缸 清·乾隆款（公元 1736—1795 年）

高 8.33 厘米，口径 11.63 厘米，底径 5.66 厘米。

山海关文物保管所藏。

直口，圆唇，微鼓腹下收，圈足。胎质洁白细润，形制规整。口沿、内壁均白素。外壁斗彩装饰：釉下青花勾绘主体纹饰轮廓线，釉上填红、绿、黄等彩。腹部主题纹饰：四组圆形开光，内饰宝相花卉，外间辅以缠枝莲花。沿口外壁饰红色平行弦纹框，框内饰链锁形开光及花卉纹。框下饰一周如意云头，用于装饰腹部主题。近足处饰一周变形仰莲花瓣。底足平宽光滑，不施釉。器底内凹施白釉，署青花篆书“大清乾隆年制”三行六字款。整器纹饰繁缛富丽，色彩浓艳，多有晕散，釉下青花与釉上彩相互陪衬烘托，争奇斗艳。

202 霁红罐 清·乾隆款（公元 1736—1795 年）

高 13.2 厘米，口径 12.6 厘米，腹径 22 厘米，底径 9.7 厘米。

山海关文物保管所藏。

敛口，圆唇，扁圆腹，卧足。内壁施白釉，外壁通体施霁红釉，釉面平润，色泽匀净。器底施白釉，署青花篆书“大清乾隆年制”三行六字款。

203 青花象鼻耳樽 清·乾隆款（公元 1736—1795 年 ）

高 27.7 厘米，口径 10.6 厘米，足径 9.65 厘米。

北戴河文物保管所藏。

撇沿口，直颈微弧，丰肩，瘦腹渐敛至足，圈足外撇。胎质致密洁白，釉面紧致肥腴。通体饰青花，色泽浓艳光润。颈部饰如意云头、变形花卉纹。肩部周饰缠枝莲和如意云头纹，一对捏塑象鼻衔环耳，高矗肩头。腹部饰两只夔凤在缠枝花海中振翅高飞，两夔凤间分别用两朵盛开的缠枝花相隔衬。近足处饰变形莲瓣纹，足饰卷草纹。器底署青花篆书“大清乾隆年制”三行六字款。器型端庄挺秀，纹饰繁缛华丽。

204 青花花卉罐 清·乾隆（公元 1736—1795 年 ）

高 14.73 厘米，口径 4.71 厘米，足径 5.87 厘米。

山海关文物保管所藏

直口，直颈，丰肩，鼓腹，高圈足外撇。釉面呈色白中稍显青。腹部主题纹饰绘六幅花树图案，花树构图简洁，根植于大地，花朵硕大，充斥画幅。各幅间用双竖线隔开。颈、肩及近足处均辅绘折枝花卉。

205 豆青釉红斑兽耳罐 清·乾隆（公元 1736—1795 年）

高 15.9 厘米，口径 5.3 厘米，底径 7 厘米。

北戴河文物保管所藏。

呈橄榄形。敛口，圆唇，天地通鼓腹。通体施豆青釉，不甚均匀，釉面有细密惊釉开片。底缘旋削，内凹。上腹部两侧对称堆塑兽头耳，两耳之间各饰有大块釉里红色斑。

206 窑变釉宝石红锥把瓶 清·乾隆（公元1736—1795年）

高39.6厘米，口径7.1厘米，足径13.3厘米。

北戴河文物保管所藏。

呈锥把形。直口，圆唇微侈，长颈，上略细，下略粗，溜肩，下垂圆腹，玉壁形砂底。胎体厚重而坚致，釉面肥腴而润滑，玻璃质感强。口沿及肩各施一道凸弦脊，颈部施一道箍状凸起宽带。釉面经高温窑变呈红、蓝、月白等色，各色与红色交融在一起肆意流淌，形成千变万化的条丝状纹理和各色斑片，犹如火焰一般绚丽，因此这种釉面也被称为“火焰红”，深得人们宠爱。

207 红釉天球瓶 清·乾隆（公元1736—1795年）

高31.65厘米，口径5.25厘米，足径12.05厘米。

北戴河文物保管所藏。

直口，长颈，丰肩，鼓腹渐收至底，圈足。外壁施薄红釉，色泽艳丽，内壁及器口施白釉。瓶口部呈月白色，俗称“灯草口”。底边沿有垂淌积釉，底施白釉。通体修胎不够细致严谨，隐约显现细密的修胎凸弦痕，在走釉的影响下红白分明，犹如装饰的道道弦纹，别有雅趣。

208 仿嘉靖款五彩游龙戏珠筒子瓶 清·乾隆（公元1736—1795年）

高45.3厘米，口径8.7厘米，底径12.9厘米。

北戴河文物保管所藏。

洗形敛口，紧束颈，小溜肩，长筒腹收至底，底微凹。胎体坚实较厚重，釉洁白光润。在洁白如雪的釉面上，用红、绿、黄、蓝、赫等色绘制纹饰。腹部主题纹饰为两条龙，躬身、曲颈、回首戏珠于三角形云纹间。肩部饰两道弦纹，内夹碎石纹。外口沿饰一单一双弦纹为框，框内饰双勾填彩链锁如意云头纹和一扇形开光，开光内由右向左署青花楷书“大明嘉靖年制”六字横款。绘画色彩斑斓，工笔娴熟，龙形轻盈挺秀，给人一种喜庆热烈之感。

209 粉彩八宝小碗 清·嘉庆款（公元1796—1820年）

高6.5厘米，口径10.6厘米，足径4.2厘米。

北戴河文物保管所藏。

敞口，圆唇，深腹，斜直壁下敛腹，圈足内敛。胎体细润坚致，胎薄釉亮，光滑如玉。内外皆施白釉，外壁饰粉彩。外口沿边饰青花弦纹框，内夹绘红彩变形回纹。腹部饰四组“八宝”图案，近足处饰青花弦纹框，内夹填黄彩衬青花乳钉纹，框外饰红彩如意云头纹。器底署青花篆书“大清嘉庆年制”三行六字款。此碗器型精致儒雅，绘画疏密有度，色彩粉润柔和，为嘉庆时期上乘佳作。“八宝”为佛教法器，由轮、螺、伞、盖、花、罐、鱼、肠组成，亦称佛家八吉祥。

210 绿地粉彩宝相花直壁洗 清·嘉庆款（公元1796—1820年）

高6.65厘米，口径22.9厘米，底径22.3厘米。

北戴河文物保管所藏。

呈圆筒状，直口，方唇，直壁，浅腹，玉壁形底。胎体较厚重，唇口施白釉，内外壁施松石绿釉。外壁轧道双勾工艺，对称饰两大四小粉彩宝相花纹。底有密集的旋修刀痕，内凹圆处施松石绿釉，釉面微缩，署红彩篆书“大清嘉庆年制”三行六字款。深沉的绿釉地，衬托清淡温润的粉彩，淳厚稳重，尽显儒雅墨韵。

211 青花鸾凤云纹盘 清・嘉庆款（公元 1796—1820 年）

高 3.65 厘米，口径 16.6 厘米，足径 9.8 厘米。

北戴河文物保管所藏。

敞口，圆唇，浅腹，弧壁，广圈足微敛。造型周正端庄，胎质细腻洁白，釉色肥润莹亮，青花色泽柔和淡雅。盘内沿口用双弦纹装饰，盘心双弦纹圆形开光内绘一对鸾凤，两首相对，展翼舒尾，呈飞翔状。中间饰两朵硕大的“壬”字形云纹。盘外壁复做一对鸾凤，亦呈飞行状，分饰两侧，之间以硕大“壬”字形云纹相隔。一对鸾凤昂首展翼飘尾，相互追逐。鸾凤形态大体一致，只是尾翼略有不同，一只似卷云，一只似拂尘。器底署青花篆书“大清嘉庆年制”三行六字款。鸾凤在朵朵祥云间翩翩舞动，呼之欲出，呈现一派永结同心、鸾凤和鸣、比翼双飞之祥瑞气象。

212 豆青青花象耳洗口瓶 清・嘉庆（公元 1796—1820 年）

高 40.2 厘米，口径 13.2 厘米，足径 12.8 厘米。

北戴河文物保管所藏。

洗形敛口，长颈，溜肩，圆鼓腹，圈足微外撇。通体施豆青釉，釉肥质坚。颈部堆塑一对象鼻形耳，施酱釉。肩部凸雕一周俯莲，上饰青花如意云纹。腹部两道褐色弦纹带间，设有椭圆形青花开光，内饰“福寿绵长，松柏齐肩”人物故事图，开光外辅饰青花仙鹤祥云纹。无底款。

213 仿成化款青花花觚 清・嘉庆（公元 1796—1820 年）

高 19.3 厘米，口径 10.3 厘米，足径 5.25 厘米。

北戴河文物保管所藏。

大撇口沿，薄唇，颈略长于腹，腹部隆起，下收敛后又外撇至足，矮圈足。口径大于腹、底径，有头重脚轻之感。胎质不尽紧密，釉面少光泽，青花浅淡干涩。通体饰青花缠枝花卉纹，肩饰一周卷云纹带。器底部双栏圈内署楷书“成化年制”二行四字款。

214 青花加白松乔之寿贯耳瓶 清・嘉道（公元 1796—1850 年）

高 22.8 厘米，口径 6.9 厘米，底径 11 厘米。

昌黎县文物研究保护所藏。

直口，侈唇，长颈，溜肩，鼓腹渐收后外撇至足，圈足。通体施豆青釉，青花加白，釉色淡雅匀净，呈青白色。长颈中部饰两周凸脊弦纹，两侧对称粘贴管状贯耳，耳上饰盛开莲花。腹饰“松乔之寿”故事图，颈饰“刘海月下戏金蟾”故事图。所绘故事情景生动传神，气韵流畅。“松乔之寿”“刘海戏金蟾”均是典型的传统民间故事题材，寓意长寿安康，财源兴旺，幸福吉祥。

215 青花夔凤穿莲纹碗 清・道光款（公元 1821—1850 年）

高 8.9 厘米，口径 23.55 厘米，足径 10.15 厘米。

北戴河文物保管所藏。

敞口，弧壁，圈足。胎质致密洁白，釉面光亮润泽，青花色翠静穆。碗内壁白釉光素，外壁腹部饰四只夔凤，展翼飞舞，穿梭在浩瀚的缠枝莲花丛中。外口沿、近足处及足墙各饰双弦纹锁边线。底署青花篆书“大清道光年制”三行六字款。青花勾勒平涂，色泽浓艳，饱满深邃。夔凤体态轻盈美妙，各展英姿，生动传神，极富艺术感染力。夔凤神鸟寓意“守护天下太平，万物安宁”。

216 斗彩暗八仙束腰碗 清·道光款（公元 1821—1850 年）

高 5.55 厘米，口径 20.35 厘米，足径 10.85 厘米。

北戴河文物保管所藏。

敞口，深弧壁，束腰，腰以下垂直至足部，高圈足。胎体质坚糯白，釉色紧致润亮，内外饰斗彩。内壁饰青花弦纹锁边框，内绘斗彩暗八仙纹，即道教八仙人所使用的法器纹饰，分别是汉钟离的扇子、张国老的渔鼓、吕洞宾的宝剑、铁拐李的葫芦、曹国舅的阴阳板、蓝采和的花篮、韩湘子的笛子和何仙姑的荷花。碗心青花双弦纹为框，绘斗彩链锁云开光，内绘束莲花蕊团花。外壁绘两组斗彩缠枝四季花卉，沿边饰青花弦纹锁口。足壁饰斗彩如意云头，衬以莲瓣纹。器底施白釉，署青花篆书“大清道光年制”三行六字款。釉下青花与釉上姹紫嫣红的色彩争奇斗艳，故称“斗彩”，创烧于明成化。即用青花勾出纹饰轮廓线，施透明釉烧成后在轮廓线内再填以红、黄、绿等色，二次入窑焙烧。暗八仙纹，寓意祈福纳祥，护佑平安。此碗紧追成化斗彩之风华，堪称隽俏。

217 茶叶末釉荸荠瓶 清·道光款（公元 1821—1850 年）

高 32.8 厘米，口径 7.55 厘米，足径 15.05 厘米。

北戴河文物保管所藏。

直口，长颈，广肩，荸荠腹，广圈足外撇。胎体厚重坚实，通体施茶叶末釉，釉色泛姜黄，釉面平净光润。器底浅刻篆书“大清道光年制”三行六字年款方章。釉面黄色釉中见隐杂黑绿色碎末点，似茶叶末，故称“茶叶末釉”。静观其器，韵味雅致，深邃苍古，隽永不俗。

218 霁蓝釉碗 清·道光款（公元 1821—1850 年）

高 5.9 厘米，口径 15.4 厘米，足径 5.3 厘米。

北戴河文物保管所藏。

敞口，斜壁下敛，圈足。胎质细腻坚硬。口沿、内壁施素白釉，外壁通体施霁蓝釉。碗底施白釉，署青花篆书“大清道光年制”三行六字款。釉面匀净，为高温单色釉，高贵雅致。

219 窑变红釉天球瓶 清·道光（公元 1821—1850 年）

高 35.9 厘米，口径 8.8 厘米，足径 11.65 厘米。

北戴河文物保管所藏。

微撇口，圆唇，长颈，丰肩，腹部圆鼓，矮圈足。通体施窑变红釉。器口沿走釉出白，俗称“灯草口”。腹底缘垂淌积釉，修足伤胎少釉。此瓶厚重、饱满、拙美，满身布满白星点点，灿若星辰，又似雪霁神州。鲜艳浓重的红色，被赋予了喜庆、祥瑞之意，深得人们喜爱。

220 青花冰梅瓶 清·道光（公元 1821—1850 年 ）

高 40.75 厘米，口径 9.75 厘米，足径 14.65 厘米。

北戴河文物保管所藏。

直口，圆唇，直颈，丰肩，瘦腹下渐收后外撇，圈足。口沿、底边施白釉，器身青花留白，青花呈冰晶状暗纹。青花留白方法绘二组盛开的梅花枝干，花枝过肩至颈部。蓝白相衬，更显梅花圣洁高雅。

221 仿康熙款哥窑铁锈花龙鹤纹瓶 清·道光（公元1821—1850年）

高45.4厘米，口径16.4厘米，足径15.3厘米。

北戴河文物保管所藏。

撇口，平唇，束颈，溜肩，瘦腹下收后外撇，矮圈足。仿哥窑，通体施青白釉，釉面金丝铁线开片。颈部两侧堆塑象鼻耳，耳边衬折枝梅花。正面雕塑二龙戏珠，背面雕塑仙鹤衔枚纹。器底施白釉，阴刻篆书“康熙年制”二行四字方款，字体草率无力。

222 五彩凤凰牡丹象腿瓶 清·道光（公元1821—1850年）

高45.2厘米，口径12.75厘米，底径13.7厘米。

北戴河文物保管所藏。

撇口，束颈，溜肩，腹微鼓，呈瘦长筒形，底微内凹。胎体较厚重坚实，釉面青白，通体饰五彩。唇口饰橘黄色釉，颈肩之间饰一周弦纹隔线。隔线之上饰高低错落锯齿状红绿蕉叶纹，之下饰变形俯莲纹。腹部主题纹饰为凤凰戏牡丹。构图舒朗，色彩浓艳，红花配绿叶，繁茂盎然，表达万物生机勃勃和花开富贵的美好寓意。此瓶一对，形制相同。

223 仿雍正款豆青釉剔花龙纹天球瓶 清·道光（公元1821—1850年）

高33.25厘米，口径5.55厘米，底径9.7厘米。

北戴河文物保管所藏。

直口，圆唇，长直颈，丰肩，圆鼓腹，卧足。胎坚质细，通体施豆青色釉，釉质肥厚滋润，极富美玉质感。回纹锦带锁口，颈部饰高低错落的蕉叶纹，肩部饰硕大的如意云纹和璎珞纹、金刚宝相花纹，腹部主题纹饰为二龙穿缠枝莲纹，颈肩之间饰一周弦纹。近足部饰一周海水江崖纹。器底署青花篆书“大清雍正年制”三行六字款。器型典雅端庄，采用剔刻覆釉法进行装饰，所刻纹饰朦胧惬意，展现出浅浮雕的艺术效果。

224 仿乾隆款青花富贵白头花鸟纹帽筒 清·道光（公元1821—1850年）

高33.3厘米，口径14.1厘米，足径13.7厘米。

北戴河文物保管所藏。

直口，直壁，矮圈足，呈圆筒状。胎体较厚，质白细。内壁白素，外壁青花，发色浅蓝。外壁口沿及近足处饰一周卷草缠枝莲纹锁边带，腹部绘富贵白头主题纹：两只白头翁栖息在枝头，相互守望，树下辅以牡丹、柱石、杂蓼。底署青花篆书“大清乾隆年制”三行六字款。白头翁与富贵牡丹组合是传统祝福图案，寓意婚姻美满，一生平平安安，白头偕老。

225 青花竹石芭蕉纹玉壶春瓶 清·同治款（公元1862—1874年）

高32.9厘米，口径8.8厘米，足径11.75厘米。

北戴河文物保管所藏。

撇口，细颈，溜肩，圆腹下垂，广圈足微外撇。胎质致密洁白，釉面莹润，青花色泽明快。腹部绘园景主题纹饰：柱石、芭蕉、毛竹、桥栏、兰草等，画面繁缛而有序。颈、肩、近足处及足墙辅助纹饰：蕉叶、缠枝花卉、如意头、变形仰莲和朵莲。各组纹饰间用弦纹相隔。底署青花楷书“大清同治年制”二行六字款。此瓶形发端于宋代，造型清丽雅致，后代多有沿袭烧造，并成为传统典型器型。因造型超然纯粹，深受人们的推崇，被赋予四季如春、冰清玉洁、光明磊落等寓意。

226 青花竹石芭蕉纹玉壶春瓶 清·同治款（公元 1862—1874 年）

高 30 厘米，口径 8.7 厘米，腹径 17.8 厘米，足径 11.6 厘米。

山海关文物保管所藏。

撇口，细颈，溜肩，圆腹下垂，广圈足微外撇。胎质致密洁白，釉面莹润，青花色泽深蓝。腹部饰毛竹、湖石、芭蕉等纹饰，颈部辅以蕉叶、卷草、如意头等纹饰，下腹辅以变形仰莲及水塘纹饰。底署青花楷书“大清同治年制”二行六字款。

227 冰梅莲花口六连瓶 清·同治（公元 1862—1874 年）

高 28 厘米，口径 3.6 厘米，足径 9.85 厘米。

北戴河文物保管所藏。

主瓶莲花口，细长颈，广平肩，腹部与五个相同小瓶组合为一体，形成一高五矮的六连体瓶造型。五个小瓶均直口，丰肩，鼓腹下敛至足。此瓶通体青花碎冰为地，留白勾勒点染，有梅花、怪石、莲瓣、如意云头、回纹等纹饰。底部为六个小平底。因六瓶腹相连，“腹”与“福”谐音，故俗称“多福瓶”。

228 青花纸槌瓶 清·同治（公元 1862—1874 年）

高 36.7 厘米，口径 3.7 厘米，足径 9.75 厘米。

北戴河文物保管所藏。

直口，圆唇，细长颈下略粗，溜肩，圆鼓腹，卧足。胎体厚重，质坚色白，青花色泽浅淡匀称。通身饰二龙戏珠纹，龙上下分布，其间点缀朵云、火焰云。口沿饰如意云纹，近足处饰海水江崖纹。

229 仿康熙款淡描红彩蝴蝶探花罐 清·同治（公元 1862—1874 年）

高 15.85 厘米，口径 16.8 厘米，足径 13 厘米。

北戴河文物保管所藏。

敛口，侈唇，丰肩，天地通鼓腹，卧足。白釉地饰矾红彩。器外口沿、近足部分别饰矾红如意云头纹、变形仰莲纹。腹部周饰成双成对的蝴蝶探花纹。器底署红彩楷书“康熙年制”二行四字款。字迹软弱无力。蝶舞花海，寓意爱情美满。

230 仿乾隆款粉彩开光六棱小瓶 清·同治（公元 1862—1874 年）

高 14.3 厘米，口径 3.5 厘米，足径 3.7 厘米。

北戴河文物保管所藏。

六棱瓶。撇口沿，侈唇，弧颈，折肩，腹渐收至足，六棱高圈足外撇。胎体厚重，釉质纤薄，施少见的淡蓝色地釉，用描金紫彩与粉彩绘画装饰。腹部、颈部各设有对称的两个扇形开光，内绘粉彩人物故事。开光外通体以紫彩为主，点缀绿、白、赭等色，用描金工艺绘制大小不一的朵朵折枝花卉。折肩处饰描金卷草纹带。足外壁饰多道描金弦纹。底署红彩篆书“大清乾隆年制”三行六字款。造型别致，技艺高超，釉色清淡优雅，其浅淡嫩蓝色犹如湖水般澄澈，倍受人们推崇喜爱。此瓶一对，形制相同。

231 仿乾隆款黄地墨彩什锦碗 清·同治（公元1862—1874年）

高6.8厘米，口径5.9厘米，足径4厘米。

北戴河文物保管所藏。

八棱碗。直口，圆唇，深腹，弧壁，八棱高圈足外撇。胎体厚重，釉质肥厚。内壁和底施松石绿釉，碗外壁饰黄地墨彩，绘双勾填彩折枝花果纹、飞鸟纹等。足外壁施绿釉地，饰缠枝纹，间衬朵花。碗底署红彩楷书“乾隆年制”二行四字方款。绘画笔法娴熟，用墨彩晕染花果、飞鸟，浓淡相宜。一派生机盎然、春华秋实的景象。

232 青花云龙赶珠纹盘 清·光绪款（公元1875—1908年）

高3.9厘米，口径16.95厘米，足径9.95厘米。

北戴河文物保管所藏。

敞口，圆唇，浅腹，弧壁，广圈足。胎体坚致润白，施釉紧密莹亮。内口沿双弦纹锁口，盘心双弦纹框内饰一条立云龙戏珠纹；外壁饰两条互相追逐的行龙赶珠纹，均辅以纤细火焰云纹。盘底署青花楷书“大清光绪年制”二行六字款。

233 白地粉彩百蝶纹赏瓶 清·光绪款（公元1875—1908年）

高39.6厘米，口径9.8厘米，足径13厘米。

北戴河文物保管所藏。

撇口，长弧颈，丰肩，圆腹，圈足。通体以白釉为地，粉彩为饰。颈、腹饰姿态各异，大小不同的百蝶图，姹紫嫣红的群蝶围绕一只较大的蝴蝶翩翩飞舞。外口沿饰如意云头纹一周，肩部描金双弦纹框，内绘缠枝花衬寿字纹，近足处饰变形莲花纹。器底署红彩楷书“大清光绪年制”二行六字款。瓶型舒展优雅，画面生动绮丽。以暖色为主色调，用藕荷、嫩黄、粉红、浅蓝、浅绿色入画，给整个画面增加了清新雅致的美感。“蝴蝶”谐音“福叠”，寓意百福叠加，福气多多。

234 粉彩百蝠二龙戏珠纹赏瓶 清·光绪款（公元1875—1908年）

高39.6厘米，口径9.85厘米，足径12.05厘米。

北戴河文物保管所藏。

撇口，长颈弧壁，丰肩，圆腹，圈足。通体以白釉为地，粉彩为饰。腹部前后主题纹饰分别绘一条红色蛟龙戏珠纹，蛟龙遒劲雄健，周间点缀褐、黄、蓝、绿色灵芝云、吉祥云、火焰云纹饰。颈部绘红色蝙蝠纹，蝙蝠姿态各异，其间点缀各色连尾祥云纹饰。口沿、肩、近足处分别绘如意云头纹、缠枝花衬寿字纹、海水江崖纹，颈肩衔接处施一道凸脊。器底署红彩楷书“大清光绪年制”二行六字款。瓶型舒展，优雅富贵。“蝠”与“福”谐音，蝙蝠与龙的组合纹饰，寓意洪福齐天。

235 白地粉彩夔凤穿莲纹碗 清·光绪款（公元1875—1908年）

高8.9厘米，口径20.8厘米，足径8.8厘米。

北戴河文物保管所藏。

敞口，深腹弧壁，圈足。胎质细腻质密，施莹润白釉，饰粉彩。内壁白釉光素，外壁腹部对称饰红、黄、蓝、绿四只夔凤，展翅飞翔，穿梭在浩瀚的缠枝莲花海中，体态轻盈典雅，极富动感。口沿、近底处各饰棕色弦纹锁边。底署青花楷书“大清光绪年制”二行六字款。粉彩色调柔和新艳，绘画采用双勾填彩法，色彩斑斓。夔凤为古代幻化神鸟，是典型的传统图案，寓意“天下太平，万物安宁”。

236 黄绿釉暗龙纹碗 清·光绪（公元 1875—1908 年）

高 7 厘米，直径 14.04 厘米，足径 7.17 厘米。

山海关文物保管所藏。

敞口，斜壁下敛腹，圈足。胎质致密轻薄，釉色均匀，内外壁均施黄绿釉。内壁光素，外壁暗刻蛟龙纹、云纹，近足处暗刻海水江崖纹，刻纹细腻流畅。威猛的蛟龙，通身布满网格状鳞片，曲颈、昂首、躬身，穿梭在云海中。底施白釉，署青花楷书“大清光绪年制”二行六字款。

237 黄地三彩二龙戏珠纹胆式瓶 清·光绪款（公元 1875—1908 年）

高 33 厘米，口径 6.85 厘米，足径 10.45 厘米。

北戴河文物保管所藏。

直口，细长直颈，溜肩，下垂腹，广圈足。胎体规整，厚薄适中，胎质细腻坚致。内外壁施黄釉，釉色明亮娇嫩，唇、底施白釉。瓶腹两侧对称绘制紫、绿彩二云龙戏珠纹，周间用紫、绿、白三色吉祥云和紫色纤细火焰云点缀。龙形遒劲，气势威严。近足处饰绿色变形海水江崖纹，瓶底署青花楷书“大清光绪年制”二行六字款。此瓶采用划画与填彩二次焙烧的技法进行装饰，线条丰富流畅，色彩饱满纯正，略有晕散。黄承天德，黄色为古代帝王专用之色，因此黄釉瓷在明清时期倍受严控，存量甚少。此瓶因器形如胆，故而得名。

238 黄地粉彩开光“万寿无疆”壶 清·光绪款（公元 1875—1908 年）

通高 11 厘米，口径 7.2 厘米，足径 8.1 厘米。

北戴河文物保管所藏。

造型独特，由壶身、把手、盖等组成，无流。壶子母口，小立沿、折肩，直腹，近足处折收，广圈足。胎质坚致洁白，施黄釉地粉彩，器表采用轧道工艺，制作精巧细致。壶盖呈头盔形，平顶折沿子口，顶立“人”字形钮。壶身两侧壁上各配有一支硕大的三角形把手，把手横梁向上翘，略高于折肩。壶面露白胎的轧道凤尾形锦地纹清晰可见，衬托形态各异的葫芦、红花、绿叶等粉彩纹饰组合。腹周饰四个大圆开光，内白釉地上红彩楷书“万寿无疆”四个大字。肩饰两道弦纹夹回纹带。下折腹至足饰莲纹。壶口径与足径大体相近。壶底施白釉，署红彩楷书“大清光绪年制”二行六字款。整器用暖色调明黄为地，色泽柔和，淡雅明快，复杂烦琐的粉彩与轧道工艺珠联璧合，锦上添花，完美地呈现出此壶之卓然不群。此壶为光绪时上乘之佳作。

239 青花开光八卦碗 清·光绪款（公元 1875—1908 年）

高 6.6 厘米，口径 13.35 厘米，足径 5.4 厘米。

北戴河文物保管所藏。

敞口，深腹，弧壁，圈足。内壁上沿饰菱格锦带纹，碗心饰水波纹。碗外壁双弦纹锁口，腹部饰八个圆形开光，内绘八卦图。开光之间用鹭鸶鸟和三出祥云纹相隔。近足处绘海水江崖纹，足外壁饰双弦纹。底署青花楷书“大清光绪年制”二行六字款。

240 宝石蓝釉描金麋鹿山水纹赏瓶 清·光绪（公元 1875—1908 年）

高 36.7 厘米，口径 10.05 厘米，足径 12.65 厘米。

北戴河文物保管所藏。

撇口，平唇，长弧颈，丰肩，圆腹，圈足。通体施宝石蓝釉，釉质滋润匀净，颜色深邃、柔美。外沿饰描金如意云头纹锁口，腹部通景饰描金麋鹿山水纹图案，颈肩有弦纹装饰。器型为清雍正始作，供赏赐之用，故称赏瓶。倍受后人尊崇，历代均有沿袭制作。此瓶造型高雅端庄、温婉华丽，以蓝色承托光彩夺目的金彩，极具艺术魅力。

241 窑变釉蒜头口瓶 清·光绪（公元 1875—1908 年）

高 22.5 厘米，口径 3.8 厘米，足径 7.5 厘米。

北戴河文物保管所藏。

蒜头口，细颈，丰肩，圆鼓腹，圈足外撇。通体施高温窑变釉，釉质肥厚光润，釉面呈细密惊釉开片。肩部饰一周凹弦纹。红、黑二色为主色调，相互交融之间产生的米黄色、赭色为辅色。在腹部、头颈部形成三块较大窑变红。晶莹剔透，美轮美奂。

242 哥瓷铁锈花干枝梅小瓶 清·光绪（公元 1875—1908 年）

高 18.6 厘米，口径 5.75 厘米，足径 5.1 厘米。

北戴河文物保管所藏。

撇口沿，小立唇，长颈，溜肩，鼓腹下渐收后外撇至足，二层台底。通体饰哥瓷釉，密布惊釉开片。腹部雕塑褐色铁锈花干枝梅。

243 墨地三彩梅竹石纹方瓶 清·光绪（公元 1875—1908 年）

高 49.7 厘米，口径 11.65 厘米，足径 11 厘米。

北戴河文物保管所藏。

圆口，撇沿，直颈，平折肩，方直腹落地，方足。胎体厚壮，质坚细腻，地釉漆黑光亮，三彩素净雅致。内施素白釉，外壁以黑釉为地，留白填彩，用绿、紫、黄等彩绘制梅、竹、石图。底施白釉，署青花树叶图记款。梅树辅以竹石，老干虬曲，新梅盛开。梅花用嫩黄点缀花蕊，娇艳欲滴，在墨地的映衬下更加突显出梅花静怡高洁的品质。

244 黄地粉彩万福万寿纹绣墩 清·光绪（公元 1875—1908 年）

高 46.7 厘米，口径 29.4 厘米，足径 27.2 厘米。

北戴河文物保管所藏。

呈腰鼓形。胎体厚重，质坚糯白。通体黄地粉彩，施以绿、粉红、蓝、藕荷等色。顶面微凹为坐面，底面内凹为假圈足。腹部纹饰分三区：中区饰主题“万福万寿”图案。墩腰两侧饰“五蝠献寿”图案，另两侧饰藕荷色镂空双钱纹，周间密布寿桃、团寿、花蝶，天地用鼓钉纹间夹一朵小白花装饰锁边，形成万福万寿之势。上区次第辅绘齿形纹、鼓钉纹、菱格锦地四开光寿桃附鼓钉纹、双叶片纹；下区次第辅绘有变形蕉叶附鼓钉纹。墩顶面中间为镂空金钱纹，周间辅饰蝙蝠、寿桃、团寿纹，外缘锦地四开光，内饰白地红彩寿桃花卉纹。此墩绘制粉彩精细艳丽，在清代晚期瓷业粗滥之风中超群脱俗。所绘图案寓意美好，如蝙蝠与钱组合，寓意“福在眼前”，蝙蝠与桃组合，寓意“福寿双全”，五只蝙蝠与寿桃组合，寓意“五蝠献寿”等。此墩集福寿吉祥于一身，表达出对美好生活的祝福与期许。

245 绿地三彩喜鹊登梅盖罐 清 · 光绪（公元 1875—1908 年）

通高 20.4 厘米，口径 7.2 厘米，足径 10.3 厘米。

北戴河文物保管所藏。

子母口，丰肩，鼓腹，卧足，配有半圆顶盖。通体施绿釉，留白处用于绘画。主题纹饰为喜鹊登梅：在山间小路边，梅花盛开，一对喜鹊嬉戏枝头。用赭色勾勒老树枝干和梅花，花蕊点嫩黄色；用墨彩绘画双鹊，鹊翅染蓝色。喜鹊作为一种“报喜鸟”深受人们喜爱，是吉祥的象征。梅花又称“报春花”。喜鹊登梅，寓示好运与福气来临。

246 粉彩暗八仙碗 清 · 光绪（公元 1875—1908 年）

高 7.5 厘米，口径 17.5 厘米，足径 10.8 厘米。

青龙满族自治县文物保护所藏。

八棱碗，撇口沿，圆唇，深腹，壁微弧，八棱圈足外撇。胎体厚重，内壁施松石绿釉，外壁饰粉彩。外壁用淡黄、草绿、松石绿、粉红、天蓝等色在各面分别绘八仙法器：葫芦、团扇、渔鼓、宝剑、荷花、花篮、横笛和阴阳板，间以折枝花卉点缀。足饰变形海水江崖纹。

247 豆青釉堆白花卉长颈瓶 清 · 光绪（公元 1875—1908 年）

高 40 厘米，口径 6.7 厘米，足径 16.6 厘米。

北戴河文物保管所藏。

直口，长颈，圆腹，广圈足微外撇。瓶体厚重，施豆青釉，釉质紧实。腹部以堆白四季花卉为主题，满饰堆白折枝花朵和枝叶。

248 仿康熙款青花应龙衔莲纹罐 清 · 光绪（公元 1875—1908 年）

高 31.9 厘米，口径 12 厘米，足径 16.3 厘米。

北戴河文物保管所藏。

子母口，溜肩，微鼓腹下敛至足，厚壮矮圈足，失盖。胎质细腻白润，满饰繁密青花图案，色泽青翠。腹部两侧各饰一应龙衔莲纹。应龙昂首衔莲，展翼、躬身、翘尾，自由翱翔，穿行在勾莲花海中。天地分别用如意云头纹、水波纹带锁边。肩部饰锦地四开光和缠枝莲衬八宝纹，近足处饰串缀花朵纹。器底署青花楷书“大清康熙年制”三行六字款。应龙鳞身脊棘，背生双翼，衔长枝花朵，足踏云气，善兴云作雨，是古代神话中唯一长翅膀的创世神龙。

249 仿康熙款青花云龙赶珠纹碗 清 · 光绪（公元 1875—1908 年）

高 6.1 厘米，口径 11.05 厘米，足径 4.15 厘米。

北戴河文物保管所藏。

撇口，深腹，弧壁，圈足。内壁为白釉素面。外壁饰两条首尾相逐的云龙赶珠纹，辅以火焰云纹；近足处饰海水江崖纹。口沿、足壁饰青花弦纹锁边。碗底饰大双栏圈，内署青花楷书“大清康熙年制”二行六字款。

250 仿康熙款绿釉地紫彩蛟龙赶珠纹碗 清·光绪（公元1875—1908年）

高5.25厘米，口径10.36厘米，足径4.8厘米。

北戴河文物保管所藏。

撇口，深腹，弧壁，圈足。内壁素白釉，外壁施绿地紫彩，饰两条首尾相逐的蛟龙赶珠纹，辅以简易云纹。近足处绘海水江崖纹。碗底施白釉，饰大双栏圈，内署青花楷书“大清康熙年制”二行六字款。

251 仿康熙款霁蓝釉瓷盘 清·光绪（公元1875—1908年）

高3.65厘米，口径17.3厘米，足径10.55厘米。

北戴河文物保管所藏。

敞口，浅腹，弧壁，广圈足。胎质坚致细润，器型规整。灯草口，内外壁施霁蓝釉，肥厚均匀。盘底施白釉，饰双栏圈，内署青花楷书“大清康熙年制”三行六字款。

252 仿雍正款淡描青花竹纹碗 清·光绪（公元1875—1908年）

高4.3厘米，口径9.45厘米，足径3.45厘米。

北戴河文物保管所藏。

敞口，深腹，弧壁，圈足。内壁白素，外壁绘两组青花淡描双勾竹子纹。碗底双栏方框内署青花楷书“大清雍正年制”二行六字年款。青花色泽清丽，竹子线条纤细工整，彰显竹子挺拔、清逸的品格。

253 仿雍正款白釉杯 清·光绪（公元1875—1908年）

高6.06厘米，口径9.16厘米，足径3.6厘米。

北戴河文物保管所藏。

敞口，深腹，斜壁，圈足。胎薄质坚，通体施白釉，釉面紧致亮洁。底部大双栏圈内署青花楷书“大清雍正年制”二行六字款。

254 仿雍正款淡蓝釉四方瓶 清·光绪（公元1875—1908年）

高24.9厘米，口径6.8厘米，足径8.65厘米。

北戴河文物保管所藏。

口微敛，圆唇外侈，矮颈，平肩，圆形底，圈足微侈。外形似玉棕，胎体较厚，通体施淡蓝釉，釉色莹润雅致，棱角处走釉泛白。足墙宽厚，足径略大于口径。底部署青花楷书“大清雍正年制”二行六字款。因施蓝釉，青花款偏黑色。

255 仿乾隆款白釉绿彩赶珠纹龙盘 清·光绪（公元1875—1908年）

高4.5厘米，口径18.1厘米，足径11.15厘米。

北戴河文物保管所藏。

撇口，浅腹，弧壁，广圈足。形制规整，施肥润白釉，白中泛青，以绿彩为饰。内沿饰一道锁口弦纹。盘心饰弦纹大栏，内绘立龙赶珠纹，衬以纤细火焰云纹。外壁饰两条头尾相逐的赶珠龙纹。底署青花篆书“大清乾隆年制”三行六字款。所绘龙纹用笔拘谨板滞，线条缺少变化，虽然张牙舞爪，但有形无神，缺少威猛气势。

256 仿乾隆款青花地红绿彩二龙戏珠纹赏瓶 清·光绪（公元1875—1908年）

高65.4厘米，口径15.6厘米，足径19.7厘米。

北戴河文物保管所藏。

撇口，长弧颈，丰肩，圆鼓腹下收，广圈足。胎体轻薄坚致，施青花地红绿彩。颈肩衔接处施一道凸脊。主题纹饰分颈、腹两区，两区间用内夹缠枝莲花衬托寿桃纹的回纹带与三角纹带相隔。颈饰云龙戏珠纹，周间点缀长结索云纹、火焰云纹；腹饰二龙戏珠纹，两条威猛的虬龙，血脉偾张，怒视火珠，欲抓又止，行于变化多端的火焰云和结索云间。口沿边饰黄、绿、紫三色如意云头纹；近足处为绿彩留白海水江崖纹。瓶底施白釉，署青花篆书“大清乾隆年制”三行六字款。青花属于高温釉下彩，红绿彩属于低温釉上彩。此瓶采用的釉下青花釉上彩工艺比刻花填彩工艺技法复杂，存量很少，是赏瓶中的佳品。

257 仿乾隆款红彩应龙纹天鸡高足盖碗 清·光绪（公元1875—1908年）

通高20.8厘米，口径15.7厘米，足径4.3厘米。

北戴河文物保管所藏。

分盖、碗两部分。盖呈圆弧形，顶塑镂空瑞鸟为钮，瑞鸟首、羽毛饰淡红彩，局部饰黄彩。瑞鸟又被称作天鸡，故此碗名为天鸡盖碗。碗子母口，折沿微侈，深腹，斜壁微弧，下承直柄式管状微侈高圈足。胎质坚致细密，体略显轻薄，均施白釉矾红彩，釉面莹润洁白。盖面与碗外壁用矾红彩各绘制两条应龙展翅飞逐火珠纹，辅以纤细火焰云纹。盖里心及碗心署红彩篆书“大清乾隆年制”三行六字方款。据清内务府档案记载，天鸡盖碗为宫中佛堂的供器，传世品稀少。本器为光绪年的作品，无论从形制、胎釉质，还是绘画用彩上考审，都略逊于康雍乾。红彩过于浓艳，覆彩不均，局部出现晕彩、缛彩，胎釉也略显苍白，但瑕不掩瑜，仍不失为这一时期难得的佳品。

258 仿乾隆款粉青釉螭龙耳鹿头樽 清·光绪（公元1875—1908年）

高30.3厘米，口径13.75厘米，足径17.4厘米。

北戴河文物保管所藏。

直口，圆唇，斜颈，溜肩，鼓腹，泥鳅脊广圈足。胎体坚致，薄厚适中，通施粉青釉，匀净、青亮、沉稳，釉下暗刻纹饰。肩饰螭龙双耳，腹部刻一周仿青铜回纹宽带，刀法流畅洒脱。颈和下腹分别刻仰、俯蕉叶纹。器底署青花篆书“大清乾隆年制”三行六字款。此樽釉色青绿淡雅，釉面润泽柔和，虽为光绪仿，但把樽尊贵内敛的个性、静谧深沉的气质表现得淋漓尽致。

259 仿乾隆款粉彩二龙戏珠纹鼻烟壶 清·光绪（公元1875—1908年）

高8.1厘米，口径1.3厘米，足径2.4厘米。

北戴河文物保管所藏。

直口，圆唇外侈，束颈，丰肩，长直腹，圈足。施白釉粉彩。腹饰二龙戏珠纹、火焰纹。色彩艳丽，有红、黑、明黄、嫩绿等色。壶底署红彩楷书“乾隆年制”二行四字款。

260 仿乾隆款绿地凸雕三彩四方笔筒 清·光绪（公元1875—1908年）

高21.85厘米，口径7.7厘米，足径8.25厘米。

北戴河文物保管所藏。

呈四棱柱体。方口，圆唇外侈，腹微鼓，方圈足，口与底大小相近。通体雕塑工艺，施绿地三彩，色浓艳。口沿处雕黄、紫色相间的如意云头纹。腹部四面均雕刻出脊长方形框，方框内凸雕黄、紫色二龙衔卷枝花争相嬉戏纹。两龙周边点缀白、黄色两朵大花及浅蓝色枝叶。其中两侧面在两龙之间雕塑紫色兽头耳。四面近足处抠小长方形横框，内雕黄色蕉叶纹。足为外二层台座式，底施绿釉，署篆书“大清乾隆年制”三行六字款。造型朴实儒雅，画面构图巧妙别致，雕塑、刻绘精美。

261 杨梅传

明·沈周 行书。

长卷。

纸本。

纵 33 厘米，横 954.5 厘米。全文 426 字。

山海关文物保管所藏。

沈周（1427—1509）字启南，号石田、白石翁、玉田翁，长洲（今江苏苏州）人，明代著名画家、书法家、文学家，与文徵明、唐寅、仇英并称“明四家”，是吴门画派的创始人。绘画造诣尤深，兼工山水、花鸟及人物，以山水和花鸟成就突出；书法学黄庭坚，遒劲奇崛。据《明史》载，他“文摹左氏，诗拟白居易、苏轼、陆游，字仿黄庭坚，并为世所爱重。尤工于画，评者谓为明世第一”。

此长卷行书《杨梅传》一文，用拟人手法为杨梅作传，随梅赋文，直道胸臆。敷陈乐天安命“淳儒”的质朴，轻执着、重“圆熟”的洒脱，屈居空山“负才不遇”的感触，进而领悟人生“豁达”的真谛。行书笔法遒劲、凝重，看似信手随意，实则墨无虚著，大字神韵，率性淋漓。书尾署名“沈周”，未署年款，钤“启南”朱文印，另钤有“清玩草堂”“章氏珍藏书画”“白石山房书画之记”三方篆书朱文收藏印。卷尾齐缝钤有一方“梅林潘氏家藏”朱文收藏印。

此书卷有一个香椿木盒子，是收藏者章瑞廷（1878—1944）所配，盒顶面刻隶书“明白石翁书杨梅卷精品章氏瑞廷藏”，盒一侧面刻隶书“明白石翁书杨梅卷精品”，署款刻“清玩草堂”隶书方章。

262 滦溪山水图

明·张凤翔 作 。

立轴。

纸本。

浅设色。

纵 92.5 厘米，横 34 厘米。

山海关文物保管所藏。

张凤翔（1577—1657），今河北滦河一带人。“滦溪”是滦河名。画面上远山峰峣叠连，涧瀑折落。平远坡下数栋村舍掩映在谷岸茂密的林荫中，山溪水从房前流过。近景巨石临水，老树枯藤，并有板桥接岸，桥上有一赶路行人。水面一叶要远行的扁舟刚刚离岸，飘荡在湍急的河水中。构图明晰严谨，用墨浓淡适宜。桥上行人与水上扁舟遥相呼应，山乡孤洁清寂的情景赫然而出。落款“丙寅长夏仿吴墨井画意少轩世台大人雅正 滦溪张凤翔”。钤“彩龟长寿”白文印，“张凤翔印”朱文印。

263 墨竹图

清·潘定澜 作。

立轴。

纸本。

水墨。

纵 83.5 厘米， 横 32 厘米。

山海关文物保管所。

潘定澜（生卒年不详）字柳塘，广东长宁人。诗书画精湛，尤擅长于画，兼工山水、人物。代表作有《北游图》《倚装独立》等。

此画为传统写意墨竹，画面简洁。两杆翠竹耸立石旁，几簇竹叶，寂然点缀，特别是石根的几叶小筱，呈现出自强不息的充沛活力。虽寥寥数笔，但竹子神形毕肖，跃然眼前。画作凸显了竹子清旷空灵的境界和顶天立地的精神品质。署款“潘定澜”。左上钤篆书“定澜”白文和“石痴”朱文两方印。右下角钤“□□江□百共南楼”印。

264 鲤鱼图

清·宋紫山 作。

横披。

绢本。

水墨。

纵 46 厘米，横 72 厘米。

山海关文物保管所。

宋紫山（生卒年不详）。画中两尾鲤鱼在水中无拘无束地追逐嬉戏，一尾跃出水面，一尾略潜水中，游潜回逐，扬鳍鼓鳃摆尾，若隐若现，栩栩如生，表现出自得其乐之态。画面通过两条鱼的白色磷光与墨色鲤脊的强烈对比，结合水流的变化，形成视觉环动，巧施疏密，独具匠心。署款“宋紫山”。钤“□山”白文印。

265 晨虎图

清·耕石 作。

条屏。

绢本。

设色。

纵 124 厘米 ，横 41.5 厘米。

山海关文物保管所藏。

耕石（生卒年不详）。画中，一只身体硕大的斑斓猛虎正从晨曦初露、草莽丛榛中蹑足而出，虎头微俯，目光炯炯，注视前方，似在寻觅。猛虎闭嘴鼓腮，仿佛内蕴刚气，其神态警觉，不怒自威，动势逼真，直扑画外，正是“虎视眈眈，其欲逐逐”。构图大胆饱满，形体真实生动，展现出猛虎的健硕雄壮和浑然大气。迎面而来的晨虎，颇具山中之君，王者之气。署款“耕石”。钤“耕石”朱文印。

266 工笔花鸟图

清·恽冰 作。

立轴。
绢本。
设色。
纵 141.2 厘米，横 45.9 厘米。
北戴河文物保管所藏。

恽冰（生卒年不详），字清於，号浩如，别号兰陵女史，亦署南兰女子。武进（今江苏常州）人。诸生恽钟隆次女，恽南田族玄孙女，一位深得家传的女画家。善花果，用粉精纯，作已辄题小诗，名著吴中。乾隆初，江苏巡抚君继善以恽冰画进呈孝圣太后，幸得乾隆帝题诗嘉奖。

此画工笔饰彩。画中绘洞石老树新丫，花枝上栖息着两只长尾兰鹊，百媚回眸；花树下绿草茵茵，彩蝶翩翩，双双追逐。画家创造了一幅和谐怡人、远离世俗浮华的大自然美景，观其画，莫名的温馨扑面而至。其笔墨精致淡雅，造型立体写实，意蕴生动传神。署“恽冰女史”款，钤印两方（不清）。

267 竹石图

清光绪·墨禅 作。
长卷。
纸本。
浅设色。
纵 43.5 厘米，横 169.5 厘米。
山海关文物保管所藏。

墨禅（1844—1911）名周镇岳，字墨禅，号梦松、仙史，北京人，清末三品官员，喜金石，善书画。此画中部洞石耸立，石旁掩映几株新竹，一丛兰草。石丑陋通透，颇得灵怪之气。幼竹穿插叠影，摇曳在微风中，浓密的兰花伴竹石茁壮成长。竹、石、兰各显现风采，独领韵味。画尾署款“时在光绪癸卯秋桂仿梅志道人草书为仁圃五兄大人清品即属 燕京竹楚僧 墨禅写于万寿之室”。尾钤“墨禅”白文印，“竹楚僧之书湊外归来”朱文印。右上钤“湊外飘香”朱文印，右下钤“结翰墨缘”白文印。

268 梅花图

清·胡峻 作。
横披。
纸本。
设色。
纵 111 厘米，横 221.7 厘米。
北戴河文物保管所藏。

胡峻（1869—1909），字雨岚，自号贞菴，四川华阳人。光绪二十一年进士，善书。1898 年授翰林院编修。著有诗文日记数十册，总编为《苍霞阁日记》。

画中兼工代写四季花卉横幅，绘两株倚洞石斜出的老干丫杈梅花，虬曲生姿，凌空绽放，交映生辉。在清劲的细枝上，勾画点染朵朵红白相间的小花，尽显温情与从容。洞石旁边辅以争相竞开的白牡丹花、南天竹，附衬红果绿叶。整幅画凝重中有婀娜，苍劲中见清新，奇古朴茂，冷香四溢。画尾署“丁亥秋日邗江胡峻”款和钤一方印。

269 松下牡丹图

现代·陈半丁 作。

立轴。

纸本。

墨彩。

纵 134.6 厘米，横 64.3 厘米。

北戴河文物保管所藏。

陈半丁（1876—1970），别名陈年，画家，浙江山阴（今绍兴）人。擅长花卉、山水，兼及书法、篆刻。有《陈半丁画集》《陈半丁花卉画谱》等著作行世。

画中左上题跋“香遍世界春满乾坤 壬寅三月朔日清明节半丁老人八十有七”，钤长方形朱文引首章一枚，署款白文、朱文方章各一枚。左下角白文压角章一枚。

270 梅花鸳鸯图

现代· 何香凝（款）。

立轴。

绢本。

设色。

纵 113.6 厘米，横 41.9 厘米。

北戴河文物保管所藏。

何香凝（1878—1972），女，原名谏，又名瑞谏，别号双清楼主。广东南海人，生于香港。是中国国民党左派的杰出代表、著名政治活动家、女权运动的先驱、画坛杰出的美术家、民革主要创始人之一、中国民主革命先驱廖仲恺的夫人。新中国成立后，曾任中央人民政府委员、全国人大常委会副委员长、政协副主席、侨务委员会主任、美术家协会主席、全国妇联名誉主席、民革中央副主席等职。擅画山水、花卉，尤工狮、虎、鹿、鹤等动物。著有《何香凝诗画集》。

左上署款楷书“香凝女士”。

271 荷花图

现代·于非厂 作。

条屏。

纸本。

设色。

纵 131.4 厘米，横 33 厘米。

北戴河文物保管所藏。

于非厂（1889—1959），满族，名照，曾用名闲人、闻人、老非、非闇。原籍山东蓬莱，生于北京并久居。精工笔花鸟，能写意山水，著有《于非闇工笔花鸟画选集》等。

此画构思巧妙，墨彩写意，把荷花含苞、绽放、结果生长过程由下向上次第展开，皴擦点染，揭示出生命的真谛。寥寥数笔，就把荷花“中通外直，不蔓不枝，出淤泥而不染，濯清涟而不妖”的高尚品格渲染得淋漓尽致。高远飞来一只蜻蜓入画，似乎在寻找“小荷才露尖尖角”的歇脚处，更增添了画幅内容和意蕴的深度，使画又平添了几分古诗的韵味。荷叶皴擦浓淡变化，枯润有致，白花红蕊淡妆素服，虚实相间，着重表现出荷花在水中生长跃动的天趣，歌颂了自然生命力的旺盛，带给人们的艺术感染力非常强烈。左上自题“冷香飞上诗句 艺圃先生博笑 甲戌中元前二日阻雨昆明湖漫写荷花四帧此其一也 非厂于□”。钤“非厂”朱文圆印，右下角钤白文压角章。

272 《北戴河》行书七言诗

现代·郭沫若 作。

横披。

纸本。

纵 65.6 厘米，横 135.3 厘米。

北戴河文物保管所藏。

郭沫若（1892—1978），字鼎堂，号尚武。四川乐山沙湾人。中国现代作家、历史学家、考古学家。

全诗如下：

满地茗秧沙岸绿，
一天霞彩海波红。
灯塔明灭东山上，
月横依稀碧落中。
一九六四年秋书为北戴河文化宫

273 高士图

现代· 溥心畬 作。

立轴。

纸本。

浅绛设色。

纵 113.7 厘米，横 33.8 厘米。

北戴河文物保管所藏。

溥心畬（1896—1963）名儒，字心畬，自比陶潜，号“羲黄上人”，又号“西山逸士”。北京人，满族，爱新觉罗氏。习天文、生物，长经史，精书画，著有《四书经义集证》《西山集》等。

此画构图搜新奇绝，平远高崖叠翠，巨石如削，幽谷藏刹，飞瀑激涧，倾泻空蒙；近景绿树掩映殿堂楼宇，清澈溪流边亭台傲岸，亭内久别重逢的两位高士隔案交谈，书童侍立一侧。深山沟壑，古刹銮台，山水、界画处理别具一格，浑然天成。静谧的山谷，精心点缀的人物，传达了寻胜访友超脱世俗的意趣。右上角自题“树古都依石山源半是云草堂有高士彝鼎供周文 心畬”。钤“旧王孙”朱文印、“溥儒”白文印各一方。

274 五牛图

现代·李可染 作。

立轴。

纸本。

水墨。

纵 136.2 厘米，横 66.2 厘米。

北戴河文物保管所藏。

李可染（1907—1989），原名李永顺，江苏徐州人，中国近代杰出的画家。擅长画山水、人物，尤其擅长画牛。有《李可染水墨写生画集》《李可染画牛》等著作行世。

画中上部自长题跋："五牛图。牛也，力大无穷，俯首孺子而不逞强，终生劳瘁，为人而安，不居功。纯厚温驯，特亦强犟；稳步向前，定不踏空；形容无华，气宇轩宏。吾素崇其性，爱其形，故屡屡不厌写之。一九六二年可染作于北戴河。"署钤"可染"长方形朱文章一枚。右下边钤"孺子牛"长方形朱文印章一枚，右下角钤"陈言务去"方形白文印章一枚。

275 鸽子图

现代 · 吴作人 作。

立轴。

纸本。

设色。

纵 100.5 厘米，横 32.8 厘米。

北戴河文物保管所藏。

吴作人（1908—1997），男，安徽宣城泾县人。中国当代著名画家、美术教育家。工诗，善书。著有《吴作人画集》《吴作人的艺术》等。

画中一对鸽子，合拢翅膀，侧身相望，翘首以盼，似要相互交流。全无衬景，一片留白。画家着意把线描和没骨结合，造成形式上的变化和对比，寥寥数笔彩墨，一气呵成，神态之惟妙，造型之纵恣，笔墨之精简，煞是耐人寻味。笔减画疏而气韵不离，形神兼具，实为罕见。左上署"一九六一 作人"款，钤"作人画"朱文篆书印。从署款看，此画应是吴作人先生中年之作。

CAPTION

1 Stone Cores

Period Paleolithic Age (ca. 10000 BP)
Dimensions length: 8.2 cm; width: 5.8 cm.
Collected by Funing Cultural Relics Protection Center.

It is made of ochre flint. The upper end is sharp and the lower end is slightly flat. Small scars, debris scars and working surface can be seen on both ends, and large strip scars can be seen on the column, which is formed by hitting the stripped stone blade tool. It was unearthed in Dasuo Village, Funing District.

2 Stone Saddle-quern, Frotton

Period Neolithic Age (ca. 10000 — 4000 BP)
Dimensions length of saddle-quern: 43 cm; width: 27.5 cm; length of millstone: 26 cm; diameter: 7cm.
Collected by Funing Cultural Relics Protection Center.

It is made of granite. The stone saddle-quern is rectangular. Due to prolonged use, it wears on the surface, which shows one thin end and the other thick end, with a thickness of 10 cm at the thin end. It is dented deeply due to abrasion and the thinnest part in the middle is 2 cm thick. The frotton is in the shape of cylinder. This group of grinders was a typical tool for grinding grains in the Neolithic Age. It was unearthed in Bingge Village, Funing District.

3 Stone Arrowhead

Period Neolithic Age (ca. 10000 — 4000 BP)
Dimensions height: 3.8 cm; thickness: 1.6 cm.
Collected by Funing Cultural Relics Protection Center.

It is in isosceles triangle shape, and made of ochre flint. The bottom edge is slightly concave, forming a two-sharp angle tail wing. The trilateral body is thin and blade-shaped, and thickening from three corners to the middle body. The entire body presents scars of different sizes that have been smashed and trimmed. It was unearthed in Licheng Site, Funing District.

4 Stone Axe

Period Neolithic Age (ca. 10000 — 4000 BP)
Dimensions length: 14.9 cm; width of blade: 4.7 cm; thickness:1.5cm.
Collected by Funing Cultural Relics Protection Center.

It is rectangular and flat in shape. The whole body is finely polished and smooth, with a regular shape. One end is ground on both sides to form an oblique arc surface cutting edge, and the other end is an elliptical section. It is a stone tool used in ancient times for cutting and smashing. It was unearthed in Weizhuang Village, Funing District.

5 Stone Axe

Period Neolithic Age (ca. 10000 — 4000 BP)
Dimensions length: 17.0 cm; width: 6.5 cm; thickness: 2.0 cm.
Collected by Qinglong Manchu Autonomous County Cultural Relics Protection Institute.

It is rectangular shaped and ground into a double side arc blade at one end. It is a stone tool used for cutting and smashing in ancient times.

6 Pentagram Stone Spinning Wheel

Period Neolithic Age (ca. 10000 — 4000 BP)
Dimensions diameter: 9 cm; thickness: 3.5 cm.
Collected by Funing Cultural Relics Protection Center.

It is a granitic stone in irregular pentagonal-star shaped. The center has a round hole with a diameter of 3.8 cm. It was unearthed in Daxinzhai Town, Funing District.

7 Cuspidate Stone Tool

Period Neolithic Age (ca. 10000 — 4000 BP)
Dimensions length: 33 cm; maximum diameter: 3.3 cm.
Collected by Funing Cultural Relics Protection Center.

It is in the shape of irregular cylindrical. Tapering at both ends, and gradually thick toward the middle. The cuspidate ends show damage trace from use. It was collected from Majia Valley, Funing District.

8 Copper Knife with Ring Head and Warped Tail

Period Shang Dynasty (1600 — 1046 BCE)
Dimensions length: 26.7 cm; width: 4 cm; ring diameter: 3.5 cm.
Collected by Qinglong Manchu Autonomous County Cultural Relics Protection Institute.

It has an oval ring top, and a long blade with a short handle. There is a small tip between the handle and the blade. The blade is thin with thick and bent ridges, and the tip of the knife is slightly warped.

9 A Pair of Wooden Barrels

Period Shang Dynasty (1600 — 1046 BCE)
Dimensions height: 18 cm; mouth diameter: ca. 22 cm;
height: 21.5 cm; mouth diameter: ca. 18 cm.
Collected by Lulong Cultural Relics Protection and Management Institute.

These two utensils are in irregular wooden barrel-shaped, with holes chiseled on both sides for tying. They were unearthed in Lihuangling, Lulong District.

10 Wooden Mallet

Period Shang Dynasty (1600 — 1046 BCE)
Dimensions length: 12.7 cm; width: 6.6cm.
Collected by Lulong Cultural Relics Protection and Management Institute.

This wooden utensil is in irregular mallet-shaped, with a rectangular hole chiseled in the middle for fixing the handle. It was unearthed in Lihuangling, Lulong District.

11 High Neck Pottery Jar with Four Handles (Pan)

Period Shang Dynasty (1600 — 1046 BCE)
Dimensions height: 27 cm; mouth diameter: 13.5 cm; base diameter: 11 cm.
Collected by Lulong Cultural Relics Protection and Management Institute.

This jar is made of gray pottery mixed with sand. It has a round mouth, a flared rim, a high neck, a slipping shoulders, bulging belly, and a flat bottom. It is applied with four columnar handles (Pan) around the abdomen. It was unearthed in Lihuangling, Lulong District.

12 Pottery Pot (Li)

Period Shang and Zhou Dynasty (1600 — 256 BCE)
Dimensions height: 17.6 cm; mouth diameter: 14 cm; abdominal diameter: 13.6 cm.
Collected by Lulong Cultural Relics Protection and Management Institute.

It is made of gray pottery and mixed with sand. It has a round mouth, a flared rim, a tied neck, a slightly bulging belly, and three feet in breast shape.

13 Tripod Copper Vessel (Yan)

Period Western Zhou Dynasty (1046 — 771 BCE)
Dimensions height: 12 cm; mouth diameter: 13 cm; abdominal diameter: 14.2 cm.
Collected by Qinhuangdao Cultural Relics Protection Center.

It is composed of two parts, the upper steamer (Zeng) and the lower tripod (li), which is plain in color and can be separated. The steamer (Zeng) has a large opening mouth, folding edge, inclined shoulders, inclined belly, and a round foot, which can be inserted into the tripod (li). The bottom is a strip grate hole, and both sides of the shoulders are applied with Pan dragon head-shaped rings as column handles. Tripod (Li) has a straight mouth, a straight short neck, a bag-shaped belly, three hoof-shaped feet, and one ring handle on each side of the shoulders.

14 Bronze Urn-shaped Vessel (Lei) with Coiling Snake Patterns

Period Spring and Autumn Period (770 — 476 BCE)
Dimensions height: 8 cm; abdominal diameter: 20.5 cm.
Collected by Qinhuangdao Cultural Relics Protection Center.

This jar is in the shape of an urn, with a cover, and the whole body is decorated with Coiling Snake patterns. It has a wide mouth, a flat-folding edge, a tied neck oblique shoulders, a belly folded, and a flat bottom. The cap is arched in a helmet shape, with a short handle of a round button in the center, and four small animal head buttons with equal distance are arranged along the mouth of the flat fold rim, for matching with the urn-shaped vessel (Lei).

15 Bronze Hatchet

Period Spring and Autumn Period (770 — 476 BCE)
Dimensions length: 18 cm; thickness: 2.6 cm; width: 3 cm.
Collected by Shanhaiguan Cultural Relics Protection and Management Institute.

It is cast into a whole by the Yuan (i.e., blade), Qiong (i.e., hole for handle)and axe, and a ridge is formed on both two sides. The Yuan part is like a dagger, and the upper and lower blades gradually become sharp like a crane's beak. The Qiong part is oval-shaped and thicker than the body, which is used to install the handle. The axe part is shorter than Yuan part and looks like an axe. It plays a balancing role and increases the chopping function of the peck. The Hatchet is a cold weapon used by cavalry, which can be used to peck, push, hook, and chop. It can be used to swipe, peck, and chop, feels chilling and pressing.

16 Straight Bronze Dagger-axe (Ge)

Period Warring States Period (475 — 221 BCE)
Dimensions length of Yuan: 12.5 cm; length of Nei: 7cm; length of Lan: 11.3 cm.
Collected by Qinglong Manchu Autonomous County Cultural Relics Protection Institute.

A ridge is formed between the upper flat and lower arcs of the double blades of Yuan, and a single Hu is even with the tail. There are three rectangles piercing the Lan part, and a rectangle piercing the middle straight inside of straight Nei. It is a long weapon that can be used for hooking, pecking, and stabbing.

17 Gold and Silver Inlaid Turquoise Copper Band Hook

Period Warring States Period (475 — 221 BCE)
Dimensions length: 21.4 cm; width: 2.6 cm.
Collected by the Great Wall Museum in Shanhaiguan.

The band hook is in the shape of an arced lute. From the head of the hook to the tail, it gradually changes from narrow to wide. The whole surface is decorated with gold and silver prismatic geometric patterns and round dots, which are inlaid with irregular turquoise in between. There are oval buttons on the back.

18 Pottery Food Container with Ball-shaped Belly

Period Warring States Period (475 — 221 BCE)
Dimensions height: 27 cm; mouth diameter: 5.5 cm; height of lid: 2.5 cm; diameter of round foot: 11.8 cm.
Collected by Funing Cultural Relics Protection Center.

It is made of mud mixed with sand and gray pottery. It has a cover and a paired mouth with one big and the other small. The lid is mushroom-shaped. The container has a straight neck, plump shoulders, a round belly, and a long handle that stretches down to form a trumpet-shaped high round foot. It was unearthed in Bingge Village, Funing District.

19 Clay Grey Pottery Food Container (Dou)

Period Warring States Period (475 — 221 BCE)
Dimensions height: 24.4 cm; mouth diameter: 16 cm; foot diameter: 13.3 cm.
Collected by Lulong Cultural Relics Protection and Management Institute.

It is made of mud mixed with sand and gray pottery. It has a paired mouth with one big and the other small, flat shoulders, and an arc-shaped belly. The abdomen is folded down to the bottom, the long straight handle is decorated with rotary profiling patterns, the bottom is turned outward with a flat foot.

20 Covered Pottery Food Container

Period Warring States Period (475 — 221 BCE)
Dimensions height: 27.5 cm; height of lid: 6.8 cm; mouth diameter: 15.2 cm; diameter of round foot: 12.8 cm.
Collected by Funing Cultural Relics Protection Center.

It is a terra brown clay pottery, with a cover and a paired mouth with one big and the other small. The cover is in the shape of a shallow reversed plate, with a round button on the top. The food container is in the shape of a shallow bowl. The handle is long and thin, and it turns downward and outward to form a trumpet-shaped high round foot. It was unearthed in Bingge Village, Funing District.

21 Pottery Basin (Jian)

Period Qin Dynasty (221 — 206 BCE)
Dimensions height: 64.8 cm; exterior mouth diameter: 120.6 cm; abdominal diameter: 120.1 cm.
Collected by Qinhuangdao Cultural Relics Protection Center.

It is a gray pottery made of clay. It has a straight mouth, a square lip turned outward, a straight body but slightly arced, and a flat bottom slightly concave. The abdomen has three ring handles (Pan). The lip is decorated with grid patterns and string patterns, the abdomen is designed with two reinforcing bands, and the upper part is decorated with diamond patterns. The words "JianYang" are engraved on the exterior rim. It was unearthed in the temporary imperial palace site of the Beidaihe Qin Dynasty Palace Ruins.

22 Eaves Tile with Kui-dragon Pattern

Period Qin Dynasty (221 — 206 BCE)
Dimensions diameter of the tile side: 52 cm; height: 37 cm; thickness: 2.5 cm.
Collected by Qinhuangdao Cultural Relics Protection Center.

It is a gray pottery made of clay. The tile side is semicircular, the side wheel is convex, and the front is decorated with two symmetrical Kui-dragon patterns in high relief. The tile top surface is connected with imbrex. It was unearthed in the temporary imperial palace site of the Beidaihe Qin Dynasty Palace Ruins.

23 Round Eaves Tile with Scallop on Cirrus Cloud Pattern

Period Qin Dynasty (221 — 206 BCE)
Dimensions diameter of the tile side: 42 cm; thickness: 2.5 cm; residual length of imbrex: 21.6 cm.
Collected by Qinhuangdao Cultural Relics Protection Center.

It is a gray pottery made of clay. The tile side is round, with a wide outline. There is a prominent round drum nail in its center. The double line boundary separates the tile into four areas. Each area is decorated with two spiral cloud patterns, which are symmetrically distributed. A shell pattern is pasted in the middle, which has highly distinctive and regional characteristics. It was unearthed in the temporary imperial palace site of Beidaihe Qin Dynasty Palace Ruins.

24 Gilded Copper Garlic-shaped Pot

Period Han Dynasty (206 BCE — 220 CE)
Dimensions height: 36.5 cm; mouth diameter: 3 cm; abdominal diameter: 22.5 cm; foot diameter: 12.5 cm.
Collected by Qinhuangdao Cultural Relics Protection Center.

The whole body is gilded, with a short and a straight small round mouth. The mouth is in the shape of an inverted garlic, with a long and thin neck, slipping shoulders, a slightly flat round belly, and a slightly flared round foot.

25 Copper Pot

Period Han Dynasty (206 BCE — 220 CE)
Dimensions height: 37 cm; mouth diameter: 16 cm; foot diameter: 18.8 cm.
Collected by Qinhuangdao Cultural Relics Protection Center.

It is straight with a slightly open mouth, tied neck, slopping shoulders, round and bulging belly, and slightly flared foot. The mouth edge, shoulders, abdomen, and lower abdomen are applied with a round of plain raised wide stripes, and the upper abdomen is applied with animal head appliques and ring handles on both sides.

26 Copper Square Pot (Fang)

Period Han Dynasty (206 BCE — 220 CE)
Dimensions height: 37.5 cm; length of mouth: 11 cm; length of base: 13 cm.
Collected by Qinhuangdao Cultural Relics Protection Center.

It has a straight mouth, square lips, an arc neck, slip shoulders, a quadrilateral tympanic abdomen, and a high square foot slightly outward curling. On both sides of the upper abdomen are applied with animal head appliques holding rings. The mouth edge is applied with a loop of convex wide band.

27 Ring-Handled Copper Ewer (You) with Hoof-shaped Feet

Period Han Dynasty (206 BCE — 220 CE)
Dimensions height: 17.5 cm; mouth diameter: 8.1 cm; abdominal diameter: 15.2 cm.

Collected by the Great Wall Museum in Shanhaiguan.

The plain ewer (You) is divided into upper and lower parts. The cover is cup-shaped, which can be used independently. It has a flared mouth, deep abdomen, and there are three annular buttons on it. The lower part is a spherical abdomen. It has a restricted mouth, a round belly. There are ring ears on both sides of the shoulder. The bottom is connected with three hoof-shaped feet.

28 Copper Gourd-shaped Ladle (Yi)

Period Han dynasty (206 BCE — 220 CE)
Dimensions height: 11.8 cm; mouth diameter: 30.5 cm.
Collected by Funing Cultural Relics Protection Center.

It has a flared mouth, an oblique edge, a deep belly, a flat bottom, with false round foot. An arc-shaped handle is extended from the mouth edge on one side, and the top of a handle is pendulous. Two string lines are decorated along the mouth. The upper abdomen is decorated with two string patterns. It is a kind of utensil for ladling water in ancient China.

29 Copper Wine-warming Burner with Four Divine Beasts

Period Han Dynasty (206 BCE — 220 CE)
Dimensions height: 11.5 cm; width:9.2 cm; length: 14 cm.
Collected by Qinhuangdao Cultural Relics Protection Center.

The whole utensil is composed of an ear cup, carbon furnace, and bearing plate. The ear cup has an oval-shaped mouth, an inclined body, a flat bottom, and folding edge-shaped ears on both sides. The upper part of the carbon furnace body is oval, and the four carved figures of Vermilion Bird, Black Tortoise, Azure Dragon, and White Tiger are on the four sides. Two small support pillars are erected along the two sides of the mouth. The lower part is rectangular, one side has a zigzag long handle, and the furnace bottom has a strip grate. Under the furnace, there are four beast faces humanoid feet with their hands behind their backs to hold the furnace bodies. The bearing plate is rectangular, which is upturned all around. It has an open mouth, trimmed edges with a flat bottom.

30 Copper Sword

Period Han Dynasty (206 BCE — 220 CE)
Dimensions length: 47.7 cm; width: 4.3 cm; length of sword body: 39 cm; length of sword handle: 8.7 cm.
Collected by Qinhuangdao Cultural Relics Protection Center.

The front end of the sword body is slightly narrow, the middle ridge of the sword should be at a level distance from the two edges til the sharp top. The sword is thinner to double edges and sharp of the edges. The handle is round and the handle has two hoops. The head is flat and the sword guard is slightly convex.

31 Double Hu Dagger-axe (Ge)

Period Han Dynasty (206 BCE — 220 CE)
Dimensions length of Yuan: 18.3 cm; length of Lan: 16.3 cm.
Collected by Qinglong Manchu Autonomous County Cultural Relics Protection Institute.

This dagger-axe has a long Yuan and a short Hu. A ridge is formed between the double blades of Yuan. Double Hu are with slipping tails. A thickened convex ridge is formed between the two Hu parts. There are two rectangular perforations on both sides of the convex ridge on the Lan part, and the internal part is missing. It is a long weapon that can be used for hooking, pecking, and stabbing.

32 Copper Gilded Seal of General Weilie

Period Han Dynasty (206 BCE — 220 CE)
Dimensions height: 2.3 cm; weight: 53.1 g; seal surface: 2.3 cm×2.3 cm.
Collected by Qinglong Manchu Autonomous County Cultural Relics Protection Institute.

The seal is made of gilded copper. It has a standing animal button. Five Seal Script characters "Seal of General Weilie" are inscribed in two columns on the seal surface.

33 Copper Kettle with Animal Head Appliques Holding Rings

Period Eastern Han Dynasty (25 — 220 CE)
Dimensions height: 46.8 cm; mouth diameter: 16.5 cm; largest abdominal diameter: 34 cm; height of round foot: 8.7 cm.
Collected by Funing Cultural Relics Protection Center.

It has a straight mouth, a flat lip, a long neck but slightly bundled, a round plump belly, an octagonal high round foot. The shoulders are applied with a pair of animal head appliques holding ring handles (i.e., ears), and the upper, middle, and lower abdomen are decorated with a group of three convex string ribbons. The outer mouth edge is applied around with a broad belt. It was unearthed in Anzhuang Village, Funing District.

34 Copper Food Vessel (Gui) with Animal Head Appliques Holding Rings

Period Eastern Han Dynasty (25 — 220 CE)
Dimensions height: 15 cm; mouth diameter: 25.6 cm; round foot diameter: 16.8 cm.
Collected by Funing Cultural Relics Protection Center.

It has an open mouth, a round lip, a deep belly but slightly plump, a flat bottom, high round foot outwards. The middle part of the abdomen is applied with two loops of convex string patterns, and iron ring handles (i.e., ears) of animal head applique are applied under the string patterns. The foot is decorated with a loop of convex string pattern. It was unearthed in Anzhuang Village, Funing District.

35 Copper Washbasin with Treasure Tripod (Ding) and Mountain and River Pattern

Period Eastern Han Dynasty (25 — 220 CE)
Dimensions height: 7.5 cm; mouth diameter: 33 cm; foot diameter: 28 cm.
Collected by Funing Cultural Relics Protection Center.

It has a restricted mouth, which has a wide rim inclined outward. The abdomen is shallow and straight, connected with a flat curved bottom and a fake round foot. Animal head appliques are applied on each two sides of the abdomen, and the inner bottom is slightly concave. It is decorated with huge treasure tripod patterns within string patterns, supplemented by mountain and river patterns. It was unearthed in Anzhuang Village, Funing District.

36 Copper Washbasin with Double Fish Pattern and Dragon-phoenix Pattern

Period Eastern Han Dynasty (25 — 220 CE)
Dimensions height: 6.1 cm; mouth diameter: 39.5 cm; foot diameter: 32 cm.
Collected by Funing Cultural Relics Protection Center.

It has an open mouth, a flat and folded outward rim, with oblique and straight abdominal body, a flat bottom, and a short round foot. The lower two sides of the folding edge are respectively applied with a downward-facing animal head appliques handles. The inner bottom is decorated with diamond patterns, with a fish on each opposite corner of the diamond pattern and a phoenix on the interior. The exterior bottom is decorated with two loops of convex string patterns, and the center of the inner loop is decorated with three convex ridge patterns. Two dragons and two phoenixes are carved symmetrically along the mouth rim. It was unearthed in Anzhuang Village, Funing District.

37 Copper Washbasin with Phoenix Climbing Tripod Pattern

Period Eastern Han Dynasty (25 — 220 CE)
Dimensions height: 9.5 cm; mouth diameter: 38.2 cm.
Collected by Funing Cultural Relics Protection Center.

It has a slightly restricted mouth, a wide inclined outward rim, a straight shallow abdomen, a flat bottom, and a short round foot.

Animal head appliques are applied on each two sides. The concave round surface at the bottom of the inner part is decorated with a phoenix spreading its wings and standing on the Treasure Tripod (Ding) within string pattern. Three loops of concave string patterns on the exterior edge. It was unearthed in Anzhuang Village, Funing District.

38 Copper Tripod (Ding) of Good Luck

Period Eastern Han Dynasty (25 — 220 CE)
Dimensions height: 19.5 cm; mouth diameter: 15.3 cm; abdominal diameter: 20 cm.
Collected by Funing Cultural Relics Protection Center.

It has an introverted mouth, a bulging belly, a round bottom, three hoof-shaped feet which are slightly outside. On both sides of the upper abdomen, there are large circular handles (i.e., ears) decorated near the edges, and higher than the edge. The upper middle part of the abdomen is applied with a wide flat ridge. One foot is engraved with the inscription: "Good luck on everything." It was unearthed in Anzhuang Village, Funing District.

39 Copper Seal of Minister of War in Ancient China

Period Eastern Han Dynasty (25 — 220 CE)
Dimensions height: 1.65 cm; length: 2.2 cm; thickness: 0.7 cm.
Collected by Funing Cultural Relics Protection Center.

It has a bridge-shaped button on the back. The Seal Script of "Seal of minister of war" (Jun Si Ma Seal) is engraved in intaglio. The font is neat, vigorous, and thick. The Seal Script of "Fan" is engraved on one side.

40 Iron Cauldron (Fu) with Triple Flat Feet

Period Liao and Jin Dynasty (907 — 1234 CE)
Dimensions height: 30 cm; mouth diameter: 25 cm.
Collected by Qinglong Manchu Autonomous County Cultural Relics Protection Institute.

It has a round lip, an open mouth, and a folded outward edge. The upper edge is applied with two standing circular handles, with a tied neck, and a round plump belly, curved bottom, and three tall flat feet are decorated. It is a utensil for cooking. It was collected from Dashizigou Village, Qinglong Manchu Autonomous County.

41 Six-handled (Pan) Iron Cauldron (Fu)

Period Liao and Jin Dynasty (907 — 1234 CE)
Dimensions height: 43 cm; mouth diameter: 65 cm.
Collected by Funing Cultural Relics Protection Center.

It has a straight mouth with square rim, a short straight neck, a bulging belly, and an arc-shaped bottom. The shoulders are applied with multiple convex strings, and the abdomen is decorated with six flat and wide handles (Pan). The bottom has a cast navel.

42 Six-handled (Pan) Iron Cauldron (Fu)

Period Liao and Jin Dynasty (907 — 1234 CE)
Dimensions height: 54 cm; mouth diameter: 68 cm; wall thickness: 3 cm.
Collected by Qinglong Manchu Autonomous County Cultural Relics Protection Institute.

It has an open mouth, a folded inward and flat along the lip, a bulging abdomen, and a round bottom. There are many spiral patterns along the exterior surface. Six flat and wide handles (Pan) are cast around the upper abdomen. It is used as a utensil for cooking, commonly known as "field cauldron". It was collected from Jiliyu Village, Qinglong Manchu Autonomous County.

43 Iron Tripod Cauldron with Two Handles

Period Liao and Jin Dynasty (907 — 1234 CE)

Dimensions height: 24 cm; mouth diameter: 40.2 cm; thickness: 1.7 cm; height of foot: 13.8 cm.
Collected by Qinglong Manchu Autonomous County Cultural Relics Protection Institute.

It has an open mouth, a square lip turned outward, an oblique body, a shallow abdomen, and a flat bottom. The mouth is decorated with circular handles, and the bottom is presents with tile-shaped tripods. It is a utensil for cooking. It was unearthed in Xiaoshipan Village, Qinglong Manchu Autonomous County.

44 Iron Strainer

Period Liao and Jin Dynasty (907 — 1234 CE)
Dimensions mouth diameter of strainer: 17 cm; length of handle: 20 cm.
Collected by Qinglong Manchu Autonomous County Cultural Relics Protection Institute.

The strainer is covered with fine holes for water leakage. Long handle with a hole (Qiong) on the end. It is a utensil for cooking. It was unearthed in Xiaoshipan Village, Qinglong Manchu Autonomous County.

45 Iron Plowshare

Period Liao and Jin Dynasty (907 — 1234 CE)
Dimensions length: 21 cm; width: 21 cm.
Collected by Qinglong Manchu Autonomous County Cultural Relics Protection Institute.

The tool is isosceles triangle shape, the front is arched, and the back is straight. The bottom end forms a crescent-shaped hole. A small triangle perforation is made on the arch ridge. It is a production tool for ploughing. It was unearthed in Shuangshanzi Town, Qinglong Manchu Autonomous County.

46 Iron Horse Pedal

Period Liao and Jin Dynasty (907 — 1234 CE)
Dimensions height: 20 cm; length of pedal: 17.5 cm.
Collected by Qinglong Manchu Autonomous County Cultural Relics Protection Institute.

It is a trapezoid shape, with an oval hole on the top, and a flat pedal on the bottom. Both sides are cylindrical beams. It was unearthed in Xiaoshipan Village, Qinglong Manchu Autonomous County.

47 Iron Ring Bell

Period Liao and Jin Dynasty (907 — 1234 CE)
Dimensions height: 14.7 cm; mouth diameter of the ring bell: 10.7 cm.
Collected by Qinglong Manchu Autonomous County Cultural Relics Protection Institute.

It is columnar and hollow. It has a flat top, and is applied with a half ring for tying up. It was unearthed in Xiaoshipan Village, Qinglong Manchu Autonomous County.

48 Iron Ladle

Period Liao and Jin Dynasty (907 — 1234 CE)
Dimensions height: 9.5 cm; mouth diameter: 21 cm; spout height: 5.5 cm, spout length: 6.5 cm, spout width: 8 cm.
Collected by Qinglong Manchu Autonomous County Cultural Relics Protection Institute.

It is round, with a bent waist and an inclined edge. It has an open mouth and deep ladle. There is a rectangular spout (Liu) on the side of the ladle. The waist of both exterior sides of this ladle is cast with a flat handle (Pan). It was collected from Dahuihe Village, Qinglong Manchu Autonomous County.

49 Copper Round Hollow Ornaments with Encircling Dragons

Period Liao and Jin Dynasty (907 — 1234 CE)
Dimensions diameter of circle: 6.1 cm; thickness: 0.35 cm; length of Chuan: 1.95 cm.
Collected by Lulong Cultural Relics Protection and Management Institute.

The outer edge of the circle is applied with five equally divided rectangle handles, named Chuan, and the inner circle is carved with two encircling dragon patterns with intersecting heads and tails. It is an ornament for chariots and horses.

50 Copper Tripod Cauldron(Fu)

Period Liao and Jin Dynasty (907 — 1234 CE)
Dimensions height: 33 cm; diameter: 25 cm; foot height: 15 cm.
Collected by Qinglong Manchu Autonomous County Cultural Relics Protection Institute.

The cauldron has a straight mouth with a cover. It has a straight belly and a slightly bulging, a flat bottom, and slightly arced, three high feet. The middle part of the abdomen is applied with a loop of the flat broad ridge, which is used as handle (Pan). There are many fine raised string patterns between the handle (Pan) and mouth. The high feet are semi-cylindrical, flat inside, drum outside, and are applied with many irregular ridges. The cover is in the shape of a hat, with a hat-shaped button on the top. It was collected from Muma Village, Qinglong Manchu Autonomous County.

51 Copper Iron

Period Liao and Jin Dynasty (907 — 1234 CE)
Dimensions height: 8 cm; mouth diameter: 20 cm; base diameter: 16 cm.
Collected by Qinglong Manchu Autonomous County Cultural Relics Protection Institute.

The iron is round, with a short upturned handle cast on the side. It has an open mouth, a square lip turned outward, a shallow arc-shaped belly, and a flat bottom but slightly bulging. A corolla-shaped fender is cast between the handle and the bucket edge.

52 Copper Iron

Period Jin Dynasty (1115 — 1234 CE)
Dimensions height: 9.2 cm; mouth diameter: 20 cm; base diameter: 16 cm.
Collected by Changli Cultural Relics Research and Protection Institute.

The iron is in a round shape, with a long upturned handle cast on the side. It has an open mouth, a square lip turned outward, a straight abdomen, and a flat bottom but slightly bulging. Two loops of string pattern on the interior wall decoration. A convex string pattern is decorated along the lower edge of the outer wall. A fender is cast at the junction of the handle and the bucket edge, with the raised cloud patterns on the inner side of the bucket.

53 Copper Iron

Period Liao and Jin Dynasty (907 — 1234 CE)
Dimensions height: 5.7 cm; mouth diameter: 18 cm; base diameter: 15.5 cm.
Collected by Qinglong Manchu Autonomous County Cultural Relics Protection Institute.

This iron is round in shape and has a short upturned hollow handle cast on the side. It has a wide mouth and square lips, a wide sloping edge, a straight abdomen, and a flat bottom. A fender is formed between the handle and a mouth rim. The inner side of the lattice is decorated with raised interlocking branches. The inner bottom of the bucket is inscribed with a Baoxiang flower pattern.

54 Copper Seal

Period Liao and Jin Dynasty (907 — 1234 CE)
Dimensions height: 3 cm; diameter of seal surface: 3.1 cm.

Collected by Qinglong Manchu Autonomous County Cultural Relics Protection Institute.

It is a lion-shaped button and a round seal surface. Embossed symbols with patterns are imprinted on the seal surface.

55 Copper Seal of Vice Marching Control

Period Jin Dynasty (1115 — 1234 CE)
Dimensions height: 5.8 cm; seal surface: 5.4 cm×5.4 cm.
Collected by Qinglong Manchu Autonomous County Cultural Relics Protection Institute.

It has a rectangular column button, with a cross mark engraved on the top. The seal surface is square, and the frame is engraved with six characters in two and three columns of the Nine Fold Seal Script "Seal of Vice marching control". This is the seal of a senior military general in the Jin Dynasty. It was unearthed in Dahuihe Village, Qinglong Manchu Autonomous County.

56 Copper Seal of Vice Marching Control

Period Jin Dynasty (1115 — 1234 CE)
Dimensions height: 5.5 cm; seal surface: 6.6 cm× 6.6 cm; weight: 120 g.
Collected by Qinglong Manchu Autonomous County Cultural Relics Protection Institute.

It is in the shape of a rectangular column button with a "+" mark on the top. The seal surface is square, and six Nine Fold Seal Script characters "Vice marching control" have been embossed on the surface with three lines. This is the seal of a senior military general in the Jin Dynasty. It was unearthed in Ganshugou Village, Qinglong Manchu Autonomous County.

57 Copper Sliding Weight (Quan) with Xijing and Huangfu

Period Liao and Jin Dynasty (907 — 1234 CE)
Dimensions height: 9 cm; foot diameter: 4.5 cm; weight: 400 g.
Collected by Qinglong Manchu Autonomous County Cultural Relics Protection Institute.

It is cast by using Hefan technique. It consists of three parts: button, body, and bottom. The flat button is inverted trapezoid with a perforation. The body has plump shoulders, bulging abdomen gradually narrows. The connection between the abdomen and the bottom forms a two-layer inverted trapezoid shape. The bottom is a three-level stepped tower. The four characters "Xijing" and "Huangfu" are respectively cast on the front and back of this sliding weight's abdomen in intaglio Regular Script.

58 Copper Sliding Weight (Quan) with Nanjing and Huangfu

Period Liao and Jin Dynasty (907 — 1234 CE)
Dimensions height: 8 cm; width:3.8 cm; weight: 220 g.
Collected by Qinglong Manchu Autonomous County Cultural Relics Protection Institute.

It is cast by using Hefan technique in the shape of a flat hexagonal prism. It consists of three parts: button, body, and bottom. The button is flat and nearly in square-shaped with a perforation in the middle. The body has flat shoulders and a straight belly, narrow on the top and wide on the bottom. The connection between the abdomen and the bottom with a ridge, and the bottom is a flat hexagon seat. The four characters "Nanjing" and "Huangfu" are respectively cast on the front and back of this sliding weight's abdomen in intaglio Regular Script.

59 Elephant Bone Counting Rod

Period Liao and Jin Dynasty (907 — 1234 CE)
Dimensions length: 12 cm; width: 0.18 cm; thickness: 0.19 cm.
Collected by Qinglong Manchu Autonomous County Cultural Relics Protection Institute.

They are made of bones, and shaped by small square sticks, in roughly the same length and thickness. In ancient times, it was used for counting operations. It was unearthed in Zhangzhangzi Village, Qinglong Manchu Autonomous County.

60 Six-handled (Pan) Copper Cauldron (Fu)

Period Yuan Dynasty (1206 — 1368 CE)
Dimensions height: 7 cm; mouth diameter: 28.8 cm.
Collected by Changli Cultural Relics Research and Protection Institute.

It has an open mouth, inner folding flat rim, deep abdomen, arc-shaped body, round bottom with a round navel. There are six flat handles attached to the upper abdomen. There is a raised casting line between the handles (Pan).

61 Jingyun Copper Blunderbuss

Period Fourth Year of Longqing, Ming Dynasty (1570 CE)
Dimensions length of breech: 64 cm; inner mouth diameter: 2 cm; length of loading: 15.1 cm; largest diameter: 5 cm.
Collected by Funing Cultural Relics Protection Center.

This copper blunderbuss is composed of two parts: breech blunderbuss and load, which has a similar function to the Western-style Franks machine. The mother blunderbuss is divided into three parts: the front chamber, the loading chamber (rear chamber), and the tail hole (Qiong). The front chamber is a long tube, which is used to launch projectiles. The loading chamber (rear chamber) is located at the rear of the front blunderbuss. The top of pipe wall is trimmed with a length of 11.8 cm and a width of 4 cm, forming a back chamber for filling the bullet. The two side walls at the tail end of the rear chamber are respectively provided with a 4.6 cm long and 1 cm wide rectangular plate hole for locking the bullet. The tail hole (Qiong) is located at the rear end of the blunderbuss. It is hollow, with an internal diameter of 3 cm. The mouth is large and the inside is small. It is used to install the handgrip. There is a 2 cm wide transverse tie on the left side of the tail hole (Qiong). The whole blunderbuss body is cast with seven raised hoops. On the wall of the mother blunderbuss, the inscription "Sheng time-honored No. 1148, craftsmen from Jingyun in the fourth year of Longqing, Xu Rong, and Hao Ying" is inscribed in black. There are multiple loads, consisting of an entrance of loads, a gunpower chamber, and a tail tap, all of which have the same shape and structure. The short body has a bulging belly, and the tail tap is semicircular, used to lock the gun barrel. Three raised hoops are cast throughout the body, with two small lifting ears cast on the body and ignition holes at the tail. Inscriptions such as "Sheng time-honored No.2682" are engraved on the walls of loading parts. All the characters are "Sheng" time-honored. This group of gun chamber and loads, with exquisite craftsmanship. It has particularly precious value for studying the history of weapons. It was unearthed in Chengziyu Village, Funing District.

62 Stone Cannon

Period Ming Dynasty (1368 — 1644 CE)
Dimensions length: 94 cm; exterior diameter: 50 cm; inner mouth diameter: 15 cm.
Collected by Funing Cultural Relics Protection Center.

It is columnar and made of sandstone. A rectangular stone groove with a shallow front and deep back is chiseled at the rear of the cannon body, and the pilot hole is located at the lower part of the front end of the stone groove and connected with the cannon chamber. A hole for tying is chiseled at the upper end of the cannon tail.

63 Stone Cannon

Period Ming Dynasty (1368 — 1644 CE)
Dimensions length: 97.8 cm; exterior diameter: 44.5 cm.
Collected by the Great Wall Museum in Shanhaiguan.

The stone cannon is carved from white sandstone, and its shape is irregularly cylindrical. The diameters of the muzzle and bottom chamber are both 11.5 cm, the depth of the chamber is 52 cm, and the maximum diameter of the middle part of the chamber is 17.2 cm. The rear of the cannon body is chiseled with a rectangular stone groove with a shallow front and deep back, and the ignition hole is located at the lower part of the front end of the stone groove and connected with the cannon chamber. A series of holes are chiseled at the upper end of the cannon tail.

64 Copper Anbian Divine Cannon

Period Third Year of Tianqi, Ming Dynasty (1623 CE)
Dimensions length: 49.5 cm; exterior mouth diameter: 12.2 cm; interior mouth diameter: 4.3 cm; weight: 38.75 kg.
Collected by the Great Wall Museum in Shanhaiguan.

This cannon consists of three parts: cannon body, chamber, and tail. The cannon body is a cylinder, cast with 4 raised hoops. The chamber is lantern-shaped, with a maximum diameter of 14.3 cm. The upper part is cast with a raised rectangular fire door. The middle part is opened with an ignition hole with a diameter of 0.4 cm. The ignition hole is 39 cm away from the muzzle. Between the single hoop cast at the end of the cannon and the hoop of the gunpowder chamber, ten inscriptions five columns of Regular Script "Tianqi Period/ Guihai Year/ Made in /Anbian / Divine Cannon" are engraved from right to left.

65 Three Hoop Flat Tail Iron Cannon

Period Ming Dynasty (1368 — 1644 CE)
Dimensions length: 89.5 cm; exterior diameter: 17 cm; interior diameter: 8 cm; tail diameter: 21 cm.
Collected by Lulong Cultural Relics Protection and Management Institute.

This cannon is divided into three parts: barrel, chamber, and tail. The muzzle has thickened lips, the exterior is cast with three raised hoops, the chamber and the tail are in waist shape. This cannon has a flat tail, and a fuse hole equipped on the waist.

66 Iron Cannon of "The Sixteenth Year of Chongzhen Period"

Period Sixteenth Year of Chongzhen, Ming Dynasty (1643 CE)
Dimensions length: 281.2 cm; exterior mouth diameter: 33.7 cm; interior mouth diameter: 10.5 cm.
Collected by the Great Wall Museum in Shanhaiguan.

It is cast twice, with a thick front and a thin back. This iron cannon has a unique shape. The near middle part is cast with columnar trunnions. The distance from the muzzle to the trunnion is 140 cm. Forge wrought iron gun tube first, then use pig iron to thicken and wrap the gun tube, and cast four bulge wide band hoops with different widths. The maximum diameter is 43.5 cm. The smallest diameter of the trunnion is 28 cm, and the diameter of the cannon tail is from thin to thick. The largest diameter of the cannon tail is 37.5cm. Two round hoops with 92 characters are cast between them. The firing hole is 230 cm from the muzzle and 0.6 cm in diameter. The tail is converged layer by layer from the tail hoop, like a bamboo hat, and a tail bead is cast behind.

67 Pottery Barrel for Trapping Horse

Period Ming Dynasty (1368 — 1644 CE)
Dimensions height: 23.5 cm; exterior diameter: 18 cm.
Collected by Lulong Cultural Relics Protection and Management Institute.

It is made of clay gray pottery as a weapon, which is used to trap horses. It is cylindrical in shape, and buried about feet deep under ground.The iron caltrops are embedded, and it is covered with a void roof. When the enemy enters, the horse foot shall be trapped by this barrel. The iron caltrops will prick the hoof and ankle by itself. It was unearthed in the east of Liujiakou Pass, Liujiaying Village, Lulong District.

68 Two Dragons Play with a Pearl Pattern Stone Medicine Cup

Period Ming Dynasty (1368 — 1644 CE)
Dimensions height: 10.5 cm; mouth diameter: 16.5 cm; thickness: 2.2 cm.
Collected by Qinglong Manchu Autonomous County Cultural Relics Protection Institute.

It is in the shape of a round pier, with a flat edge and straight mouth, a thick body, a deep belly, and an arc-shaped bottom. There is a spout on the outside. The whole body is decorated with high relief "Two Dragons Play with a Pearl". It is a utensil for mashing and stirring.

69 The Great Wall Brick “Made by Yanhe Road in the Twelfth Year of Wanli”

Period Ming Dynasty (1584 CE)
Dimensions length: 37.6 cm; width: 18 cm; thickness: 9.5 cm.
Collected by the Great Wall Museum in Shanhaiguan.

The brick of the Great Wall is rectangular, with a rectangular frame and characters stenciled on the side, and nine characters “Made by Yanhe Road in the twelfth year of Wanli” are stenciled vertically inside the frame in Regular Script. This is one of more than ten kinds of Great Wall year title bricks of the Ming Dynasty.

70 Iron Dovetail Tenon

Period Ming Dynasty (1368 — 1644 CE)
Dimensions length: 20 cm; widest width: 11 cm; height: 6 cm.
Collected by the Great Wall Museum in Shanhaiguan.

The shape is wide on both sides and narrow in the middle, such as the swallow tail. It is a kind of connecting latch for linking the building components.

71 Copper Fire-pan with Three Hoof-shaped Feet

Period Ming Dynasty (1368 — 1644 CE)
Dimensions height:17 cm; mouth diameter: 48 cm; base diameter: 34 cm.
Collected by Changli Cultural Relics Research and Protection Institute.

It has a straight mouth, a flat-folding edge, slightly up warping along the edge, a shallow abdomen, and a straight body, and a flat bottom. It is decorated with the animal’s face as three hoof-shaped feet. The animal’s face is with stared eyes and teeth, and the hoof is strong and hollow inside.

72 Gild-copper of Zhangcang Reclining Buddha

Period Ming Dynasty (1368 — 1644 CE)
Dimensions length: 12 cm; width: 5.8 cm; height: 4 cm; weight: 650 g.
Collected by Changli Cultural Relics Research and Protection Institute.

This statue is reclining on the right side with a square flower pillow under the head. The stature’s hair is fashioned as a topknot, shaped in a spiral shell with jewels on the head, a high nose and big ears, curved eyebrows and kind eyes, and a plump cheek, looks perfectly calm. The right hand is resting on the pillow under the head, and the left hand is resting on the waist, with a string of black rosary beads in hand, passed away peacefully on the rectangular bed. The upper body is exposed, the lower body is covered with the monk quilt with bare feet. The quilt surface is golden yellow, and the lining is in vermilion color. The statue is realistic in exquisite and vivid workmanship. It was unearthed in Yuanying Temple Pagoda, Changli District.

The bed of Zhangcang Reclining Buddha is 12 cm long, 5.8 cm wide, and 0.6 cm thick. On the back of the base of Zhangcang Reclining Buddha, there is an inscription inscribed in Regular Script of 38 characters: “In the spring of the 26th year of Jiajing Period of Ming Dynasty, the head monk of Shuiyan Temple in the north of Changli County, Jing Shi, set his intention to make Zhangcang Reclining Buddha. It is made by copper-smith Gaocong”.

Shuiyan Temple in Changli County today was named Shuiyan Temple in the 26th year of Jiajing (1547) Period of Ming Dynasty.

The box of Zhangcang Reclining Buddha is 18.5 cm long, 7.5 cm wide, and 7.2 cm thick. It is made of silver. The surface of this box is smooth, and some parts are slightly oxidized. The box cover is designed as a push-pull type. Both ends of the cover plate are decorated with leaf patterns, and one end is provided with a lock catch. The box is padded with cotton. In addition to placing Zhangcang Reclining Buddha, there are also copper coins of “Xining Ingot Treasure”, “Jianyan Tongbao”, “Yuanfeng Tongbao” and “Yuanyou Tongbao” .

73 Elephant-shaped Cloisonne with Meaning of Peace and Ceremony

Period Qianlong Reign, Qing Dynasty (1736 — 1795 CE)
Dimensions height: 61.1 cm; length: 56 cm; width: 35.6 cm.
Collected by Beidaihe Cultural Relics Protection and Management Institute.

It is divided into two parts, the recumbent elephant and the Sumeru throne. The upper part is a recumbent elephant, lying on the ground, looking back, with large fan ears, long tusks, and a rolled nose. The elephant is applied with a broad dragon suit, with a brocade cloth-wrapper on its back, a saddle on its back, and a ribbon vase on the saddle. The elephant body, brocade cloth-wrapper, saddle and vase are all decorated with fine cloisonne enamel. Elephant's body is covered with ruby red enamel glaze. Brocade cloth-wrapper and vase are covered with light blue enamel glaze, decorated with auspicious patterns such as bats and interlocking lotus. The saddle is made of black enamel glaze and decorated with interlocking lotus patterns. The lower part is a lotus Sumeru throne. The platform is designed in curtain shaped. There are gilt fence posts and hollow fence boards around the abutment top. The lotus and the fence post are gilded, and the rest are enamel glazed, decorated with cloisonne enamel flower patterns. It is a paired utensil, with a large body, exquisite workmanship, elaborate but not chaotic patterns, gorgeous but not vulgar colors, and elegant demeanor. It should be the exquisite enamel ware used by the imperial court.

74 Cloisonne Hollowed-out Globular Vase with Kaiguang Cloud Dragon Pattern

Period Qianlong Reign, Qing Dynasty (1736 — 1795 CE)
Dimensions height: 34 cm; mouth diameter: 9 cm; base diameter: 10.5 cm.
Collected by Changli Cultural Relics Research and Protection Institute.

It is made of copper. It has a flared mouth, a round lip, a thin neck, a sloping shoulder, a round belly, a round foot turned outward. Taking black color as the ground color, it is decorated with a variety of enamel patterns, fine filigree, full filling, which is extremely beautiful. The neck and shoulder are decorated with patterns of hanging flowers and Ruyi (i.e., as ones wish) clouds, interlacing Baoxiang flowers, and banana leaves. The belly is the theme decoration area, which is decorated with entwined flower patterns against four sides of circular Kaiguang patterns. Interior of each Kaiguang pattern is hollowed out with embossed a dragon among clouds pattern, and Kaiguang patterns are separated by three different colors of flowers which arranged vertically. The lower abdomen is decorated with a beaded lotus for a loop. The round foot is decorated with four sets of intertwined flowers and a hoop band around the bottom. The most exquisite and unique design is that the abdomen is designed to be double-layered and rotatable. After rotating, through the circular Kaiguang patterns, you can see the dragon flying and hovering among the auspicious clouds. The four sides of the circular Kaiguang technique are all gold-plated, which makes it more resplendent and luxurious.

75 Copper Box in the Shape of Ship

Period Qing Dynasty (1616 — 1911 CE)
Dimensions length: 12.8 cm; width: 6.2 cm; height: 7.8 cm.
Collected by Lulong Cultural Relics Protection and Management Institute.

It is cup-shaped with a top lid. The upper part is shaped like a ship which is wide at one end and narrow at the other. A horizontal axis in the middle connecting with both sides, which one side is fixed, and the other is a movable cover. The cover edge is decorated with a circle of teeth pattern, the lower part is a trumpet-shaped base, which is applied with three layers of outward folding edges. It is a utensil for using in Yongping Mansion Church.

76 Copper Tripod Fire-pan

Period Qing Dynasty (1616 — 1911 CE)
Dimensions height: 18.4 cm; mouth diameter: 34 cm.
Collected by Funing Cultural Relics Protection Center.

It has a straight mouth, which is folded outward along the flat edge, the rim is upturned, the abdomen is deep and straight, and the bottom is flat. Three hollow hoof-shaped feet are riveted on the abdominal body.

77 Bucket Shaped Copper Seal

Period Qing Dynasty (1616 — 1911 CE)
Dimensions height: 4.8 cm; length: 6.8 cm; width: 4.9 cm; length of top: 5.6 cm; width of top: 3.9 cm.
Collected by Qinglong Manchu Autonomous County Cultural Relics Protection Institute.

It is engraving Zhuge Liang's "Northern Expedition Memorial" on the seal surface.

78 Micro Carving Ox Horn Seal

Period Qing Dynasty (1616 — 1911 CE)
Dimensions height: 3.7 cm; length of base: 5.7 cm; width of base: 3.7 cm; length of top: 4.4 cm; width of top: 3.1 cm.
Collected by Qinglong Manchu Autonomous County Cultural Relics Protection Institute.

It is engraved micro carving words on the seal surface.

79 Golden Hairpin with Tianhui Interlocking Branches Pattern

Period Qing Dynasty (1616 — 1911 CE)
Dimensions length: 13 cm; width: 1.5 cm; thickness: 0.1 cm; weight: 31 g.
Collected by Changli Cultural Relics Research and Protection Institute.

It has a flat body and a mushroom-shaped cap. The body is carved with flowers like hemlock and interlocking lotus. Round double happiness pattern is carved on one end.

80 Copper Mirror with Five Mountain Character Pattern

Period Warring States Period (475 — 221 BCE)
Dimensions diameter: 22 cm; thickness of edge: 0.5 cm.
Collected by Funing Cultural Relics Protection Center.

It is round. Three string-shaped bridge buttons connect with a round button seat. The mirror edge is plain. The back of the mirror is decorated with two circles of concave rings patterns, which one is decorated around the button seat, and another is decorated around the mirror edge. The theme decoration area is located between the two bands, which is composed of thin and densely feathery patterns, long-stemmed Begonia flowers patterns, and five sloping "mountain" characters patterns stacked together. The five mountain characters are arranged in a left-handed way around the buttons, with thin strokes, long in middles, and large gradient. The mountain characters divide the theme pattern area into five equal sections, and distributed with long-stemmed Begonia flowers patterns.

81 Copper Bo-ju Mirrors with Four Divine Beasts Designs

Period Han Dynasty (206 BCE — 220 CE)
Dimensions diameter: 18 cm.
Collected by Qinhuangdao Cultural Relics Protection Center.

It is round. It has a round button and a square button base interior with a persimmon pattern. Twelve drum nails are arranged between the two convex stripe lines shaped pattern, and twelve terrestrial branch inscriptions are decorated between them. The exterior of this frame is decorated with eight drum nail patterns and the pattern of Bo Ju pattern, which divide the inside into four sides of eight directions, respectively: Azure Dragon on the left, White Tiger on the right, Vermilion Bird in the front, Black Tortoise on the back, and supplemented with patterns such as phoenix, unicorn, bird, toad, etc. The space of each party shall be filled with regular T-shaped, L-shaped, and V-shaped patterns. The exterior is decorated with a loop of inscription with multi-characters. The outermost circle is decorated with a loop of short diagonal lines and zigzag lines. The outer edge is decorated with cloud and air patterns. This type of mirror is named because of the words "Bo Ju" inscription.

82 Copper Mirror with Chinese Alligator Pattern

Period Tang Dynasty (618 — 907 CE)

Dimensions diameter: 13.6 cm; thickness: 0.6 cm.
Collected by Changli Cultural Relics Research and Protection Institute.

It is round. It has a round button and a round button base. The mirror edge is plain. The inner area is decorated with four Chinese alligator patterns. They all look vividly but different, which is to bend down and crawl, or curl neck and open mouth angrily, or roll head and look back, or bow head and dive to swing tail. The outer area is decorated with comb pattern, zigzag pattern, water ripple pattern and one thick and two fine concave string patterns for separating these patterns.

83 Copper Mirror with "Zhenzi Feishuang" Pattern

Period Tang Dynasty (618 — 907 CE)
Dimensions diameter: 15.6 cm; thickness: 0.5 cm.
Collected by Shanhaiguan Cultural Relics Protection and Management Institute.

This mirror is in the shape of six sunflowers, with tortoise buttons and a lotus leaf base. There are four groups of themed decorations, which are distributed on the left, right, upper, and lower of the turtle button. The content is the common folk stories in the Tang Dynasty mirrors. The decoration configuration is: Distinguished men playing qin in a bamboo forest; Phoenix spreading its wings fairy tree; Phoenix flying among mountains and clouds under sunlight; Strange rock with a pond lotus. It has a plain edge. It has fine decoration and vivid stories. In particular, it is interesting and ingenious to use the leaves of lotus out of water and turtles as a button. Some Tang Dynasty mirrors were named due to the inscription of "Zhenzi Feishuang".

84 Copper Mirror with Four Auspicious Animals and Grapes Pattern

Period Tang dynasty (618 — 907 CE)
Dimensions diameter: 11.4 cm; thickness: 0.9 cm.
Collected by Qinglong Manchu Autonomous County Cultural Relics Protection Institute.

It is a round shape, with a crouching animal button. A loop of raised high ridge string pattern divides the theme pattern into internal and external areas. The inner area is decorated with four auspicious animals climbing and playing around the crouching animal button, interspersed with winding leaf vines and full grape grains. In the outer area, birds with different attitudes shuttle between the vine and fruit, while bees, dragonflies, and butterflies fly and play. The mirror edge is decorated with a circle of petal patterns. The crouching animal looks forward with its head raised, which is vivid and interesting. Patterns of this mirror are delicately depicted, vivid and interesting.

85 Straight Handled Copper Mirror with Children Playing Pattern

Period Liao and Jin Dynasty (907 — 1234 CE)
Dimensions diameter: 9 cm; thickness: 0.4 cm; handle length: 8.1 cm.
Collected by Qinglong Manchu Autonomous County Cultural Relics Protection Institute.

It is a round shape, with a plain edge and straight handle. There is a tree on the right. The branches are hung with lanterns covering the upper part of the mirror. Three naughty children are playing under the tree, or jumping with their hands raised, or cheering with their arms outstretched. One of them prostrated himself on the ground, reaching out to light the big firecracker in front of him. On the left side, an adult carrying a table is coming to the child and raising his left leg for fear of being blown up by firecrackers. The lines are simple, but the dynamic portrayal of the characters is subtle. The scene of arrogant and naive, lovely naughty children playing together, supplemented by a tree full of lanterns, presents a lively and festive atmosphere, giving people a peaceful, joyful feeling, and more importantly, an artistic conception of praying for happiness and peace.

86 Copper Mirror with Double Fishes Pattern

Period Liao and Jin Dynasty (907 — 1234 CE)
Dimensions diameter: 10.5 cm; thickness: 0.6 cm.
Collected by Qinglong Manchu Autonomous County Cultural Relics Protection Institute.

This copper mirror is round, with a round button and a plain edge. The pattern is two fishes folded around the mirror button. Two fishes are swaying their tails to play with each other in the rushing water.

87 Copper Mirror with Two Cranes among Auspicious Clouds Pattern

Period Liao and Jin Dynasty (907 — 1234 CE)
Dimensions diameter: 9.4 cm; thickness: 0.5 cm.
Collected by Qinglong Manchu Autonomous County Cultural Relics Protection Institute.

It is a round shape, with a round button and a plain edge. The pattern is two chasing cranes flying freely under the three auspicious clouds.

88 Copper Mirror with Mythical Animal in the Ocean and Phoenix Pattern

Period Liao and Jin Dynasty (907 — 1234 CE)
Dimensions diameter: 13.0 cm; thickness: 0.4 cm.
Collected by Qinglong Manchu Autonomous County Cultural Relics Protection Institute.

It is a round mirror with a round button and a plain edge. The water below the button is boiling in shock, the mythical animals gallop on the ocean. Above the button, the red phoenix spreads its wings and looks down, adorned with divine trees on both sides Phoenix and mythical animals echo from afar to symbolizes the auspicious and harmonious.

89 Copper Mirror with Hundred Birds Pay Homage to the Phoenix Pattern

Period Liao and Jin Dynasty (907 — 1234 CE)
Dimensions diameter: 9.4 cm; thickness: 0.5 cm; handle length: 8.2 cm.
Collected by Qinglong Manchu Autonomous County Cultural Relics Protection Institute.

It is a round mirror with a plain edge and a handle. The back of the mirror is divided into two areas with a raised ridge . In the inner area, a standing phoenix looks back, decorated with flowers and plants. Hundreds of birds in the outer area shuttle among the flowers and branches, and form a pattern of birds paying homage to the phoenix in the inner area. The handle top and end are provided with lace guards. "Hundred birds pay homage to the phoenix" is a popular theme for folk decoration.

90 Copper Mirror with Two Dragons Play with a Pearl and Curly Leaves Pattern

Period Jin Dynasty (1115 — 1234 CE)
Dimensions diameter: 18.5 cm; thickness: 0.8 cm.
Collected by Qinglong Manchu Autonomous County Cultural Relics Protection Institute.

It is a round shape, with a round button and a plain edge. The theme decoration on the back of the mirror is two dragons playing with a pearl, benting necks and raising heads. They are opening mouths with flying manes. The two dragon forelimbs that meet each other are in a press and dance shape, and the buttons are used as beads to play. One dragon has a bowed body, strong and powerful limbs. One front limb is pressing and another is waving, while one hind limb is kicking the ground and the other is stretching back, which is entangled by the tail. The other dragon is straight and relatively weak, which has a twisted body, pressing one of the front limbs, and waving the other, the hind limbs are straight. The two dragons chase each other and are full of moving sense. The proximal edge is decorated with a loop of curly leaves pattern.

91 Copper Mirror of "Wu Zi Deng Ke"

Period Ming Dynasty (1368 — 1644 CE)
Dimensions diameter: 17.3 cm; thickness: 0.7 cm.
Collected by Qinglong Manchu Autonomous County Cultural Relics Protection Institute.

The mirror is a round shape, connected with a round flat button. Four raised rhombic pattern frames are cast on the top, bottom, left, and right of the button, with the four-character auspicious wishes of "Wu Zi Deng Ke" written in Regular Script. The outer edge is decorated with a high and low double ridge ring belt.

92 Copper Mirror of "Wu Zi Deng Ke"

Period Ming Dynasty (1368 — 1644 CE)

Dimensions diameter: 24.7 cm; thickness: 0.7 cm; inner diameter: 7.5 cm.
Collected by Shanhaiguan Cultural Relics Protection and Management Institute.

The mirror is a round shape, connected with a round flat button. It has a plain wide edge. The top surface of the flat round button is cast with seven-character inscription "Made by Xue Jinhe, Huzhou" in three lines with small Regular Script. It has a plain wide edge on the back, and four-character Official Script inscription "Wu Zi Deng Ke" is cast around the button. Each word is surrounded by a diamond-shaped frame. It is a symbol of good fortune for many children and grandchildren. It means good luck and happiness.

93 Stone Statue of Avalokitesvara (Guanyin Bodhisattva)

Period Tang Dynasty (618 — 907 CE)
Dimensions height: 58 cm; width: 17.5 cm; thickness: 14 cm; height of throne: 11 cm.
Collected by Shanhaiguan Cultural Relics Protection and Management Institute.

This statue wears a crown of Buddhist treasures on the top. The head is slightly tilted, with a solemn expression, wide forehead, drooping eyes, shows solemn and kind. It wears a collar on the neck, bracelets on the wrists, and beads on the chest and dress. The right hand is holding a vase in front of the chest, and the left hand is tied at the side of body. Stand with bare feet on the lotus Sumeru throne with curly cloud patterns. The silk belt falls from the shoulders and arms on both sides of the throne. The modeling is dignified and atmospheric, the lines are simple and smooth.

94 Copper Statue of Sakyamuni

Period Jin Dynasty (1115 — 1234 CE)
Dimensions height: 11 cm; width: 2.6 cm; weight: 100 g.
Collected by Changli Cultural Relics Research and Protection Institute.

The statue's hair is fashioned as a topknot, shaped in a spiral shell with jewels on the topknot. The front of the bun is inlaid with bun beads, the big ears are prolapsing to the shoulders. The cheeks are plump, the eyes are looking down with a kindly and amiable expression. The arms are bent in front of the abdomen and applied with certain gestures. It is wearing a round neck square placket long-sleeved full-length robe. The four groups of curved garment folds from the front of the chest to the bottom form the Futian lattice. The big sleeve, which is bent and dropped by the forearm, gushes down like a waterfall, is realistic in concise and accurate lines. It is wearing a skirt, standing barefoot on the rectangular lotus Sumeru throne.

95 Gild-copper and Colored Decoration Statue of Samantabhadra Sitting on Elephant

Period Ming Dynasty (1368 — 1644 CE)
Dimensions height: 35.5 cm; width: 28.3 cm.
Collected by the Great Wall Museum in Shanhaiguan.

This statue wears a crown and a bodhisattva costume. It wears double high buns with a plump face, curved eyebrows, and kind eyes. Long hair with ribbons covers both ears, falling over shoulders. The shoulders are full and the waist is tied with silk. The neck is decorated with beads, and the chest and body are covered with pearls and jade necklace. The right arm is raised on the chest with the elbow bent, and the palm of the hand is bound outward and applying the abhaya mudra gesture. The left bent arm is placing in front of the abdomen and knotted with the mudra of supreme generosity. It has a blue skirt around its waist, trousers, and bare feet. It sits on the six-tooth white elephant with its right foot on the lotus flower and its left leg on the elephant's back. The white elephant knelt on the oval single-layer lotus platform. This statue is exquisitely made, gilded, and painted. It is very rare because it is basically well preserved.

96 Gild-copper and Colored Seated Statue of Sakyamuni

Period Ming Dynasty (1368 — 1644 CE)
Dimensions height: 41.5 cm; width: 28 cm; thickness: 20.5 cm; height of throne: 10 cm.
Collected by Shanhaiguan Cultural Relics Protection and Management Institute.

The statue's hair is fashioned as a topknot, with blue hair shaped in spiral shell and jewels on the head. The eyes are slightly closed, the chin is slightly down, the big ears are prolapsing to shoulders, which is wide but with tied waist. It is vivid of quiet expression, and the expression is more solemn, giving people a quiet and solemn look. The upper body is wearing a cassock that exposes the right shoulder, the right shoulder is covered with the corners of the cassock, and the lower body is wearing a skirt, which is realistic. This figure is sitting on the huge lotus Sumeru throne with waist tied and leaning forward in a lotus position, and applying with a dhyana-mudra gesture. The shape proportion is symmetrical with smooth lines, and the workmanship is exquisite, which represents the style of Buddha statues in the Ming Dynasty.

97 Copper Seated Statue of Sakyamuni

Period Ming Dynasty (1368 — 1644 CE)
Dimensions height: 16.8 cm; width: 13.2 cm.
Collected by Qinglong Manchu Autonomous County Cultural Relics Protection Institute.

This statue's head is decorated with spiral shell-shaped hair, with a jewel on the top. It has big ears that are prolapsing to shoulders, and it has a dignified expression. Wearing a topless cassock, with the right shoulder half exposed. It wears a robe with double pendulous, sitting in lotus position with both hands in front of the lower abdomen and applying with dhyana-mudra gesture. The overall line is concise and straightforward, natural and smooth.

98 Copper Statue of Ananda

Period Ming Dynasty (1368 — 1644 CE)
Dimensions height: 28.7 cm; width: 11.3 cm; thickness: 9.9 cm.
Collected by Shanhaiguan Cultural Relics Protection and Management Institute.

The forehead of this statue is round with a wide face, the eyes are looking down, the big ears are prolapsing to shoulders, the body is covered with cassock. This statue is standing on lotus Sumeru throne with folded hands. The shape is refined and vivid, and the ingenious technology depicts Ananda's dignified and intelligent characteristics, giving people a sense of sculpture beauty. Ananda is the smallest of the ten disciples of Sakyamuni Buddha, also called Duo Wen Di Yi.

99 Copper Statue of Maha Kasyapa Coated by Powdered Gold

Period Ming Dynasty (1368 — 1644 CE)
Dimensions height: 18.7 cm; width: 7.6 cm.
Collected by Qinglong Manchu Autonomous County Cultural Relics Protection Institute.

This statue has round but slightly square physiognomy. It has plump cheeks. Its eyes are slightly closed, its big ears are down, and it looks kind and smiling. It has a headband, and bun beads. It is wearing a long skirt inside and a kapok cassock with the right full shoulder exposed. The hands are held in front of the chest. It stands barefoot on the lotus covered sumi seat, practicing humility and leading the posture of "picking flowers and smiling". The draped ribbon falls down the shoulders and arms, with one side hanging on the lotus platform. It is designed in a beautiful shape and realistic style, full of strong artistic appeal. Maha Kasyapa is one of the ten disciples of Sakyamuni Buddha.

100 Stone Seated Statue of Sakyamuni

Period Ming Dynasty (1368 — 1644 CE)
Dimensions height: 116 cm; width: 65 cm; thickness: 41 cm.
Collected by Funing Cultural Relics Protection Center.

This statue is carved from granite. The hair on the head is fashioned in spiral shell-shaped, with plump cheeks, slightly closed eyes, and the big ears hanging down. It is wearing a coat used to cover shoulders, the garment folds are gathered on the left arm, and the right shoulder spreads the fold angle. The chest collar is symmetrical and sagging, then it is curved and connected, and the waist knot is flowered. The lower body is wearing a skirt. The left hand is placed in front of the lower abdomen with dhyana-mudra, the right hand is placed on the leg with bhtunyakramana gesture. The statue is sitting on the lotus throne. The lines are simple and bright, and the shape is solemn and dignified.

101 Gold Coating Copper Seated Statue of Sakyamuni

Period Ming Dynasty (1368 — 1644 CE)

Dimensions height: 10 cm; weight: 314 g.
Collected by Funing Cultural Relics Protection Center.

The whole body of this statue is golden paint, with its head decorated with a high bun of spiral shell-shaped hair and big earlobes hanging down to the shoulders. The face is square and round, the eyes are kind and looking down, and the expression is solemn. It is wearing a round collar, thin clothes with folds, which are hanging down curved and symmetrical. The lower body is wearing a skirt. Both hands are placing in front of the lower abdomen with dhyana-mudra gesture and sitting and leaning forward in a lotus position. The patterns are concise and straightforward, and the lines of the round neckline are smooth and attracting attention.

102 Copper Seated Statue of Avalokitesvara (Guanyin Bodhisattva)

Period Ming Dynasty (1368 — 1644 CE)
Dimensions height: 15.8 cm.
Collected by Qinglong Manchu Autonomous County Cultural Relics Protection Institute.

This statue has a square and round face. Wearing a crown of Buddhist treasures, the top of the bun is decorated with jewels, the ears are decorated with round Baoxiang flowers pendants, and the chest is decorated with wreaths. It is placing the left hand to hold the bottle in front of the abdomen, and the right bent arm to hold the bottle. It is wearing a bodhisattva costume on the upper part and a long skirt on the lower part, sitting on the throne of lotus. The collar of the dress is chisel carving with exquisite patterns.

103 Gild-copper Seated Statue of Sakyamuni

Period Qing Dynasty (1616 — 1911 CE)
Dimensions height: 33.5 cm; thickness: 14 cm; width: 21 cm.
Collected by Shanhaiguan Cultural Relics Protection and Management Institute.

The hair of this statue is shaped in a spiral shell on the head, with a high bun of topknot and jewels on the top. The eyes are slightly closed, the big ears are prolapsing to the shoulders, and the neck is decorated with a set of collars. The upper body is wearing a cassock that exposes the right shoulder, the right shoulder is covered with the corners of the cassock, and the lower body is wearing a skirt. This figure is sitting on the huge lotus Sumeru throne with waist tied and leaning forward in a lotus position, placing the left hand on the lower abdomen with a dhyana-mudra gesture, and putting the right hand on the knee with bhtunyakramana gesture. The gilding of the statue is basically fall off, the overall line is designed with a dignified appearance and smooth contours.

104 Gild-copper and Colored Seated Statue of Sakyamuni

Period Qing Dynasty (1616 — 1911 CE)
Dimensions height: 24.5 cm; width: 16 cm; thickness: 10.2 cm.
Collected by Shanhaiguan Cultural Relics Protection and Management Institute.

The statue's hair is fashioned as a topknot, with blue hair shaped in a spiral shell. It is in a solemn atmosphere, which has a square and round face, slightly closed eyes, big ears prolapsed to shoulders. It is wearing a cassock, exposing the upper chest, sitting in lotus position, and applying with dhyana-mudra gesture. The head has a large proportion and leans forward slightly, forming a shape of looking down posture. It is not paired with Sumeru throne.

105 Gild-copper Figure of Ushnishavijaya

Period Qing Dynasty (1616 — 1911 CE)
Dimensions height: 17.5 cm; width: 11.4 cm; thickness: 8 cm; height of Sumeru throne: 3.2 cm.
Collected by Shanhaiguan Cultural Relics Protection and Management Institute.

Ushnishavijaya is portrayed as one with three heads and eight arms. The three faces are one front and two lateral sides. They are all wearing five-leaf corolla beads on their heads. The two ears are decorated with Baoxiang flowers earrings. Their faces are dignified and kind. The eight arms are all bent with elbows and hand mudras. The main arm and hands are used to be the chest, with the left hand standing on the palm of the index finger, and the right hand pinching the finger with the right hand holding the palm horizontally, and applying the abhaya mudra gesture. The other six arms extend to both sides of the body. The first hand on the left side is raised in a lifting shape, the second hand pinches the palm outward, and the third hand puts the palm upward on the knee. The palm of the index finger of the first hand on the right side is upward, in a lifting shape, the palm of the middle finger of the second hand is outward, and the third hand is knotted with the mudra of supreme generosity. The arms are staggered in height and in various postures, which are very exquisite.

The whole figure is dressed in gorgeous and exquisite clothes, wearing necklaces and bracelets, with flexible and elegant belts around arms, and sitting and leaning up on a lotus Sumeru throne. The figure is elegant with smooth curves, which can be called superb in craftsmanship. This statue has a shaped body for Tibetan Buddhism. Together with Namas Amitayus Buddha and White Tara Buddha, they form the "Three Honors for Longevity".

106 Gild-copper Seated Statue of Green Tara Buddha

Period Qing Dynasty (1616 — 1911 CE)
Dimensions height: 10.5 cm; width: 8.5 cm; thickness: 8.5 cm.
Collected by Changli Cultural Relics Research and Protection Institute.

This green Tara is the embodiment of Avalokitesvara (Guanyin Bodhisattva). It looks like a young woman, wears a five-leaf corolla, and is decorated with gourd shaped beads on the top of a high bun. The face is solemn and beautiful, with slim eyebrows, long eyes, a wide forehead, full cheeks, and round pendants hanging down shoulders. Necklaces and collars are decorated on necks, bracelets and bangles are decorated on arms, wrists and ankles. It has an exposed upper body, wearing a waist tied silk dress, head slightly to the right, waist slightly to the left, thin waist and shoulders, shows graceful and elegant The right hand is knotting with mudra of supreme generosity, and the left hand is applying with Sanbao gesture and holding the willow branch to stretch shoulders along arms. It is sitting comfortably on the lotus moon wheel carried by the auspicious animal Dangkang, bending bare feet to the left and stretched right leg outward. The auspicious animal Dangkang is lying on the ground with its head held high. The whole statue is simple in style, realistic in technique, beautiful and dignified in shape, and gentle and natural in appearance.

107 Gild-copper Seated Statue of Sakyamuni

Period Qing Dynasty (1616 — 1911 CE)
Dimensions height: 13.2 cm; width of throne: 8.6 cm.
Collected by Funing Cultural Relics Protection Center.

The statue's hair is fashioned as a topknot, with hair shaped in a spiral shell and jewels on the head, the big ears are hanging down. The face is square and solemn. It is wearing a cassock with the right shoulder exposed and a skirt. The left hand is placed on the front of the abdomen with a dhyana-mudra gesture, and the right hand is placed on leg with a bhtunyakramana gesture. This statue is sitting on a double layer lotus Sumeru throne.

108 Gild-copper Seated Statue of Mahasthamaprapta with Boat-shaped Mandorla

Period Qing Dynasty (1616 — 1911 CE)
Dimensions height: 12.3 cm; weight: 206 g.
Collected by Funing Cultural Relics Protection Center.

This statue is wearing a corolla, with hair tied in a high bun, lotus beads on top, ears, and round pendants hanging down to shoulders. It has a beautiful face, with eyes looking down, looks kind and quiet. It folds its palms in front of the abdomen with a dhyana-mudra gesture with a flower vase. Necklaces and collars are decorated on necks, bracelets and bangles are decorated on arms, wrists, and ankles. The shoulders are draped with silk, twined and turned down around the arms. The tail of the silk ends float upward from both sides of the body. The lower body is wearing a long skirt, the thigh is crossed with colorful silk, and hang on both sides of the table. The front of the lower leg is displayed with a lotus shaped ribbon. The statue is sitting on the throne with lotus waist tied up. The top and bottom of the throne are decorated with a loop of beads. There is a beautifully carved boat-shaped mandorla behind. On the raised mandorla edge around the main statue, the convex string pattern is decorated with a bead pattern in the middle, and the curly leaf pattern is decorated outside. It is designed as elegant shape, gorgeous and exquisite decoration.

109 Stone Statue of Songzi Avalokitesvara

Period Qing Dynasty (1616 — 1911 CE)
Dimensions height: 47.8 cm; width: 15 cm; thickness: 14.8 cm.

Collected by the Great Wall Museum in Shanhaiguan.

This statue wears a lotus crown with a high bun, two earlobes hanging down to the shoulders. It has plump cheeks, a kind face with a smile. Pearl and jade necklace hangs on the neck. It wears long clothes and a skirt with bare feet. It is sitting on the lotus platform with a square pedestal raised. It steps on the small lotus platform with its right leg bent, holds its left leg high with its right hand, and puts its left hand on the lotus platform. A golden monster Hou is lying under the lotus platform, twisting its neck forward.

110 Copper Statue of Taoist

Period Qing Dynasty (1616 — 1911 CE)
Dimensions height: 39.5 cm; length of throne: 14 cm; width of throne: 11.2 cm.
Collected by Qinglong Manchu Autonomous County Cultural Relics Protection Institute.

This Taoist's hair is tied in a high bun which is covered with a lotus crown. It has a square face, curved eyebrows and round eyes, a smiling face, drooping ears, and three long beards. It is wearing a pair of front facing robes, wide sleeved linings, and long skirts and shows boots. With both hands folded, holding an object in front of chest, it shows peace and looks at the front horizontally, and stands on a square pedestal. Exquisite flowers and cloud patterns are carved on the cuffs and robe surface.

111 White Crystal Sitting Statue of Taoist

Period Qing Dynasty (1616 — 1911 CE)
Dimensions height: 11.8 cm; width: 7 cm; width of throne: 6.1 cm.
Collected by Shanhaiguan Cultural Relics Protection and Management Institute.

The material is crystal clear, and carved the whole statue. It is a Taoist image, with hair tied and a scarf worn, and clothes wide and straight. It has square cheeks, slender eyebrows, eyes slightly open, the mouth slightly closed, three long beards hanging down on the chest, modest expression. The left hand holding the mountain stone, the right hand holding a horsetail whisk on the arm bend, cross the legs and sit on a dangerous rock.

112 Toad-shaped Jade Ornament

Period Warring States Period (475 — 221 BCE)
Dimensions length: 6.7 cm; width: 6.3 cm; thickness: 0.3 cm.
Collected by Funing Cultural Relics Protection Center.

It is made of soft jade by cutting it into thin pieces and hollowing it out. It is yellowish brown, mixed with purple and brown spots. Without polishing, the surface still has cut line marks. The shape of the toad is round, with legs in four directions, which is abstract and patterned. It is symmetrically applied with a small perforation for fixing and binding on both sides. It was unearthed in Bingge Village, Funing District.

113 Dragon-shaped Jade Ornament

Period Warring States Period (475 — 221 BCE)
Dimensions length: 9.8 cm; width: 7 cm; thickness: 0.2 cm.
Collected by Funing Cultural Relics Protection Center.

It is made of soft jade by cutting it into thin pieces and hollowing it out. It is yellowish brown, mixed with purple and brown spots. Without polishing, the surface still has cut line marks. The dragon shape turns back and turns into an abstract pattern. It is symmetrically applied with a small perforation for fixing and binding on both sides. It was unearthed in Bingge Village, Funing District.

114 White Jade Decoration Belt Plate with Dragon Tail Pattern

Period Tang Dynasty (618 — 907 CE)
Dimensions length: 12.44 cm; width: 3.41 cm; thickness: 0.95 cm.
Collected by Shanhaiguan Cultural Relics Protection and Management Institute.

This jade is fine and smooth. This jade belt plate is in the shape of a long strip, with a square corner at one end and a half circle at the other. The front is embossed with simple lines to describe a dragon with a tail. The back is plain, and applied with 10 small symmetrical holes for sewing around.

115 Green Jade Belt Hook in the Shape of Dragon Head and a Small Dragon

Period Ming Dynasty (1368 — 1644 CE)
Dimensions length: 13.5 cm; width: 2.6 cm; height: 3 cm.
Collected by Lulong Cultural Relics Protection and Management Institute.

It is carved out of green jade and has a texture with tufts. It is in a long strip shape. It has a flat abdomen and a round button. It is carved in a dragon head shape on top of the belt, and with horns, nose, mouth, ears and eyes. A small dragon is carved on the belly, and look at the big dragon head.

116 Light Green Jade Belt Hook in the Shape of Dragon Head and a Small Dragon

Period Ming Dynasty (1368 — 1644 CE)
Dimensions length: 12.62 cm; width: 2.88 cm; thickness: 2.95 cm.
Collected by Shanhaiguan Cultural Relics Protection and Management Institute.

It is made of light green jade, with grain inside. The hook is in the shape of a lute, with a flat broad belly and round button. The hook head is carved with a vertical dragon head, which has good horns, ears, eyes, and nose. A small dragon is carved on the belly, and look at the big dragon head. The curves are beautiful, the body is agile, and the head, tail, and limbs are clearly dynamic. It is an exquisitely crafted product.

117 White Jade Hollow Double Badger Pendant

Period Ming Dynasty (1368 — 1644 CE)
Dimensions length: 4.13 cm; width: 3.41 cm; thickness: 1.24 cm.
Collected by Shanhaiguan Cultural Relics Protection and Management Institute.

This jade is delicate and smooth. The vertical sculpture is hollowed out, with symmetrical layout. The shape selects the scene of two naughty badgers playing and fighting. The four feet lift each other, vividly portraying the badger's temperament. The folk custom has the meaning of the homophonic "Happy together".

118 White Jade Pendant of Happiness and Longevity

Period Qing Dynasty (1616 — 1911 CE)
Dimensions length: 7.3 cm; width: 4.9 cm; thickness: 0.5 cm.
Collected by Lulong Cultural Relics Protection and Management Institute.

This jade is clean and flawless. Curly clouds located in "Pin" character are embossed on the head of the pendant, with a small hole for tying in the middle. The pendant body is square with rounded corners. The outer edge frame is carved with ridge lines, the middle line is carved with a rectangular double line frame, and the inner relief is carved with the words "Happiness and Longevity" (Fu and Shou). Between the outer frame and the inner frame, the corners of the upper and lower branches are decorated with a single branch slanting out with tangled branches and rolled leaf patterns inward. Two diagonal twisted branches and curled leaf patterns upwards are decorated the bottom edge. The tail of the pendant is embossed with four symmetrical double-knot curly clouds. It is elegant and beautiful, stable and grand.

119 Green Jade Embossed Plum Blossom Ruyi Tile

Period Qing Dynasty (1616 — 1911 CE)
Dimensions length: 8.9 cm; width: 7.5 cm; thickness: 1.76 cm.
Collected by Lulong Cultural Relics Protection and Management Institute.

It is a Ruyi accessory. It is in a tile shape, which is concave on one side and convex on the other. The convex surface is embossed with dried plum branches, supplemented by bamboo and stones. The plum trees are exquisite and convoluted, light and flexible. The scene is supplemented by plum trees, stones, and bamboo to form, which is pleasing to the eyes.

120 Green Jade Pendant Carved in Concentric Circle Shape with a Rotating Hub

Period Qing Dynasty (1616 — 1911 CE)
Dimensions diameter: 5.9 cm; thickness: 0.4 cm.
Collected by Lulong Cultural Relics Protection and Management Institute.

This pendant is round and shaped in concentric circles, carved with green jade. It is composed of an outer ring, an inner ring, and a central hub. The inner and outer rings are engraved and linked by eight spokes. The outer ring shows sunflower-shaped edges, and the two sides are carved with cloud patterns. The two sides of the inner ring are carved with Hui patterns. The middle hub is slightly plump, embedded in the notch, which can rotate, and is carved with grain seedling patterns.

121 Light Green Jade Pendant with Auspicious Double Kui-dragon Design

Period Qing Dynasty (1616 — 1911 CE)
Dimensions length: 5.8 cm; width: 4 cm; thickness: 0.55 cm.
Collected by Lulong Cultural Relics Protection and Management Institute.

It is made of light green jade but in cyan color. It is rectangular, with two symmetrical carved standing Kui-dragons that are grabbing the sky, with auspicious clouds overhead. The Seal Script "Good luck" (Da Ji) are carved between the dragons. It is delicate and graceful.

122 White Jade Pendant in the Shape of Child Holding Lotus and Petting Dog

Period Qing Dynasty (1616 — 1911 CE)
Dimensions length: 3.92 cm; width: 3.8 cm; thickness: 1.98 cm.
Collected by Shanhaiguan Cultural Relics Protection and Management Institute.

It is designed as a child with his head combed into two side buns, squatting down, holding a large lotus leaf in his left hand to cover his back, and petting a puppy with his right hand, which has a strong atmosphere of life. The carving is delicate and smooth, and the shape is vivid and interesting.

123 Jadeite Belt Hook in the Shape of Dragon Head and a Small Dragon

Period Qing Dynasty (1616 — 1911 CE)
Dimensions length: 8.8 cm; width: 1.9 cm; thickness: 2.55 cm.
Collected by Shanhaiguan Cultural Relics Protection and Management Institute.

It is made of jadeite in dexterous color, which is the original jade color. It has a flat and wide abdomen, and a round button. It is applied with the dragon head. A small dragon is carved on the belly, which is looking ahead. The dragon head and Kui-dragon are red, and the whole body is gray and green.

124 Jadeite Belt Hook in the Shape of Ruyi

Period Qing Dynasty (1616 — 1911 CE)
Dimensions length: 7.16 cm; width: 1.7 cm; thickness: 2.34 cm.
Collected by Shanhaiguan Cultural Relics Protection and Management Institute.

It is made of jadeite in dexterous color, which is the original jade color. The body is in the shape of a lute. It has a Ruyi-shaped top, a flat and bulging belly, and a round button. A frog sitting on lotus leaves are embossed on the ventral surface. Ruyi top and frogs are both in red color, and the whole body is gray and green.

125 Light Green Jade Belt Hook in the Shape of Dragon Head and Ram's Horns

Period Qing Dynasty (1616 — 1911 CE)
Dimensions length: 11.9 cm; width: 2.59 cm; thickness: 2.9 cm.
Collected by Shanhaiguan Cultural Relics Protection and Management Institute.

The jade is smooth and warm. The belt body is in the shape of a lute, with a round belly and round button. It is applied with a dragon head with ram's horns. The whole body is plain.

126 White Jade Hollow Double Happiness Pendant

Period Qing Dynasty (1616 — 1911 CE)
Dimensions height: 5.7 cm; width: 4.13 cm; thickness: 0.54 cm.
Collected by Shanhaiguan Cultural Relics Protection and Management Institute.

This jade is delicate and smooth. The pendant is rectangular and flat, with a pair of "Xi" characters carved on the whole body, and a perforation at the upper end. The word "double happiness" is a traditional auspicious pattern in folk customs, which means happiness and blessing, and good luck comes in pairs.

127 White Jade Chi-dragon Pattern Ring

Period Qianlong Reign, Qing Dynasty (1736 — 1795 CE)
Dimensions height: 2 cm; external diameter: 3.36 cm; internal diameter: 1.96 cm.
Collected by Shanhaiguan Cultural Relics Protection and Management Institute.

This ring is made of white jade with a partial coating. The ring is embossed with a Chi-dragon pattern, which is in a circular shape. The dragon's body is curved and protruding, with its head connected to its tail.

128 Jade Pendant with Hollow Melon and Butterfly Patterns

Period Qing Dynasty (1616 — 1911 CE)
Dimensions diameter: 5.4 cm; thickness: 0.6 cm; weight: 40 g.
Collected by Changli Cultural Relics Research and Protection Institute.

This pendant is round and hollow, and the jade is clean and smooth. The upper half is decorated with melons and vines, and a butterfly with spreading wings covers the lower half of this round jade. It is intaglio carved double knife lines to draw the detailed veins on the plates, melons, and leaves. This picture is decorated with a strong traditional pastoral atmosphere, implying many children, and long fortune.

129 White Jade Lotus Seedpod and Water Chestnut Pendant

Period Qing Dynasty (1616 — 1911 CE)
Dimensions length: 5.5 cm; width: 4.1 cm; thickness: 2.2 cm.
Collected by Changli Cultural Relics Research and Protection Institute.

This jade is clean and smooth. It is shaped like a lotus seedpod, round plump lotus seeds inlaid with the receptacle, and the surrounding is decorated with water chestnut. It means perfection and beauty, good match as if made in heaven, and having many children and grandchildren.

130 Agate Snuff Bottle with Handles in Animal Head Applique Shaped

Period Qing Dynasty (1616 — 1911 CE)
Dimensions height: 6.2 cm; mouth diameter: 2 cm; longer foot diameter: 3.2 cm.
Collected by Changli Cultural Relics Research and Protection Institute.

It is in oblate shape, with hard texture, which is smooth and bright. It has a mouth inlaid with copper, a straight neck, a slipping shoulder, a flat abdomen, a short and flat foot in oval-shaped. It is paired with a red material round cover inlaid with silver bottom, and animal head appliques are embossed on both sides of the shoulder. It is elegant and interesting. All over the body shows the natural green Sardonyx in earthworm pattern. The patterns flow like waterfalls, with clear layers and rich colors.

131 Agate Snuff Bottle with Bird and Beast Pattern

Period Qing Dynasty (1616 — 1911 CE)
Dimensions height: 6.6 cm; mouth diameter: 2.1 cm; longer foot diameter: 3 cm.
Collected by Changli Cultural Relics Research and Protection Institute.

It is in oblate shape. It is hard and brittle, fine and translucent. The whole body is in natural beige color in an oblate shape. It has a copper lace mouth, a straight neck, a smooth shoulder, a flat abdomen, a short and flat foot in oval-shaped. It is paired with a red material round cover inlaid with silver bottom, and animal head appliques are embossed on both sides of the shoulder. On the upper left side of the front, an eagle standing on a huge rock looks down at the earth, and on the lower right corner, a cliff stream is carved.

132 Agate Snuff Bottle with Plain Surface

Period Qing Dynasty (1616 — 1911 CE)
Dimensions height: 7.9 cm; mouth diameter: 2.4 cm; longer foot diameter: 3.6 cm.
Collected by Changli Cultural Relics Research and Protection Institute.

It is in oblate shape. The texture is hard and brittle, clear, fine and translucent. It has a straight mouth, a straight neck, sloping shoulders, a flat abdomen, a short and flat foot in oval-shaped. Large animal head appliques are embossed on both sides of the shoulders. The surface of this bottle is plain, and the irregular natural texture appears indistinctly. The whole body is yellowish brown with a single color. The color is quiet and warm, giving people a feeling of plentiful, happiness and well-being.

133 Mother-of-pearl Snuff Bottle with Portrait and Characters Pattern

Period Qing Dynasty (1616 — 1911 CE)
Dimensions height: 5 cm; mouth diameter: 1.3 cm; foot diameter: 1.3 cm.
Collected by Changli Cultural Relics Research and Protection Institute.

It is in oblate shape. The clam snail has a circular pattern, flashing the light of clam. It has a small straight mouth, a straight neck, a plump shoulders, a flat abdomen, and gradually close, a short and flat feet. Both sides are decorated with double incised carving lines of Kaiguang Pattern along the rim of the bottle. On one side, the interior Kaiguang decoration is embossed a portrait to wear embroidered robe, and on the other side, the interior Kaiguang decoration is incised with Running Script poetry, "Falling flowers and flowing shadows are articles Chi calligraphy".

134 Sardonyx Snuff Bottle

Period Qing Dynasty (1616 — 1911 CE)
Dimensions height: 5 cm; abdominal diameter: 3.62 cm; thickness: 2.76 cm.
Collected by Shanhaiguan Cultural Relics Protection and Management Institute.

The whole body is of a natural spiral texture, and various colors are intertwined with each other. It has a straight mouth and the flat edge, a straight neck, a sloping shoulder, a bulging belly, and a round flat bottom. The snuff bottle is ingenious in color and elegant in pattern.

135 White Jade Embossed Floral Snuff Bottle

Period Qing Dynasty (1616 — 1911 CE)
Dimensions length: 6 cm; width: 5.54 cm; thickness: 2 cm.
Collected by Shanhaiguan Cultural Relics Protection and Management Institute.

It is in oblate shape. The jade is a fine and smooth bas-relief. The snuff bottle has a straight mouth, a flat round lip, a tied neck, sloping shoulders, and a flat body with a round belly. The body is carved with plum blossom, bamboo and stone patterns, and the side is decorated with a Hui pattern. The layout is clear and fresh, the patterns are quiet and concentrated.

136 Coral Emerald Beaded Necklace

Period Qing Dynasty (1616 — 1911 CE)
Dimensions length: 52 cm.
Collected by Shanhaiguan Cultural Relics Protection and Management Institute.

This necklace consists of one hundred and eight coral beads of the same size, three positioning emerald beads, one three-way tubular emerald piece combined together, and three jade pendants with leaf-shaped engraved patterns.

137 Three-feet Pottery Dresser Set Box with Brown Glaze

Period Eastern Han Dynasty (25 — 220 CE)
Dimensions height: 24 cm; mouth diameter: 14.5 cm; base diameter: 15 cm.
Collected by Changli Cultural Relics Research and Protection Institute.

This box is made of ceramic, with brown glaze interior and exterior. It has a round lip, a straight mouth, a cylindrical abdomen, a flat bottom, and three bear-shaped feet. There are three sets of concave string lines on abdomen.

138 Yellow Ground Glazed and Green Colored Jar with Three Animal-shaped Legs

Period Tang Dynasty (618 — 907 CE)
Dimensions height: 14.45 cm; mouth diameter: 14.3 cm; belly diameter: 20.5 cm.
Collected by Shanhaiguan Cultural Relics Protection and Management Institute.

This jar has a flared mouth, a round lip turned outward, a short neck, a bulging belly, a round arc bottom, and three animal-shaped legs. It has a thick ceramic clay body but with light white color. A layer of engobe coating is applied on the surface of the whole jar, and a light yellow glaze is applied on the lower abdomen. The mouth, shoulder, and abdomen are decorated with green color in a vertical flowed shape. The color blocks are scattered in appropriate, and the flavor is very rich. The mouth rim and three feet are incomplete.

139 Cyan Glazed Plate with Incised Decoration of Longquan Kiln

Period Song Dynasty (960 — 1279 CE)
Dimensions height: 5 cm; mouth diameter: 26.5 cm.
Collected by Qinglong Manchu Autonomous County Cultural Relics Protection Institute.

It has an open mouth, a sloping belly, a wide round foot. The texture is white, delicate, and thick. This plate is covered with bean-green glaze, which is thick and moist. This plate has a high degree of vitrification. A string pattern is engraved on the circumference of the interior bottom, and a flower pattern is engraved inside.

140 Dark Brown Glazed Vase in the Shape of Chicken Leg

Period Liao and Jin Dynasty (907 — 1234 CE)
Dimensions height: 37 cm; mouth diameter: 5.5 cm.
Collected by Qinglong Manchu Autonomous County Cultural Relics Protection Institute.

It has a flared mouth, an outward lip, a tied neck, and a sloping shoulder. Its abdomen is long and slender, and gradually draws down like a chicken leg. The round foot is small. The texture is hard and thick. It is applied with black-brown glaze, and scraped a loop of glaze on the shoulder. The abdomen is densely covered with convex string patterns. The bottom is concave, and the foot is flat. It was collected from Zhushiling Village, Qinglong Manchu Autonomous County.

141 Four-handled Vase with the Design of Black Colored Phoenixes

Period Liao and Jin Dynasty (907 — 1234 CE)
Dimensions height: 38 cm; mouth diameter: 7.7 cm; foot diameter: 12 cm.
Collected by Qinglong Manchu Autonomous County Cultural Relics Protection Institute.

It has a flared mouth, an outward lip, a short neck, a sloping shoulder, a bulging belly, and a round foot. The texture is relatively hard, with white glaze applied on the upper part and black glaze applied from the lower abdomen to the feet. Four flat ribbon handles are designed on the neck and shoulder. It is carved with a phoenix (Luan) and a phoenix (Feng) in freehand style on the abdomen. The shoulder is decorated with four day lily patterns. The shoulders and abdomen are zoned with two sets of string lines, each set of three strings. The foot is irregular and, the bottom is concave. The patterns are abstract, with one phoenix (Luan) and one phoenix (Feng) connected at the head and tail, echoing and calling each other, symbolizing harmony between husband and wife, and the prosperity of family and everything. It was unearthed in Luzhangzi Village, Qinglong Manchu Autonomous County.

142 Four-handled Vase with the Design of Black Colored Dragon among Clouds

Period Liao and Jin Dynasty (907 — 1234 CE)
Dimensions height: 32 cm; mouth diameter: 4.7 cm; foot diameter: 10.5 cm.
Collected by Qinglong Manchu Autonomous County Cultural Relics Protection Institute.

It has a flared mouth, an outward lip, a tied neck, a sloping shoulder, a bulging belly that gradually narrows, and a wide round foot. Four flat ribbon handles are designed on the neck and shoulder. On the mid-belly area, white ground glaze is painted with a black-brown freehand cloud dragon pattern. It is complemented by multiple brownish string lines on the shoulder. It is applied with black-brown glaze to the lower abdomen until the foot. It was unearthed in Qinglong First Experimental Primary School, Qinglong Manchu Autonomous County.

143 Four-handled Vase with the Brown Colored and Large Leaf Pattern Curled Stems

Period Liao and Jin Dynasty (907 — 1234 CE)
Dimensions height: 26 cm; mouth diameter: 5.9 cm; foot diameter: 9.8 cm.
Collected by Qinglong Manchu Autonomous County Cultural Relics Protection Institute.

It has a flared mouth, an outward lip, a short neck, a sloping shoulder, a bulging belly, and a round foot. Four flat ribbon handles are designed on the neck and shoulder. This vase is applied with ivory white glaze on the belly and neck, and black-brown glaze on the lower abdomen to the foot. The shoulders and lower abdomen are each decorated with two dark brown colored string patterns, and black-brown freehand curled stems and large leaf patterns are painted between the string patterns. The foot is trimmed irregularly, and the bottom is concave. It is an old collection.

144 Four-handled Vase with the Brown Colored Grass and Leaf Pattern

Period Liao and Jin Dynasty (907 — 1234 CE)
Dimensions height: 30 cm; mouth diameter: 5 cm; base diameter: 9.5 cm.
Collected by Changli Cultural Relics Research and Protection Institute.

It has a flared mouth, an outward lip, a short neck, sloping shoulders, a long bulging belly, and a round foot. White glaze is applied to the upper part and the lower part is applied with brown glaze. The theme pattern is painted on the upper part of the abdomen, which is a freehand grass and leaf pattern, decorated with black brown wide band pattern and two water ripple lines. Four flat handles are designed on the neck.

145 Four-handled Vase with the Brown Colored Grass and Leaf Pattern

Period Jin Dynasty (1115 — 1234 CE)
Dimensions height: 26 cm; mouth diameter: 4.3 cm; abdominal diameter: 14 cm; foot diameter: 8.3 cm.
Collected by the Great Wall Museum in Shanhaiguan.

It has a flared mouth, an outward lip, a restricted neck, a sloping shoulder, an arc-shaped belly, a round foot, and the abdomen is olive-shaped. The round foot is thick. The upper part is applied with white glaze, and the lower part is applied with dark brown glaze. There are four strap-shaped handles (i.e., ears) at the junction of the shoulder and neck. The shoulder is applied with two dark brown string patterns, and the upper white-glazed area is decorated with a concise dark brown grass and leaf pattern.

146 Four-handled Olive-shaped Vase with Yellowish Green Glaze

Period Liao and Jin Dynasty (907 — 1234 CE)
Dimensions height: 40 cm; mouth diameter: 8.2 cm; foot diameter: 9 cm.
Collected by Qinglong Manchu Autonomous County Cultural Relics Protection Institute.

It is in olive shaped. It has a straight mouth, a round lip, a straight neck, a sloping shoulder, a bulging belly and gradually tapering to small round foot. The round foot is slightly out. The texture is hard and brownish-red. Yellowish green glaze is applied between the shoulder and neck, applied with four dragon head appliques holding rings, and the four characters "Wei Jia De Shi" in Regular Script are engraved around the circumference.

147 Two-handled Vessel (Zun) with Black Glaze

Period Liao and Jin Dynasty (907 — 1234 CE)
Dimensions height: 10 cm; mouth diameter: 4.5 cm; foot diameter: 5.8 cm.
Collected by Qinglong Manchu Autonomous County Cultural Relics Protection Institute.

It has a straight mouth, a flat lip, a short neck, a sloping shoulder, a dropping belly, and a wide round foot. There are two large handles (Pan) (i.e., Pan ears) on the shoulder. The lower abdomen and feet are not glazed.

148 Dark Brown Glazed Two-handled Jar

Period Liao and Jin Dynasty (907 — 1234 CE)
Dimensions height: 14.7 cm; mouth diameter: 17.4 cm; foot diameter: 8 cm; abdominal diameter: 63 cm.
Collected by Qinglong Manchu Autonomous County Cultural Relics Protection Institute.

It has a straight mouth, a round lip, a short and straight neck, weak shoulders, a slightly bulging belly that narrows to the bottom, and a round foot. The texture is exquisite and soft, and the body is covered with a uniform dark brown glaze, with unglazed bottom and foot. Between the neck and shoulders, there are two flat and wide handles. The surface of this jar has convex string patterns of different shades. It was collected from Lamagou Village, Qinglong Manchu Autonomous County.

149 Dark Brown Glazed Two-handled Jar with Vertical Stripes

Period Jin Dynasty (1115 — 1234 CE)
Dimensions height: 31 cm; mouth diameter: 21 cm; foot diameter: 12 cm.
Collected by Changli Cultural Relics Research and Protection Institute.

It has a straight mouth, an outward lip, a stubby neck slightly bunched, a sloping shoulder, a round belly tapering below, and a round foot. The texture is fine and glossy but hard, presents greyish white color. The dark brown glaze is applied until of the whole body. Lower abdomen and foot is applied with transparent glazed. The neck is applied with two wide and flat band-shaped handles (i.e., ears), which are basically as the same level as the mouth. The abdomen is decorated with dense vertical ridge stripes, like wicker, so it is commonly known as a "Wicker Jar".

150 Two-handled Jar with Black Glazed

Period Jin Dynasty (1115 — 1234 CE)
Dimensions height: 10.3 cm; mouth diameter: 12.4 cm; base diameter: 7.1 cm.
Collected by Changli Cultural Relics Research and Protection Institute.

It has a straight mouth, a round lip, a short and straight neck, a wide shoulder, a round belly and gradually restricted, and a round foot. The texture is hard and covered with engobe clay on the surface. It is applied with black glaze, the upper part is glazed but the lower part is exposed. The glaze surface is bright and soft. Two strap-shaped handles (i.e., ears) are applied on the shoulder that are almost level with the mouth. There are dark swirls hidden throughout the whole body.

151 Two-handled Jar of Jun Kiln

Period Jin Dynasty (1115 — 1234 CE)
Dimensions height: 14.3 cm; mouth diameter: 12 cm; abdominal diameter: 18.1 cm; foot diameter: 9 cm.
Collected by the Great Wall Museum in Shanhaiguan.

This jar has a paired mouth which one is big and the other is small. It has a short neck, a round belly which is downward convergence, and the round foot is not glazed. It has two flat handles (i.e., ears) on the shoulder. The whole body is applied with goose-egg-green color as ground glaze, with irregular flambé glazed reddish patches. This is a defective jar.

152 Wide Round Foot Large Bowl with White Glaze

Period Liao Dynasty (907 — 1125 CE)
Dimensions height: 5.5 cm; mouth diameter: 19.5 cm; foot diameter: 7.7 cm.
Collected by Changli Cultural Relics Research and Protection Institute.

It has a mouth without any glaze on the edge, a deep abdomen, an arc-shaped body, a wide round foot. The texture is coarse and soft, and applied with white glaze. There are obvious irregular swirls marks on the surface, and a string pattern is engraved on the upper abdomen.

153 Deep Belly Bowl with White Glaze

Period Liao Dynasty (907 — 1125 CE)
Dimensions height: 4 cm; mouth diameter: 8 cm; foot diameter: 3.3 cm.
Collected by Changli Cultural Relics Research and Protection Institute.

It has an open mouth, thin lip, deep abdomen, arc-shaped body, and round foot exposed with ceramic clay. The texture is fine and dense, applied with white glaze. There are obvious irregular swirled marks on the surface.

154 Deep Belly Small Bowl with White Glaze

Period Liao Dynasty (907 — 1125 CE)
Dimensions height: 4.2 cm; mouth diameter: 6.8 cm; foot diameter: 2.2 cm.
Collected by Changli Cultural Relics Research and Protection Institute.

It has an open mouth, thin lip, a deep abdomen, a straight body slightly in arc-shaped, and a small round foot. The texture is light and thin, applied with white glaze, of which color is grayish white.

155 Double Circle Pattern Bowl of Cizhou Kiln

Period Liao and Jin Dynasty (907 — 1234 CE)
Dimensions height: 8.4 cm; mouth diameter: 20.5 cm; foot diameter: 8.4 cm.
Collected by Qinglong Manchu Autonomous County Cultural Relics Protection Institute.

It has an open mouth, a round lip, a sloping body, a deep belly, and a round foot. The texture is thick. The body is half covered with slightly yellowish-white glaze, and the lower abdomen to the foot is not glazed. The interior is decorated with two loops of brown string patterns, the exterior is decorated with multiple raised string patterns. It was collected from Lamagou Village, Qinglong Manchu Autonomous County.

156 Black and White Glazed Bowl

Period Liao and Jin Dynasty (907 — 1234 CE)

Dimensions height: 7.4 cm; mouth diameter: 19.8 cm; foot diameter: 7.1 cm.
Collected by Qinglong Manchu Autonomous County Cultural Relics Protection Institute.

It has an open mouth, a round lip, a deep abdominal oblique body, and a round foot. It has a plain surface, with yellow-brown glaze on the mouth, white glaze interior, and black-brown glaze exterior. It was collected from Zengzhangzi Village, Qinglong Manchu Autonomous County.

157 White Glazed Large Bowl of Cizhou Kiln

Period Song Dynasty (960 — 1279 CE)
Dimensions height: 7.1 cm; mouth diameter: 20.9 cm; foot diameter: 5.8 cm.
Collected by Qinglong Manchu Autonomous County Cultural Relics Protection Institute.

It has an open mouth, a round lip, a sloping belly, and a round foot. The texture is coarse and soft. It is semi-glazed. The glaze is white and slightly yellow. It was unearthed in Xiaoshipan Village, Qinglong Manchu Autonomous County.

158 Ding Kiln Mold Printing Plate with Lotus Pond Fish Jumping

Period Song Dynasty (960 — 1279 CE)
Dimensions height: 2 cm; mouth diameter: 11.6 cm; foot diameter: 5.5 cm.
Collected by Qinglong Manchu Autonomous County Cultural Relics Protection Institute.

This plate has a mouth without any glaze on the edge, a shallow sloping belly and a wide round foot. The texture is soft. The whole body is covered with yellowish white glaze. The exterior is plain with some sand holes. The interior is embossed with a loop of chrysanthemum petals, and the bottom center is embossed with a four-diamond flower frame. The interior of the frame is decorated with fish jumping in a lotus pond pattern, and the exterior is decorated with a loop of curled leaves. It was unearthed in Tumenzi Village, Qinglong Manchu Autonomous County.

159 Ding Kiln Mold Printing Plate with Lotus

Period Liao and Jin Dynasty (907 — 1234 CE)
Dimensions height: 3.2 cm; mouth diameter: 18.5 cm; foot diameter: 5.7 cm.
Collected by Qinglong Manchu Autonomous County Cultural Relics Protection Institute.

This plate has a mouth without any glaze on the edge, a sloping belly, and a round foot. The whole body is covered with yellowish white glaze, the mouth rim is adhered with water scale in brown color, with a plain exterior. The interior is embossed with broken branches floral pattern. It was unearthed in Xiaoshipan Village, Qinglong Manchu Autonomous County.

160 Ding Kiln Mold Printing Plate with Lotus

Period Liao and Jin Dynasty (907 — 1234 CE)
Dimensions height: 5.1 cm; mouth diameter: 18.9 cm; foot diameter: 5.7 cm.
Collected by Qinglong Manchu Autonomous County Cultural Relics Protection Institute.

It has a mouth without any glaze on the edge, a deep oblique belly, and a round foot. The whole body is applied with white and slightly grey glaze, while the rim is adhered with water scale in color. The interior is embossed with a broken branches floral pattern. The exterior is white-glazed plain surface. It was unearthed in Xiaoshipan Village, Qinglong Manchu Autonomous County.

161 Round Foot Plate with White Glaze

Period Liao Dynasty (907 — 1125 CE)
Dimensions height: 3.2 cm; mouth diameter: 13.9 cm; foot diameter: 4.7 cm; weight: 100 g.
Collected by Changli Cultural Relics Research and Protection Institute.

It has a mouth without any glaze on the edge, a shallow abdomen, a sloping arc-shaped body, and a small round foot. The texture is coarse and soft, and is applied with white glaze, of which layer is slightly thicker and yellowish. The exterior is looming with swirls that are produced when pulling ceramic clay and slight scratches can be seen inside the plate. The foot is slightly trimmed inward and flat.

162 Black Glazed Porcelain Jar

Period Liao and Jin Dynasty (907 — 1234 CE)
Dimensions height: 46.2 cm; mouth diameter: 32.3 cm; abdominal diameter: 161 cm; base diameter: 20.5 cm.
Collected by Qinglong Manchu Autonomous County Cultural Relics Protection Institute.

It has a flared mouth, an outward lip, a short neck, sloping shoulders, a bulging belly that gradually narrows down, and a small flat bottom. The whole body is applied with thick and uniform black glaze, and a number of dense spiral patterns on the lower abdomen.

163 Black Glazed Gourd-shaped Vase

Period Liao and Jin Dynasty (907 — 1234 CE)
Dimensions height: 31 cm; mouth diameter: 2.8 cm; foot diameter: 9.6 cm.
Collected by Qinglong Manchu Autonomous County Cultural Relics Protection Institute.

The vase is in the shape of a gourd, with a small straight mouth. The upper small belly and the lower large belly are connected with a round foot. The texture is exquisite and soft, with hidden swirl marks on the surface. It is applied with black glaze until the lower abdomen, the foot is exposed without any glaze.

164 Tri-color Bowl with Engraved Floral Pattern

Period Liao Dynasty (907 — 1125 CE)
Dimensions height: 5 cm; mouth diameter: 13.5 cm; foot diameter: 5.8 cm.
Collected by Qinglong Manchu Autonomous County Cultural Relics Protection Institute.

This bowl has a straight mouth, a deep belly, a sloping wall, and a round foot. It is carved with floral pattern decoration in the middle. The texture is raw in brown-red color, with a layer of white engobe clay applied. It is semi-glazed, mainly in green glaze, supplemented by yellow glaze, which are dispersed each other, forming stains. The lower abdomen and foot reveal a more solid red ceramic clay body. It was unearthed in Lamagou Village, Qinglong Manchu Autonomous County.

165 Green Glazed Censer

Period Liao and Jin Dynasty (907 — 1234 CE)
Dimensions height: 6.9 cm; mouth diameter: 8.3 cm; height of foot: 1 cm.
Collected by Qinglong Manchu Autonomous County Cultural Relics Protection Institute.

It has a mouth with folded edge, a straight mouth, a round lip thick and straight neck, a round belly, an arc-shaped bottom, and three drum nail shaped feet are pinched. The texture is firm, applied with engobe clay and green glaze. The glaze is thin and dispersed each other, slightly shimmering yellow color. The lower abdomen and feet are not glazed.

166 Azure Glazed Dish of Jun Kiln

Period Song Dynasty (960 — 1279 CE)
Dimensions height: 2.7 cm; mouth diameter:12.9 cm; foot diameter: 4 cm.
Collected by Qinglong Manchu Autonomous County Cultural Relics Protection Institute.

It has a flared mouth, a round rim, a shallow arc abdomen of inclined body, and a small round foot. The texture is fine and hard, applied with light greyish azure glazed. It has cracked glaze on surface, presented with irregular reddish spots. It was unearthed in Xiaoshimen Village, Qinglong Manchu Autonomous County.

167 Azure Glazed Bowl with Red Colored Patch of Jun Kiln

Period Yuan Dynasty (1206 — 1368 CE)
Dimensions height: 8.5 cm; mouth diameter: 18.7 cm; foot diameter: 7.3 cm.
Collected by Qinglong Manchu Autonomous County Cultural Relics Protection Institute.

It has a straight mouth, a round lip, a deep oblique belly, a small round foot. The texture is hard, with light greyish azure glaze applied, and ceramic clay exposed foot. There are irregular cracks on the surface and flambé glazed reddish patches on the surface. It has chicken heart-shaped bottom.

168 Azure Glazed Bowl with Deep Belly of Jun Kiln

Period Yuan Dynasty (1206 — 1368 CE)
Dimensions height: 9.5 cm; mouth diameter: 22.7 cm; foot diameter: 6.5 cm.
Collected by Changli Cultural Relics Research and Protection Institute.

It has an open mouth, a round lip, a deep abdomen, an oblique arc-shaped body, and the round foot is turned outside. The texture of this bowl is delicate and hard, applied with light greyish azure glaze, and there are light red spots revealed on the surface. Black brown glaze is applied on the mouth rim, and glaze accumulated at the intersection with the foot.

169 Azure Glazed Dish with Shallow Belly of Jun Kiln

Period Yuan Dynasty (1206 — 1368 CE)
Dimensions height: 2.5 cm; mouth diameter: 14.3 cm; foot diameter: 5.8 cm.
Collected by Changli Cultural Relics Research and Protection Institute.

It has a straight mouth, a round lip, a shallow abdomen, an oblique body. The texture is delicate and hard, applied with light greyish azure glaze, and brown glaze applied to the mouth, and glaze accumulated at the intersection with foot. The round foot is trimmed with ceramic clay body exposed.

170 Azure Glazed Cup with Straight Belly of Jun Kiln

Period Yuan Dynasty (1206 — 1368 CE)
Dimensions height: 5cm; mouth diameter: 10.6 cm; foot diameter: 5.6 cm.
Collected by Changli Cultural Relics Research and Protection Institute.

It has a slightly convergent mouth, a round lip, a deep abdomen, a straight body but slightly curved, an oblique retracted lower abdomen, and a flared round foot. The texture is fine and hard, shows greyish white color. The whole body is applied with azure glaze. The surface has fine cracking pieces. There is glaze accumulated at the intersection with the foot. The round foot is exposed without any glaze.

171 Azure Glazed Cup with Straight Belly of Jun Kiln

Period Yuan Dynasty (1206 — 1368 CE)
Dimensions height: 4.6 cm; mouth diameter: 7.9 cm; foot diameter: 4.4 cm.
Collected by Changli Cultural Relics Research and Protection Institute.

The mouth is slightly convergent, with a round lip, a deep abdomen, a straight body, and a round foot. The texture is fine and hard. The whole body is covered with azure glaze, of which color is elegant and soft. There are fine cracking pieces on the surface, and partial accumulated glaze marks. The round foot is connected with residual sagger.

172 White Glazed Sculpture Vessel (Zun) of Two Crabs Delivering Reed

Period Chenghua Reign (1465 — 1487 CE), Ming Dynasty
Dimensions height: 22.25 cm; mouth diameter: 11.55 cm; foot diameter: 11.45 cm.

Collected by Beidaihe Cultural Relics Protection and Management Institute.

This vessel has a wavy ware mouth, a short neck, sloping shoulders, a sagging abdomen shaped, and a wide round foot. The whole body is designed by high floating sculpture with a pearl patterned bottom. The texture of this vessel is solid and thick. The whole body is covered with thick transparent white glaze, and the interior and exterior of rim are symmetrically and densely decorated with two loops of drum nail patterns of alternate sizes. The body is decorated with a pair of crabs, supplemented with fleabane pattern. The other side is decorated with lotus leaves and fleabane pattern. The foot rim is trimmed and regular. The bottom of this vessel has a concave square seal, and the inside is engraved with the four- character mark of "Made in Chenghua Period" in Regular Script. The shape is exquisite, the life is full of interest, and the crabs are portrayed in a charmingly naive and lifelike manner. Two crabs are delivering bunch of reeds, is the homophonic phrase with "Er Jia Chuan Lu (Reed)", which carries the meaning of being succeed in the examination.

This vessel (Zun) is designed in a pair, with roughly the same in shape but different in decoration.

173 Blue-and-white Glazed Small Mortar Jar with the Design of Dragon and Phoenix

Period Chenghua Reign (1465 — 1487 CE), Ming Dynasty
Dimensions height: 13.08 cm; mouth diameter: 18.65 cm; foot diameter: 12.03 cm.
Collected by Shanhaiguan Cultural Relics Protection and Management Institute.

This jar has a straight paired mouth, a deep straight abdomen, a flat bottom, a wide round foot, and a regular shape. It is applied with bluish-white glaze and plain surface interior. The exterior is painted with greenish white glaze. Blue-and-white cloud dragon and flying phoenix patterns are drawn on the whole body. The front and back of the exterior are decorated with dragon among clouds and flying phoenix patterns, and the string pattern locks the edges. The bottom is decorated with double blue hoops, and is printed with six blue-and-white Regular Script characters "Made in Chenghua Period of Ming Dynasty" in three lines inside. The dragon is powerful, vigorous and vivid. The phoenix spreads its wings, and its feathers soar, light and elegant. The dragons and phoenixes chase through the clouds, forming a momentum of flying dragons and dancing phoenixes, presenting an auspicious atmosphere.

174 Cyan Glazed Bowl with Incised Floral Pattern

Period Ming Dynasty (1368 — 1644 CE)
Dimensions height: 11 cm; mouth diameter: 19.5 cm, abdominal diameter: 6.6 cm.
Collected by Lulong Cultural Relics Protection and Management Institute.

It has a flared mouth, a round rim, a deep abdomen, an arc-shaped body, and a round foot. The texture of this bowl is tight. Interior and exterior are covered with cyan color glaze. The glaze is thick, and companied with crackings. The exterior is carved with simple patterns and double vertical zoning lines.

175 Cyan Glazed Bowl with Hui Pattern

Period Ming Dynasty (1368 — 1644 CE)
Dimensions height: 11 cm; mouth diameter: 19.5 cm, foot diameter: 6 cm.
Collected by Lulong Cultural Relics Protection and Management Institute.

It has a straight mouth, a round rim, a deep belly, an arc-shaped wall, a small round foot, and the bottom is slightly convex. The texture is fine and delicate. The Cyan glaze is applied interior and exterior, and the whole body is cracked on the surface. A loop of Hui pattern can be vaguely seen on the exterior mouth rim.

176 Azure Glazed Bowl with High Foot

Period Ming Dynasty (1368 — 1644 CE)
Dimensions height: 8 cm; mouth diameter: 14.6 cm; base diameter: 5.5 cm.
Collected by Changli Cultural Relics Research and Protection Institute.

It has a flared mouth, a round rim, a deep abdomen, an arc-shaped body folded down slightly, and a high round foot turned outward. The texture is dense, applied with uneven bluish-white glaze. There are obvious irregular swirled marks on the surface and densely small pores.

177 White Glazed High Foot Bowl

Period Ming Dynasty (1368 — 1644 CE)
Dimensions height: 8 cm; mouth diameter: 14.6 cm; base diameter: 5.5 cm.
Collected by Changli Cultural Relics Research and Protection Institute.

It has a flared mouth, a thin rim, a deep abdomen, an arc-shaped body folded down slightly, and a high round foot turned outward. The texture is fine and dense, applied with white glaze. The color is yellowish white, and there are accumulated glaze like tears on the belly. There are obvious irregular swirled marks on the surface.

178 Small Porcelain Jar with the Design of Polychrome Phoenix and Peony Pattern

Period Ming Dynasty (1368 —1644 CE)
Dimensions height: 9.1 cm; mouth diameter: 4.9 cm; abdominal diameter: 9 cm; foot diameter: 6.2 cm.
Collected by the Great Wall Museum in Shanhaiguan.

It has a straight mouth, a short neck, a slipping shoulder, a bulging belly, and a round foot. It is applied with multiple colors, are mainly divided into different areas separated by multiple pairs of blue lines. The belly is designed with phoenix and peony motifs pattern. The neck is designed with deformed banana leaf patterns. The shoulder is designed with polychrome auspicious clouds pattern. The lower abdomen is decorated with deformed banana leaves.

179 Fahua Color Jar with Lotus Pond and Egret Design

Period Ming Dynasty (1368 —1644 CE)
Dimensions height: 42.5 cm; mouth diameter: 23.8 cm; foot diameter: 22.7 cm.
Collected by Qinhuangdao Cultural Relics Protection Center.

It has a slightly flared mouth, a straight neck, plump shoulders, a bulging belly restricted to the bottom, a wide round foot, and a flat bottom without any glaze. The texture is glutinous white, slightly hard and tight. Green glaze is applied interior the mouth. The surface is applied with blue ground glaze, and the outline is made by the technique of piling raw materials and filling with color, such as yellow and light green glaze to form the patterns. The neck is decorated with auspicious clouds pattern, the shoulders are decorated with brown Ruyi (i.e., as one wishes) cloud patterns separated by a loop of Yingluo pattern and a wide green plain ribbon pattern. The abdomen is decorated with patterns of lotus pond with egrets. A loop of shore waves is decorated near the bottom. The lotus pond scenery is the most captivating among the decorations, with many egrets flying or playing in the water, complemented by blooming lotus flowers, creating a spring filled garden. The jar is dignified and majestic, with elegant and eye-catching fahua color tones and strong three-dimensional sense, making it a rare and excellent product.

180 Blue-and-white Glazed Jar with the Design of Interlocking Branches of Lotus

Period Chongzhen Reign, Ming Dynasty (1628 — 1644 CE)
Dimensions height: 17.8 cm; mouth diameter: 7.1 cm; foot diameter: 10.15 cm.
Collected by Beidaihe Cultural Relics Protection and Management Institute.

It has a straight mouth and a slightly flared rim. The neck is tied and short, connected with drum shoulders. It has a slightly bulging belly and wide round foot. The texture is dense and hard with thick and heavy body. The top of this jar is slightly outward extension, applied with yellowish-brown glaze. The shoulders are decorated with lotus floral spray patterns, the abdomen is decorated with interlocking branches of lotus patterns, and the lower abdomen is decorated with grass leaves. Each area is separated by double string lines. The round foot is wide and thick. The bottom of the vessel is decorated with a blue-and-white pattern inscribed with a rabbit. The texture is clear and broad, with pure and deep blue-and-white tones.

181 Blue-and-white Glazed Jar with the Design of Figures

Period Chongzhen Reign, Ming Dynasty (1628 — 1644 CE)
Dimensions height: 17.95 cm; mouth diameter: 7.05 cm; foot diameter: 9.85 cm.
Collected by Beidaihe Cultural Relics Protection and Management Institute.

It has a straight mouth with a slightly flared rim. It is designed into slightly bunched short neck, a plump shoulders, a slightly bulging belly, and a wide round foot. The texture is dense and hard with thick and heavy body. The top of this jar is outward extension, applied with brown-yellow glaze. The shoulder is complemented with flowers in Kaiguang Pattern, and is separated by fish scales patterns. It is ornamented with figures, pavilion, flowers and plants. The lower abdomen is supplemented with grass leaf pattern. Each area is separated by single or double string lines. The bottom is decorated with three horizontal patterns of blue-and-white glaze in solid brush painting skills. The color is dark blue, with gray and scattered tones.

182 Blue-and-white Glazed Plate with the Design of Landscape Pattern

Period Kangxi Reign, Qing Dynasty (1662 — 1722 CE)
Dimensions height: 11.8 cm; mouth diameter: 55.4 cm; foot diameter: 31.4 cm.
Collected by Beidaihe Cultural Relics Protection and Management Institute.

It has an open mouth, a round lip, an arc-shaped body, and a wide round foot. The texture is white and hard, covered with bright and clear glaze. Three sets of broken branch flowers pattern is decorated on the exterior, while landscape and portraits in the interior. The close view is intertwined streams, shades by trees, two red deer play freely on the water bank. In the distant view, there are towering mountains and ridges, with overlapping peaks and peaks, and two people are walking and talking on the mountain path. The picture is rich in layers, full in composition, and interesting in content. The beautiful scenery in the mountains and wild areas is impressive. The six blue-and-white Seal Script characters "Made in Kangxi Period of Qing Dynasty" has signed in three lines. The composition of the picture is full, with rich layers, clear and lively blue-and-white separation, and rich and pure color. The content is extremely rich in rural mountain and wilderness charm, and the tranquil mountains and rivers are vividly displayed in front of us. It is produced palace furnishings for Jingdezhen's official kiln in Kangxi Period.

183 Yellow Glazed Bowl with Green Colored Peach Trees and Birds Patterns

Period Kangxi Reign, Qing Dynasty (1662 — 1722 CE)
Dimensions height: 6.35 cm; mouth diameter: 12.35 cm; foot diameter: 5.15 cm.
Collected by Beidaihe Cultural Relics Protection and Management Institute.

It has a flared mouth, a round lip, a deep abdomen, an arced oblique body, and a round foot which turns slightly inwards. The texture of this bowl is fine and firm, with yellow round glaze green color on the exterior surface, and plain yellow glaze on the interior surface. The exterior rim is decorated with two pairs of string patterns, and the surface is decorated with green peach trees, rocks, flowers and birds. The bottom is applied with yellow glaze and an ochre glazed double column circle, with the six ochre color characters in Regular Script "Made in Kangxi Period of Qing Dynasty" in two lines. The yellow ground glaze is clean and fresh, and the green color is slightly blurry. The glaze surface is thick, smooth and bright. The decorative patterns are first carved on the plain ceramic clay body, and then burned with transparent glaze after carefully carving the lines, and then apply colored glaze and fire it in the kiln for the second time. On the basis of following the process of yellow glazed porcelain in the Ming Dynasty, the technique of carving and decorating color was applied to change the appearance of the monochrome yellow glaze before, forming another peak in the development history of yellow glazed porcelain.

184 Bowl with the Design of Two Yellow-colored Dragons Chasing a Pearl on Blue-and-white Ground Glaze

Period Kangxi Reign, Qing Dynasty (1662 — 1722 CE)
Dimensions height: 6.45 cm; mouth diameter: 13.35 cm; foot diameter: 6 cm.
Collected by Beidaihe Cultural Relics Protection and Management Institute.

It has a flared mouth, a thin lip, a deep abdomen, a slightly bulging arc-shaped body, and a slightly introverted round foot. The interior of this bowl is coated with plain white glaze. The texture is white and dense, the glaze is smooth and bright, decorated with blue-and-white ground in yellow color in the exterior, which is to draw patterns on the blank areas of the blue-and-white paint, fill them with low-temperature yellow glaze color after baking, and then burn them in the kiln again. The outer edge of the mouth is decorated with a loop of blue-and-white string patterns, and the abdomen is decorated with two dragons that bow and bend their necks and raise their heads and feet. Dragons are through the flame cloud patterns, each chasing a fire pearl. The near lower abdomen is decorated with three layers of lotus petals, and the foot is decorated with small lotus leaves and two strings. The bottom of the bowl is white glazed with double blue circles. Marked by six blue-and-white characters, inscribed in two lines in Regular Script, which is "Made in Kangxi Period of Qing Dynasty".

185 Peacock-blue Glazed Pigeon

Period Kangxi Reign, Qing Dynasty (1662 — 1722 CE)
Dimensions height: 17.1 cm; length: 20.4 cm; width: 9 cm.
Collected by Beidaihe Cultural Relics Protection and Management Institute.

Pigeons stand on the rock base with their heads turned sideways. Their wings are closed, their eyes are round and their beaks are sharp. They've got sharp eyes. The ceramic clay is dense and gray, with a unique shape and accurate shape, and the whole body is covered with peacock-blue low-temperature monochrome glaze, shows a brilliant blue color, which is bright and glorious. There are two small holes on the front of the base, and two small holes on both sides for suspended installation.

186 Sacrificial-red-glazed Beaker Vase

Period Kangxi Reign, Qing Dynasty (1662 — 1722 CE)
Dimensions height: 27.5 cm; mouth diameter: 15.15 cm; foot diameter: 10.35 cm.
Collected by Beidaihe Cultural Relics Protection and Management Institute.

The rim slanted outward, forming a large edge, a round lip. It has a long cylindrical body, and the waist has a loop of wide band collar. The ceramic clay is white, fine, and hard, thick texture. The white glaze is applied inside, and the sky-cleaning-red glaze is applied outside. Appearance looks uneven in color, with partly dull. A thick glaze is accumulated on the outside near the bottom. It has a double layer platform circle foot, and the foot is flush and without any glaze.

187 Blue-and-white Dish with the Design of Hundred Bats

Period Yongzheng Reign, Qing Dynasty (1723 — 1735 CE)
Dimensions height: 4.1 cm; mouth diameter: 20.9 cm; foot diameter: 13 cm.
Collected by Beidaihe Cultural Relics Protection and Management Institute.

This dish has an open mouth, a round lip, a shallow abdomen, a slightly curved sloping, and a widely round foot. The texture is hard and clean, covered by light and blue glaze. It feels wide and smooth. The blue-and-white color is light, slightly faint. The center of this plate is decorated with five bats connected to form a group of bat patterns, and the interior is decorated with twelve bats patterns in different postures. The two groups of patterns are separated by double-string line patterns. The upper and lower part is each decorated with a set of double-string line patterns, with eight bats in between. The round foot in loach spine foot, which is decorated with Hui patterns, and the bottom is decorated with double-column circles. There are six characters located in two lines on the bottom, which is "Made in Yongzheng Period of Qing Dynasty" in blue-and-white Regular Script. "Bat" is a homonym for "happiness" in Chinese, so it is commonly known as "hundred bats" dish. This dish is thin but feeling a sense of solidity, the pattern is clear and sparse, and the bat pattern composition has a large curve, which makes the picture flexible and elegant.

188 Sacrificial-blue-glazed Plate

Period Yongzheng Reign, Qing Dynasty (1723 — 1735 CE)
Dimensions height:4.16 cm; mouth diameter: 15.7 cm; foot diameter: 9.9 cm.
Collected by Shanhaiguan Cultural Relics Protection and Management Institute.

This plate has a flared mouth, a round lip, a sloping belly, and a wide round foot. The exterior is covered with sacrificial blue glaze, and the interior is covered with bluish-white glaze. The bottom is covered with bluish-white glaze, decorated with double blue circles, and six blue-and-white Regular Script characters "Made in Yongzheng Period of Qing Dynasty" are signed inside in three lines.

189 Light Greenish-blue Glazed Cong-shaped Vase with the Design of the Eight Diagrams

Period Yongzheng Reign, Qing Dynasty (1723 — 1735 CE)
Dimensions height: 30.06 cm; mouth diameter: 9.3 cm; foot diameter: 11.45 cm.
Collected by Beidaihe Cultural Relics Protection and Management Institute.

It has a straight mouth, a round lip, a low neck but outward sloping. The shoulder is flat. It has a long abdomen which is in rectangular column shape. The exterior of this rectangular-shape vase is embossed with raised Eight Trigrams. The texture is solid and white, and the whole body is covered with light greenish-blue glaze, which is plump and bright, and the edges and corners are white. The round foot is broad and strong, and the exposed body is finely polished and sliced. The round foot is light greenish-blue glazed. There are six characters located in three lines on the bottom, which is "Made in Yongzheng Period of Qing Dynasty" in blue-and-white Regular Script. The mouth and foot of this vase are the same size, and the abdomen imitates the tubular form of an ancient jade Cong. It is simple and elegant, reflecting a humanistic theory that "the earth was square and heaven was round" "human is an integral part of nature".

190 Famille-rose Glazed Brush Holder with the Design of Flower and Butterfly

Period Yongzheng Reign, Qing Dynasty (1723 — 1735 CE)
Dimensions height: 12 cm; mouth diameter: 7.2 cm; foot diameter: 6.7 cm.
Collected by Qinglong Manchu Autonomous County Cultural Relics Protection Institute.

It is cylindrical in shape. It has a straight mouth, a squared lip, and a straight column body, with double layer platform circle short base. The texture is white and firm, and in regular shape. Using a multi-layered famille-rose glazed technique, flowers are drawn on white ground glaze in red, green, yellow, blue, and purple. The bottom is signed a six-character in two lines, "Made in Yongzheng Period of Qing Dynasty" in blue-and-white Regular Script inside a double blue circles.

191 Blue-and-white Glazed Bobbin-shaped Vase

Period Yongzheng Reign, Qing Dynasty (1723 — 1735 CE)
Dimensions height: 19.95 cm; mouth diameter: 4.65 cm; base diameter: 5.1 cm.
Collected by Beidaihe Cultural Relics Protection and Management Institute.

This vase has an outward mouth, a round lip, a tied neck, slip shoulders, a long straight belly, and a flat bottom. The ceramic clay of this vase is hard, with blue-and-white glazed. The pattern covered on the abdomen is blooming flowers and full moon, means perfect conjugal bliss, and the neck is supplemented by two groups of orchid patterns.

192 Famille-rose Beaker Vase with the Design of Phoenix-tail

Period Yongzheng Reign, Qing Dynasty (1723 — 1735 CE)
Dimensions height: 44.8 cm; mouth diameter: 21.4 cm; foot diameter: 14.05 cm.
Collected by Beidaihe Cultural Relics Protection and Management Institute.

The mouth is outward, the mouth surface is large, with a long neck. The shoulder slightly bulging, a bulging belly that is gradually restricted to the bottom. The bottom is a double layer platform circle base but very short. It is dense and white texture, with white glaze and bright luster. The body is painted with a tall peony flower and bird, supplemented by grass insects, butterflies and cave stones. The composition of the picture is from shoulder to neck. The neck and abdomen are decorated with green glazed ribbon pattern. The caliber is larger than the belly and base diameters. The bottom of this vase is decorated with blue-and-white double column circles without any inscription.

193 Famille-rose Beaker Vase with the Design of Phoenix-tail

Period Yongzheng Reign, Qing Dynasty (1723 — 1735 CE)
Dimensions height: 44.8 cm; mouth diameter: 21cm; foot diameter: 14.2 cm.
Collected by Beidaihe Cultural Relics Protection and Management Institute.

The mouth is outward, the mouth surface is large, with a long neck. The shoulder slightly bulging, a bulging belly that is gradually restricted to the bottom. The bottom is a double layer platform circle base but very short. It is dense and white ceramic clay, with cyan white glaze and bright luster. The body is painted with a tall peony flower and two birds are resting on the branches, supplemented by grass, insects and cave stones. The composition of the picture is from shoulder to neck, supplemented by a deer. The neck and abdomen are decorated with turquoise green ground glaze with brown colored floral pattern. The caliber is larger than the belly and base diameters. The bottom of this vase is decorated with blue-and-white double column circles without any inscription.

194 Blue-and-white Glazed Covered Jar with Plum Pattern

Period Yongzheng Reign, Qing Dynasty (1723 — 1735 CE)

Dimensions height: 24.9 cm; mouth diameter: 8.45 cm; foot diameter: 12.85 cm.
Collected by Beidaihe Cultural Relics Protection and Management Institute.

This jar is divided into two parts which are the cover and the jar. The blue-and-white glaze is left blank, and the color surface shows a broken ice crystal pattern. The lid shape is in a straight body but with an arc top, decorated with broken plum branches. It has a paired mouth with one big and the other small. It has a plump shoulder, bulging belly, and lying foot. The shoulder is decorated with a loop of geometric patterns, and the abdomen is decorated with four white plum blossoms and branches. The bottom is decorated with double-blue rings.

195 Blue-and-white Glazed General Jar with the Design of Lions Playing among Flowers

Period Yongzheng Reign, Qing Dynasty (1723 — 1735 CE)
Dimensions height: 33 cm; mouth diameter: 15.1 cm; foot diameter: 15 cm.
Collected by Lulong Cultural Relics Protection and Management Institute.

The jar has a cover, a short neck, a sloping shoulder, a bulging belly that is gradually restricted to the bottom, a flat round foot, and a slightly concave bottom. The texture is hard and heavy, and the glaze color is greenish white. The lid is concave, with a column button on top, decorated with a pattern of dragon chasing bead. The design on abdomen is decorated with two lions, walking through the interlocking peony flowers. The neck is decorated with deformed seawater, river, and cliff patterns. It is decorated with dark Eight Immortals pattern with flame cloud patterns near foot. Three sets of decorative patterns are separated by string belt patterns. The blue-and-white colors are bright, clear, and smooth. The fierce lion contrasts sharply with the enchanting peony, shows the meaning is to exorcise evil spirits and disasters, and prosperity and auspiciousness.

196 Blue-and-white Glazed High-footed Bowl with the Design of Sanskrit Inscriptions

Period Qianlong Reign, Qing Dynasty (1736 — 1795 CE)
Dimensions height: 13.75 cm; mouth diameter: 14.75 cm; foot diameter: 7.4 cm.
Collected by Beidaihe Cultural Relics Protection and Management Institute.

This bowl has a flared mouth, a thin lip, a deep belly, an arc-shaped body, a flat bottom, and a high round foot is in flared shape. The texture of this bowl is fine, white, and firm, with smooth and clean ground glaze, and covered by pure blue-and-white color glaze, which is slightly hazy. The interior is decorated with string patterns, and a lotus flower is inscribed in the string pattern frame around the middle of this bowl. On the exterior belly is eight Baoxiang patterns interlocking lotus flowers with Sanskrit characters, and string patterns are decorated on the edge of the mouth and the bottom edge of the belly. There is a raised ridge ribbon on the foot of the handle, and the upper part of the adjacent ridge is decorated with four flower patterns, and the lower part is decorated with Yingluo and double-string pattern. The interior of the round foot is inscribed from right to left in blue-and-white Seal Script, which are "Made in Qianlong Period of Qing Dynasty" six horizontal characters. This bowl is often used in religious rituals in elegant shape and the layout of the picture is exquisite. Warm and bright white glaze relieves against the blooming lotus graceful posture.

197 Blue-and-white Glazed Bowl with Three Fruits Pattern

Period Qianlong Reign, Qing Dynasty (1736 — 1795 CE)
Dimensions height: 5.05 cm; mouth diameter: 12.05 cm; foot diameter: 4.55 cm.
Collected by Beidaihe Cultural Relics Protection and Management Institute.

It has an open mouth, a round lip, a deep belly, convergent belly under the oblique body, and a round foot. The color is pure. The texture of this bowl is fine, smooth, and white, and the glaze color is rich and firm. The interior and exterior sides of this bowl are decorated with wave patterns as borders, the center of this bowl is decorated with double-string circles, and the interior is painted with three fruit patterns. The exterior belly is decorated with three groups of with floral sprays and fruit patterns of peaches offered as a birthday present, water melon and pomegranate. The lower abdomen is decorated with lotus pattern. The round foot is decorated with double-string patterns. There are six characters located in three lines on the bottom, which is "Made in Qianlong Period of Qing Dynasty" in blue-and-white Seal Script. The fruits are used as decorations to imply auspiciousness, which is to have more children, more blessings, and more longevity, and express people's vision for a better life.

198 Blue-and-white and Alum Red-colored Glaze Small Bowl with Baoxiang Flowers Pattern

Period Qianlong Reign, Qing Dynasty (1736 — 1795 CE)

Dimensions height: 4.35 cm; mouth diameter: 8.28 cm; foot diameter: 3.4 cm.
Collected by Beidaihe Cultural Relics Protection and Management Institute.

It has an open mouth, a round lip, a deep abdomen, a convergent belly under the oblique body, and a round foot. The texture of this bowl is delicate, light and thin. The ground glaze is lustrous white and solid. It is decorated with blue-and-white and retouched with a bit of alum red-colored. The bowl is made of sweet white glaze, the exterior mouth is decorated with blue- and-white double-string patterns, the abdomen is decorated with four symmetrical blue-and-white flowers and alum red-colored Baoxiang flowers pattern. The bottom of the vessel is signed in the blue-and-white Seal Script "Made in Qianlong Period of Qing Dynasty" is signed in six characters in three lines. The pattern is sparse and clear, the color is elegant and beautiful. Red highlights the flower, blue leaves relieve against red color and complement each other.

199 Blue-and-white Glazed Dish with the Design of Red Dragon Crossing the Ocean in Blank

Period Qianlong Reign, Qing Dynasty (1736 — 1795 CE)
Dimensions height: 4.15 cm; mouth diameter: 17.65 cm; foot diameter: 10.75 cm.
Collected by Beidaihe Cultural Relics Protection and Management Institute.

It has a flared mouth, a round lip, a shallow abdomen, a slightly curved sloping body. The wide round foot is slightly restrained. The texture of this dish is white, firm, and bluish-white, and decorated with blue-and-white ground glaze with ocean in blank, and retouched in alum red color. The inner mouth is bordered with blue-and-white double-string patterns, the body is plain white. It is decorated with blue-and-white double-string patterns in the middle of this plate, and the interior is painted with a red-colored dragon crossing in the blue-and-white with ocean in blank patterns. The exterior is adorned with nine red colored small dragons with different postures, complemented by blue-and-white with ocean in blank patterns and white string frames on top and bottom, with blue and white ribbon patterns along the mouth and locking edges. The bottom of the plate is inscribed in blue-and-white Seal Script with six characters in three lines of "Made in Qianlong Period of Qing Dynasty". The red-color is rich and delicate, the blue-and-white color is deep and dignified. The white ocean wave pattern is used as a foil to highlight nine dragons leaping out of the ocean, which is extremely good to hear or see.

200 Yellow Ground Glaze Chrysanthemum Petal-shaped Dish with the Design of Green-colored Dragon

Period Qianlong Reign, Qing Dynasty (1736 — 1795 CE)
Dimensions height: 2.8 cm; mouth diameter: 13.2 cm; foot diameter: 7.45 cm.
Collected by Beidaihe Cultural Relics Protection and Management Institute.

It has a chrysanthemum petal-shaped mouth, a flared rim, a shallow abdomen, a micro arc-shaped oblique body, and a wide round foot. This dish is fine and firm texture. The glaze is thick, smooth and bright. Both inside and outside are applied with yellow ground green color glaze, and engraved with decorative patterns, that is, the dragon's head, claw, body, and scale of this dragon are first carved on the ceramic clay, and then fired with transparent glaze. Finally colored glaze is fired in the kiln for two times according to the figure. The mouth rim of this dish is black ochre color, and both the interior and exterior body are decorated with two green- colored dragons chasing fire beads. In the middle of this interior dish is a green dragon holding a twig and catching fire bead pattern in a single-string pattern. The bottom of this Plate is covered with white glaze, and the blue-and-white six characters Seal Script "Made in Qianlong Period of Qing Dynasty" is arranged in three lines. Because of the continuous dragons, agile walking, yellow glaze delicate and fresh, green and lush green, slightly scattered, with engraved patterns changing in depth, enhancing the three-dimensional sense of the picture.

201 Doucai (Contrasting-colors) Jar with Flowers and Interlocking Lotus Pattern

Period Qianlong Reign, Qing Dynasty (1736 — 1795 CE)
Dimensions height: 8.33 cm; mouth diameter: 11.63 cm; foot diameter: 5.66 cm.
Collected by Shanhaiguan Cultural Relics Protection and Management Institute.

It has slightly a straight mouth, a round lip with a slightly bulging belly, and a round foot. The texture is white and delicate in regular shape. It is covered with plain white glaze interior and lip rim. The exterior is decorated with Doucai (contrasting- colors) on a white ground glaze. Outlines of the main decoration are applied with blue-and-white under glazed, and the glaze on the surface is mainly filled with red, green, and yellow color. The theme decoration on the abdomen is multiple groups of circular Kaiguang Patterns. Baoxiang flowers pattern is intertwined with lotus branches and flowers inside. A set of red parallel string patterns is decorated on the upper part of the belly. The chain-shape Kaiguang pattern are decorated between parallel strings, and the interior is decorated with various flowers. The frame is designed with a loop of Ruyi (i.e., as ones wish) cloud pattern is to decorate motif pattern of abdomen. Near the foot is decorated with a loop of deformed lotus petals. The foot is flat and wide, smooth, and without any glaze. The bottom is covered with white glaze, and signed with a blue-and-white inscription "Made in Qianlong Period of Qing Dynasty" in six-character and three-line Seal Script. The decoration of the whole tank is rich and colorful, bright and eye- catching. The blue-and-white under-glazed color and over-glazed colors set off each other, competing for beauty.

202 Sacrificial-red-glazed Mortar Jar

Period Qianlong Reign, Qing Dynasty (1736 — 1795 CE)
Dimensions height: 13.2 cm; mouth diameter: 12.6 cm; abdominal diameter: 22 cm; base diameter:9.7 cm.
Collected by Shanhaiguan Cultural Relics Protection and Management Institute.

This jar has a round lip, a convergence mouth, a flat but bulging belly, and a recumbent foot. The interior is applied with white glaze, and the exterior is decorated with sacrificial-red-glaze, with smooth glaze and uniform color. The bottom is applied with white glaze, and it is signed with six blue-and-white Seal Script characters "Made in Qianlong Period of Qing Dynasty" in three lines.

203 Blue-and-white Wine Vessels (Zun) with Elephant-trunk Handles

Period Qianlong Reign, Qing Dynasty (1736 — 1795 CE)
Dimensions height: 27.7 cm; mouth diameter: 10.6 cm; foot diameter: 9.65cm.
Collected by Beidaihe Cultural Relics Protection and Management Institute.

It has a flared mouth, a slightly outward arc-shaped neck, and a plump shoulders. The abdomen below the shoulders gradually converges to the foot, and the round foot is turned outward. The texture of this vessel is fine and white, covered with firm and plump glaze. The whole body is decorated with blue-and-white floral patterns, and the color is deep and natural. The neck is decorated with Ruyi clouds and Baoxiang pattern. The shoulders are decorated with interlocking lotus and Ruyi cloud patterns. A pair of kneading elephant-trunk handles (i.e., ears) are carved with two rings on each side and above shoulders. The abdomen is decorated with intertwined flowers, and two Kui-phoenixes standing and walking through it. Two Kui-phoenixes are separated by two larger blooming flowers. Near the foot is decorated with deformed algae patterns. The foot is decorated with a loop of curly grass pattern. The bottom of this vessel is marked with six characters in three lines in blue-and-white Seal Script "Made in Qianlong Period of Qing Dynasty". The vessel is dignified and elegant, with intricate and gorgeous decorations.

204 Blue-and-white Jar with Floral Pattern

Period Qianlong Reign, Qing Dynasty (1736 — 1795 CE)
Dimensions height: 14.73 cm; mouth diameter: 4.71 cm; foot diameter:5.87 cm.
Collected by Shanhaiguan Cultural Relics Protection and Management Institute.

This jar has a straight mouth and neck, a wide shoulder, a bulging belly, and a high round foot turned outward. The glaze is bluish-white and slightly azure in color. Several groups of blue-and-white ornaments are painted, separated by double-string patterns. The abdomen motif is designed with six pictures of flowers and peony trees, each separated by double vertical lines. The composition of flowers and trees is simple but exaggerated and deformed. They are rooted on the earth. The peony flowers are huge and full of the whole design. The neck, shoulders, and lower abdomen are supplemented with fold branches and flowers.

205 Bean-green Glazed Jar with Animal-shaped Handles

Period Qianlong Reign, Qing Dynasty (1736 — 1795 CE)
Dimensions height: 15.9 cm; mouth diameter: 5.3 cm; base diameter: 7 cm.
Collected by Beidaihe Cultural Relics Protection and Management Institute.

This jar is olive-shaped. The lip is rounded with the convergent mouth, the top and foot are both bulging. It is covered with bean-green glaze, which is uneven thickness, and finely cracks on the glaze surface. The foot edge is trimmed, and slightly concave. The two sides of the upper abdomen are symmetrically shaped with animal-shaped handles (i.e., ears), with large underglaze red spots between the two handles (i.e., ears).

206 Ruby Glazed Vase in the Shape of Awl Handle

Period Qianlong Reign, Qing Dynasty (1736 — 1795 CE)
Dimensions height: 39.6 cm; mouth diameter: 7.1 cm; foot diameter: 13.3 cm.
Collected by Beidaihe Cultural Relics Protection and Management Institute.

It is in an awl handle shaped. It has a straight mouth, a round lip but slightly flared, a long neck slightly thicker below, a sloping shoulders, a drooping abdomen, and bottom without any glaze. The texture of this vase is thick, applied with firm, smooth, and even glaze, and shows strong glass texture. A raised string pattern is applied to the mouth and shoulders, and a raised hoop-shaped wide rib is applied to the lower part of the neck. The glaze becomes red, blue, moon white and other colors after high temperature kiln. Various colors and red blend together and flow recklessly, forming ever-changing filamentous textures and color patches, which are as gorgeous and dazzling as flames. Therefore, this kind of glaze is known as "flame red" and is deeply loved by people.

207 Red Glazed Globular Vase

Period Qianlong Reign, Qing Dynasty (1736 — 1795 CE)
Dimensions height: 31.65 cm; mouth diameter: 5.25 cm; foot diameter: 12.05 cm.
Collected by Beidaihe Cultural Relics Protection and Management Institute.

It has a straight mouth, a long neck, plump shoulders, a bulging belly gradually retracted to the bottom, and a round foot. The exterior is covered with red glaze, and the interior and mouth rim are applied with white glaze. Its red color is strong and bright, with a glass texture, as gorgeous as a ruby. The mouth is glazed to form a moon-shaped white glazed mouth, commonly known as "Dengcaokou". The bottom edge has a vertical flow of glaze, and is covered with white glaze. The whole body is not trimmed meticulously enough, and repair swirl marks are vaguely displayed. Under the influence of glaze removal, red and white are distinct, like decorative string patterns, with a unique elegance.

208 Bobbin-shaped Vase with the Design of Famille Verte Dragon Chasing Pearls as an Imitation of Jiajing Reign Style

Period Qianlong Reign, Qing Dynasty (1736 — 1795 CE)
Dimensions height: 45.3 cm; mouth diameter: 8.7 cm; base diameter: 12.9 cm.
Collected by Beidaihe Cultural Relics Protection and Management Institute.

This vase has a plate-shaped convergence mouth, tightly bound neck, small sloping shoulders, cylindrical abdomen slightly retracted to the foot, and a slightly concave bottom. The texture of this vase is solid and thick, covered by white and smooth ground glaze. On the glazed surface as white as snow, red, green, yellow, blue and other colors are used to describe decorative patterns. The belly is decorated with two standing dragons with the theme pattern, bowing, bending the neck, looking back, and chasing through the flame-shaped cloud patterns, playing with fire beads. The shoulder is supplemented with gravel patterns and double-string patterns. The exterior mouth rim is decorated with two single and double-string patterns as a frame. The double-line Ruyi cloud pattern and a fan-shaped Kaiguang Pattern. Between the frames, which is signed with six characters, in blue-and-white Regular Script "Made in Jiajing Period of Ming Dynasty" are inscribed from right to left as an imitation. The painting is colorful and gorgeous, the lines are skillful, the pattern of the dragon is light, standing and lively, giving people a festive and warm feeling as a whole.

209 Famille-rose Glazed Small Bowl with the Design of Eight Buddhist Ritual Instruments

Period Jiaqing Reign, Qing Dynasty (1796 — 1820 CE)
Dimensions height: 6.5 cm; mouth diameter:10.6 cm; foot diameter: 4.2 cm.
Collected by Beidaihe Cultural Relics Protection and Management Institute.

It has an open mouth, a round lip, a deep belly, a sloping straight body below the belly, and convergence round foot. The texture of this bowl is as fine as jade. The white glaze is applied interior and exterior. The exterior is decorated with famille-rose glaze. The exterior rim is decorated with red-colored deformed Hui patterns with upper and lower blue-and-white string patterns as borders, and the abdomen is decorated with four pairs of Buddhist Ritual Instruments patterns. Near the foot is described with red-colored Ruyi cloud pattern with blue-and-white string pattern filled with yellow color lined with blue-and-white drum nail patterns. Six blue-and-white colored Seal Script characters in three lines, "Made in Jiaqing Period of Qing Dynasty", are inscribed on the bottom. The shape of this bowl is exquisite and elegant, the color is smooth and soft, and the painting layout is reasonable, delicate and vivid. It is a superior product in Jiajing period. The eight auspicious objects are eight instruments used in a Buddhist such as the Buddhist wheel, Buddhist conch, Chattra, canopy of Chattra, lotus flower, treasure vase, Buddhist twin fishes, and Pan Chang knot, also known as the Eight Buddhist Emblems.

210 Green Ground Glazed Writing-brush Washer with the Design of Famille-rose Glazed Baoxiang Flowers

Period Jiaqing Reign, Qing Dynasty (1796 — 1820 CE)
Dimensions height: 6.65 cm; mouth diameter: 22.9 cm; base diameter: 22.3 cm.
Collected by Beidaihe Cultural Relics Protection and Management Institute.

It has a straight mouth, a square lip, a straight body, a shallow belly. The flat bottom is in the shape of a Jade Bi. The texture of this cylindrical washer is thick. The mouth rim is applied with white glaze, the interior body is decorated with turquoise glaze. The exterior body is applied with turquoise green ground glaze with the design of famille-rose glazed interlacing flowers by using a unique grilling flower technique. It has a visible bottom trimming rotary knife mark. The round concave part of the bottom is covered with turquoise green glaze, and the glaze surface is slightly crawling. Six red-colored Seal Script characters in three lines, "Made in Jiaqing Period of Qing Dynasty", are inscribed on the bottom. The deep turquoise green ground glaze makes prominent the light and warm famille-rose glaze, decorates the simple and steady writing-brush washer, and shows both charm and elegance.

211 Blue-and-white Glazed Plate with the Design of Phoenix among Clouds

Period Jiaqing Reign, Qing Dynasty (1796 — 1820 CE)
Dimensions height: 3.65 cm; mouth diameter:16.6 cm; foot diameter: 9.8 cm.
Collected by Beidaihe Cultural Relics Protection and Management Institute.

It has an open mouth, a round lip, a shallow abdomen, an arc-shaped body, wide round foot. This plate is designed as delicate ceramic clay body, covered in rich, smooth and bright white glaze, and modeled in a dignified and regular shape. The color is gentle. The interior rim of this dish is decorated with double-string patterns, and the center of this plate is decorated with a set of double-string patterns for round Kaiguang Pattern. A pair of symmetrical double phoenix patterns are painted on each inside. The two phoenix heads face each other, and the wings and tails are stretched out to make a flying shape. They are separated by a large "Ren" shaped cloud pattern. The exterior body of this dish is redone with a pair of phoenix images, head to tail connected, head held high, wings spread, tail floating, flying among clouds. The shape of the two groups of phoenix is basically the same, except that the tail wings are slightly different, one like cirrus clouds and the other like horsetail whisk. Six blue-and-white colored Seal Script characters in three lines, "Made in Jiaqing Period of Qing Dynasty", are inscribed on the bottom. The symmetrical and regular twin phoenixes are dancing among the auspicious clouds. They are vividly portrayed, presenting an auspicious scene.

212 Bean-green Ground Glazed Plate-shaped Mouth Vase with Elephant-trunk Handles

Period Jiaqing Reign, Qing Dynasty (1796 — 1820 CE)
Dimensions height: 40.2 cm; mouth diameter: 13.2 cm; foot diameter: 12.8 cm.
Collected by Beidaihe Cultural Relics Protection and Management Institute.

This vase has a plate-shaped convergence mouth which is inwardly convergent, a long neck, sloping shoulders, a round and bulging belly and a flared round foot. The whole body of this vase is covered with bean-green glaze, and the glaze is rich and with firm texture. A pair of elephant-trunk shaped ears are sculpted on each side of the neck, which is applied with brownish glaze. The shoulders are embossed with a blue-and-white Ruyi cloud pattern on the lotus petals. The pattern abdomen is a character story of "As longevity as pine tree which lives longer than Nan mountain", drawing in blue-and-white glaze, in a Kaiguang Pattern. And the exterior of this consecrated pattern is decorated with blue-and-white cranes and auspicious cloud patterns. The interior is decorated with "happiness and longevity, as long as pine and cypress". The exterior foot is finished without any glaze, without any inscription on the bottom.

213 Blue-and-white Glazed Beaker Vase as an Imitation of Chenghua Reign Period Style

Period Jiaqing Reign, Qing Dynasty (1796 — 1820 CE)
Dimensions height: 19.3 cm; mouth diameter: 10.3 cm; foot diameter: 5.25 cm.
Collected by Beidaihe Cultural Relics Protection and Management Institute.

It has a large flared mouth, a thin rim, the neck is slightly longer than the abdomen. The abdomen is slightly bulging, and after converging, it is turned outward to the feet, and short round foot. The texture is not very dense and white, and the glaze is not very bright and lustrous. The mouth diameter is larger than the diameter of the abdomen and the bottom. It has a feeling of top heavy and bottom light. The whole body is decorated with blue-and-white interlocking flower patterns. The whole body is decorated with blue-and-white floral patterns, and the shoulder is adorned with a circular cloud pattern. In the blue-and-white double column circle at the bottom of this vase, there are four characters and two lines of "Made in Chenghua Period" in Regular Script.

214 Blue-and-white Double Tubular Handled Vase with the Design of as Longevity as Song Qiao

Period Jiajing and Daoguang Reign, Qing Dynasty (1796 — 1850 CE)
Dimensions height: 22.8 cm; mouth diameter: 6.9 cm; base diameter: 11 cm.
Collected by Changli Cultural Relics Research and Protection Institute.

It has a straight mouth, and a flared lip. It has a long neck, a slip shoulder, a bulging belly that gradually retract to foot and turned outward, and a round foot. The whole vase is applied with bean-green glaze, the glaze color is elegant and uniform, and it is blue-white. The middle of long neck is decorated with two convex string patterns, and the two sides are symmetrically connected with tubular handles. The handles are decorated with blossomed lotus petals. The belly is decorated with "As longevity as Song Qiao", the neck is decorated with "Liuhai playing with golden toad under moonlight". The painted scenes are smooth and vivid, both of them are typical traditional folk stories, which are wishing longevity, wealth and auspiciousness.

215 Blue-and-white Glazed Bowl with the Design of Kui-phoenix Crossing Lotus

Period Daoguang Reign, Qing Dynasty (1821 — 1850 CE)
Dimensions height: 8.9 cm; mouth diameter: 23.55 cm; foot diameter: 10.15 cm.
Collected by Beidaihe Cultural Relics Protection and Management Institute.

It has an open mouth, an arc-shaped body, and a round foot. The clay texture of this bowl is delicate and white, and the glaze is bright and lustrous. The interior of this bowl is brightly glazed with only white glaze, and the exterior rim, near the bottom and the foot rim are decorated with double-string patterns. The abdomen is decorated with Kui-phoenixes, which are shuttling in the vast sea of interlocking lotus flowers, spreading their wings. Double string pattern locking edges are decorated on exterior rim, abdomen near the foot, and foot wall. The bottom of this bowl is marked with a six-character three-line year mark "Made in Daoguang Period of Qing Dynasty" in blue-and-white Seal Script. The blue-and-white outline is painted flat, with a rich and vibrant color, full and profound. Kui-phoenix has a graceful and beautiful posture, showcasing his heroic figures vividly, with a strong artistic appeal. Kui-phoenix pattern means "Peace in the world, and peace in all things".

216 Doucai (Contrasting-colors) Bamboo Hat Shaped Bowl with the Eight Immortals' Ritual Instruments

Period Daoguang Reign, Qing Dynasty (1821 — 1850 CE)
Dimensions height: 5.55 cm; mouth diameter: 20.35 cm; foot diameter: 10.85 cm.
Collected by Beidaihe Cultural Relics Protection and Management Institute.

It has an open mouth, a deep arc-shaped body, a girdle waist, vertical below waist to foot, and a high round foot. The texture is neat and beautiful, and the glaze is clear, smooth, and elegant. The interior of this bowl is decorated with blue-and-white double- string as Kaiguang Pattern, and is painted with Eight Immortals' Ritual Instruments in Doucai (Contrasting-Colors), that is, the ritual instruments used by the eight Taoist immortals are used as the decora tive content without describing characters. They are Han Zhongli's fan, Zhang Guolao's fishing drum, Lyu Dongbin's sword, Tieguai Li's gourd, Cao Guojiu's yin and yang board, Lan Caihe's flower basket, Han Xiangzi's flute and He Xiangu's lotus flower. The blue-and-white double-string pattern in the center of this bowl leaves blank frame, and is painted with Doucai interlocking branches and stamen-shaped as Baoxiang Pattern in the blank. The exterior of this bowl is painted with two sets of Doucai interlacing branches four seasons flowers, with blue-and-white string patterns along the rim, and Doucai Ruyi cloud patterns along the foot. The bottom is decorated with white glaze, and it is marked with six characters in three lines in blue-and-white Seal Script "Made in Daoguang Period of Qing Dynasty". The outline of the decoration is drawn with blue-and-white color, and then filled with red, yellow, green and other colors in the outline. The underglazed blue-and-white color and brilliant multi-color glaze contrast with each other, closely following the elegance of the Doucai technique in Chenghua Period, which can be called extremely beautiful. The composition is full and orderly, which means blessing for good luck, and praying for peace and safety.

217 Tea-dust Glazed Biqi-shaped (water chestnut shaped) Vase

Period Daoguang Reign, Qing Dynasty (1821 — 1850 CE)
Dimensions height: 32.8 cm; mouth diameter: 7.55 cm; foot diameter: 15.05 cm.
Collected by Beidaihe Cultural Relics Protection and Management Institute.

It has a straight mouth, a long neck, wide shoulders, a Biqi-shaped abdomen, a wide round foot and outward curling. This vase is made by thick and solid ceramic clay, and is in a simple and elegant shape. The whole body is covered with tea-dust glaze, the glaze color is turmeric color, and the surface is smooth. Six Seal Script characters in three lines, "Made in Daoguang Period of Qing Dynasty", are shallow inscribed on the bottom in a square seal. In the yellow glaze, there are hidden green fragments, which are like tea dust but not the real, therefore, it is called Tea-dust Glaze. When you look at this vase, it feels profound and ancient, magnificent, elegant and meaningful.

218 Sacrificial-blue-glazed Bowl

Period Daoguang Reign, Qing Dynasty (1821 — 1850 CE)
Dimensions height: 5.9 cm; mouth diameter: 15.4 cm; foot diameter: 5.3 cm.
Collected by Beidaihe Cultural Relics Protection and Management Institute.

It has an open mouth, an inclined body which curves downward, and a round foot. The texture is fine and hard. The interior rim is made of plain white glaze. The exterior is made of sacrificial-blue-glazed (i.e., Ji-blue glaze). At the bottom of the bowl, there are six characters in three lines of blue-and-white Seal Script "Made in Daoguang Period of Qing Dynasty" on white ground glaze. The high-temperature colored glaze is as blue as deep ocean. It is full of color and elegance.

219 Red Flambé Glazed Globular Vase

Period Daoguang Reign, Qing Dynasty (1821 — 1850 CE)
Dimensions height: 35.9 cm; mouth diameter: 8.8 cm; foot diameter: 11.65 cm.
Collected by Beidaihe Cultural Relics Protection and Management Institute.

It has a slightly flared mouth, a round lip, a long neck, abundant shoulders, a drum belly, and a short round foot. It is applied with flambé red glaze, and the glaze is colorful and dazzling. The glaze along the mouth rim leaves blank, commonly known as the "Dengcaokou". The bottom edge of the abdomen is dripping with accumulated glaze, and there is a lack of glaze when trimming the foot. This bottle is thick, full, clumsy and beautiful. It is full of white stars, shining like stars and resembling a snowy paradise. The bottom rim of this vase shows tear stain-shaped glaze, and the foot is lack of enamel. The bright and thick red color, which is endowed with auspicious omens, is deeply loved by people.

220 Blue-and-white Glazed Prunus Vase with the Design of Ice Crystal Structure

Period Daoguang Reign, Qing Dynasty (1821 — 1850 CE)
Dimensions height: 40.75 cm; mouth diameter: 9.75 cm; foot diameter: 14.65 cm.
Collected by Beidaihe Cultural Relics Protection and Management Institute.

It has a straight mouth, a round lip, a straight neck, abundant shoulders, gradually retracting under the contracted abdomen, and then turning away near the round foot. White glaze is applied on the mouth and bottom rim, and blue glaze is applied on the whole. The glaze color is ice crystal structure with dark crinkles. Three groups of plum blossom branches are painted with the method of leaving blank, and the flower branches are over the shoulder to the neck. The blue ground glaze sets off the white plum blossom, which is holy and elegant.

221 An Imitation of Ge Kiln Vase in the Kangxi Period Style with the Design of Rust-red Colored Dragon and Crane

Period Daoguang Reign, Qing Dynasty (1821 — 1850 CE)
Dimensions height: 45.4 cm; mouth diameter: 16.4 cm; foot diameter: 15.3 cm.
Collected by Beidaihe Cultural Relics Protection and Management Institute.

It has a flared mouth, a flat lip, a bound neck, a sloping shoulders, contracted abdomen close to the foot and then turns outward to the foot, and a short round foot. This vase imitates Ge kiln ware and is covered by greyish-white glaze, which has slight iron thread cracking and chipping throughout. The neck is molded with elephant-trunk handles (i.e., ears), and the handles are lined with two plum blossoms and floral sprays. The front is sculptured with the pattern of two dragons play with a pearl, and the back is sculptured with the pattern of a crane holding a Mei. The bottom is covered with greyish-white glaze, and is imitatively engraved with the four-character in two lines mark of "Made in Kangxi Period" in Seal Script inside. The font is sloppy and weak.

222 Bobbin-shaped Vase with the Design of Famille Verte Phoenix and Peony

Period Daoguang Reign, Qing Dynasty (1821 — 1850 CE)
Dimensions height: 45.2 cm; mouth diameter:12.75 cm; base diameter: 13.7 cm.
Collected by Beidaihe Cultural Relics Protection and Management Institute.

It has a flared mouth, a tied neck, a slipped shoulder, and a slightly bulging abdomen. It has a cylindrical belly, and slightly concave bottom. This vase is designed as heavy, solid and smooth ceramic clay body, covered in bluish-white glaze. The patterns of the vase are colored. The mouth rim is decorated with orange color glaze, the neck is decorated with well-arranged deformed red and green banana leaves, the lower part is decorated with a loop of string pattern, the shoulder is decorated with a deformed lotus petal pattern, and the theme on abdomen is decorated with Phoenix among peony. The pattern is exquisite, with rich and colorful color glaze. The red flowers and green leaves are luxuriant, expressing the beautiful implication of everything is vibrant, rich and honored, being in full flower. This bottle is a pair of identical shapes.

223 Bean-green Glazed Globular Vase with the Graffito Dragon Design as an Imitation of the Yongzheng Period Style

Period Daoguang Reign, Qing Dynasty (1821 — 1850 CE)
Dimensions height: 33.25 cm; mouth diameter: 5.55 cm; foot diameter: 9.7 cm.
Collected by Beidaihe Cultural Relics Protection and Management Institute.

It has a straight mouth, a round lip, a long thin straight neck, a plump shoulders, a drum belly, and a recumbent foot. The whole body is covered with bean-green glaze. The glaze is thick and smooth, and the texture is firm and fine. The mouth is decorated with Hui pattern. The upper neck is decorated with well-arranged banana leaf patterns, and the lower shoulders are decorated with a huge Ruyi cloud pattern. The cloud pattern is decorated with Yingluo and Jingang Baoxiang flowers Pattern. The theme pattern on the abdomen is a design of two dragons intertwined with lotus branches. The neck and shoulders are decorated with a loop of string patterns as partitions. Near the bottom is a loop of seawater pattern. This vase is imitated with six Seal Script characters in three lines, "Made in Yongzheng Period of Qing Dynasty", which is inscribed on the bottom. The shape of this vase is regular, elegant and dignified, it is decorated with the method of graffito design to show the artistic effect of bas-relief, and the engraved patterns are faintly visible.

224 An Imitation Hat Stand of the Qianlong Period Style with the Design of Blue-and-white Glazed "Wealthy and Happiness" Flower-and-bird Pattern

Period Daoguang Reign, Qing Dynasty (1821 — 1850 CE)
Dimensions height: 33.3 cm; mouth diameter: 14.1 cm; foot diameter: 13.7 cm.
Collected by Beidaihe Cultural Relics Protection and Management Institute.

It has a straight mouth, a straight body, a short round foot. This is a cylindrical hat stand, with thick texture, white and fine texture. Both the interior and exterior are decorated with thick and bright white glaze. The blue-and-white glaze is light blueish. The rim of the exterior body and the part near the foot is decorated with a brocade belt-shaped pattern with curled grass and interlocking lotus branches. The "Wealthy and Happiness" theme pattern is depicted on the belly, which describes two white-headed birds perching on the branches, whispering to each other, supplemented below the two birds by peonies, pillar stones and Polygonum flowers. At the bottom of this ware, there are six characters in three lines of blue-and-white Seal Script "Made in Qianlong Period of Qing Dynasty". The combination of white headed birds and wealthy peony is a traditional auspicious pattern, implying a happy marriage and a happy life.

225 Blue-and-white Pear-shaped Vase with the Design of Bamboo, Stone and Plantain

Period Tongzhi Reign, Qing Dynasty (1862 — 1874 CE)
Dimensions height: 32.9 cm; mouth diameter: 8.8 cm; foot diameter: 11.75 cm.
Collected by Beidaihe Cultural Relics Protection and Management Institute.
It has a flared mouth, a thin neck, a sloping shoulder, a drooping belly, and a wide round foot towards outside. This pure and elegant

shaped vase is made by white ceramic clay body, covered by bright and lustrous glaze, and bright color. The abdomen is painted with motifs of landscape pictures, including pillar stones, plantains, moso bamboo, hedges, orchids, etc., the picture is abundant and orderly. The auxiliary decorative patterns of the neck, shoulder, near foot and foot body are: plantain, intertwined flowers, Ruyi cloud pattern, deformed Lotus petals and lotus flower decoration. Each group was separated by string patterns. Six blue-and-white Regular Script characters "Made in Tongzhi Period of Qing Dynasty" arranges in two lines on the bottom. This kind of vase shape originated from the Song Dynasty, and it has been modified and fired, finally becomes traditional typical utensils by later generations. Because of its detached and pure shape, it is endowed with the meanings of "It's like spring all the year round", "As clean as ice crystal and as pure as jade", and "Open and aboveboard". It is highly praised by people.

226 Blue-and-white Pear-shaped Vase with the Design of Bamboo, Stone and Plantain

Period Tongzhi Reign, Qing Dynasty (1862 — 1874 CE)
Dimensions height: 30 cm; mouth diameter: 8.7 cm; abdominal diameter: 17.8 cm; foot diameter:11.6 cm.
Collected by Shanhaiguan Cultural Relics Protection and Management Institute.

This vase has a flared mouth, a thin and tied neck, a sloping shoulder, a round drooping belly, and a wide round foot towards the outside. The texture is firm and pure white, the glaze is smooth, and the blue-and-white color is deep blue. The abdomen is drawn with bamboo, lake stone, plantain, etc. The neck is supplemented by banana leaf and curly grass patterns, and the lower abdomen is supplemented by deformed lotus petals and pond patterns. It is signed with six blue-and-white Regular Script characters "Made in Tongzhi Period of Qing Dynasty" in two lines on the bottom.

227 Six-linked Vase with the Design of Ice Crystal Structure and Plum Blossoms Pattern with a Lotus Shaped Mouth

Period Tongzhi Reign, Qing Dynasty (1862 — 1874 CE)
Dimensions height: 28 cm; mouth diameter: 3.6 cm; foot diameter: 9.85 cm.
Collected by Beidaihe Cultural Relics Protection and Management Institute.

The main bottle has a lotus-shaped mouth, a slender neck, and wide flat shoulders. Five identical vases are adhering to a combination of one belly, which all have straight mouths, abundant shoulders, and plump bellies that converge to the feet, forming a novel linked vase shape with one high and five short vases. It has six small flat bottoms. The whole body is covered by blue-and-white ground glaze, and the white blank outline is dotted for decoration. There are ice crystal structure and plum blossoms, strange stones, flower Ruyi clouds, and Hui patterns (i.e., deforming from cloud patterns but look like a Chinese character "Hui"). Due to the connection between the belly of the six chambers and the homophonic sound of "belly" and "fu", it is commonly known as a "multi fu vase".

228 Blue-and-white Glazed Vase in the Shape of Mallet

Period Tongzhi Reign, Qing Dynasty (1862 — 1874 CE)
Dimensions height: 36.7 cm; mouth diameter: 3.7 cm; foot diameter: 9.75 cm.
Collected by Beidaihe Cultural Relics Protection and Management Institute.

It has a straight mouth, a round lip, a slender neck, sloping shoulders, a round plump belly, and a recumbent foot. The texture is thick, firm, and white in color. The color of blue-and-white is well-proportioned and light. The whole body is decorated with the theme of two dragons play with a pearl. The dragon tossed up and down, dotted with clouds, and flame clouds. The mouth is decorated with Ruyi cloud patterns. Near the bottom is decorated with seawater, river, and cliff pattern.

229 An Imitation of the Kangxi Period Style Jar with the Design of Butterfly-touching-flower in Pastel Shade

Period Tongzhi Reign, Qing Dynasty (1862 — 1874 CE)
Dimensions height: 15.85 cm; mouth diameter: 16.8 cm; foot diameter: 13 cm.
Collected by Beidaihe Cultural Relics Protection and Management Institute.

It has a restricted mouth, a flared lip, abundant shoulders, slightly retract under the bulging abdomen, and a recumbent foot. This jar is white ground glazed and decorated with red color. Both the exterior rim and foot part are decorated with red Ruyi cloud patterns and deformed Lotus petals pattern. The abdomen is using pastel shade with red colors to describe butterfly-touching-flower patterns. The bottom is decorated with a four-character of red color Regular Script "Made in Kangxi Period". The font is sloppy and weak. The butterflies dancing among flowers means happiness in love.

230 Famille-rose Glazed Hexagonal-sided Vessel with the Kaiguang Pattern as an Imitation of the Qianlong Period Style

Period Tongzhi Reign, Qing Dynasty (1862 — 1874 CE)
Dimensions height: 14.3 cm; mouth diameter: 3.5 cm; foot diameter: 3.7 cm.
Collected by Beidaihe Cultural Relics Protection and Management Institute.

This vessel has six edges. It has an outward mouth, a flared rim, an arc-shaped neck, a folded shoulders, a gradually retracted abdomen, and towards outward high hexagonal-side foot. It has thick texture. It is a very unique and rare light green (water green) glaze ground, and decorating a combination of purple and pastel painting. There are two fan-shaped Kaiguang Pattern in the abdomen and neck, with pastel character stories painted inside. It used gold painting techniques to draw flowers of different sizes with folded branches outside the Kaiguang Frame, and mainly in purple color glaze, with embellishments of green, white, ochre and other colors,. The shoulder folds are decorated with gold scrolled grass patterns. The exterior decoration of the feet is adorned with multiple gold string patterns. The bottom is signed with six Seal Script characters in three lines "Made in Qianlong Period of Qing Dynasty" in red color. The craftsmanship of this vessel is unique, the craftsmanship is superb, the glaze color is light and elegant, and its light and tender blue color is as clear as the lake water, which is highly praised and loved by people. This bottle is a pair of identical shapes.

231 Assorted Bowl Painted in Black Color as an Imitation of the Qianlong Period Style on a Yellow Ground Glazed

Period Tongzhi Reign, Qing Dynasty (1862 — 1874 CE)
Dimensions height: 6.8 cm; mouth diameter: 5.9 cm; foot diameter: 4 cm.
Collected by Beidaihe Cultural Relics Protection and Management Institute.

This bowl has eight edges. It has a straight mouth, a round lip, a deep belly, an arc-shaped body, eight-sided trimmed high-footed outward. The interior body and bottom of this bowl are painted with turquoise green glaze, and the exterior body of this bowl is decorated with ink color on yellow ground glaze, painted with floral sprays, fruits, flowers, and birds. The foot is decorated with curling leaves and twigs, and flowers are interspersed. At the bottom of this bowl is an imitation of four red-colored characters "Made in Qianlong Period" in Regular Script. This ink color painting is in a deep or light orderly manner. It uses black and white colors to dye flowers, fruits and birds. The brushwork is skillful with smooth lines. The picture is natural and vivid, delicate and natural.

232 Blue-and-white Glazed Plate with the Design of Dragons Chasing Pearls

Period Guangxu Reign, Qing Dynasty (1875 — 1908 CE)
Dimensions height: 3.9 cm; mouth diameter: 16.95 cm; foot diameter: 9.95 cm.
Collected by Beidaihe Cultural Relics Protection and Management Institute.

This plate has a flared mouth, a round lip, a shallow belly, an arc-shaped body, and a round foot. The texture is firm and white,with tightly glazed and shiny appearance. The interior is decorated with double-string patterns. It is drawn a double strings Pattern in the middle, with a single dragon playing with a pearl inside. The exterior is decorated with two dragons chasing pearls pattern, both of them are in the direction of head-to-tail, and are supplemented by fine flame cloud patterns. Six blue-and-white Regular Script characters "Made in Guangxu Period of Qing Dynasty" is placed inside in two lines on bottom.

233 White Ground Glazed Ornamental Vase with the Design of Hundred Butterflies

Period Guangxu Reign, Qing Dynasty (1875 — 1908 CE)
Dimensions height: 39.6 cm; mouth diameter: 9.8 cm; foot diameter: 13 cm.
Collected by Beidaihe Cultural Relics Protection and Management Institute.

This vase has a flared mouth, a slender neck with arc-shaped, abundant shoulders, a round belly and round foot. The whole body is applied with white ground glaze and decorated with famille-rose glaze. The neck and abdomen are decorated with hundreds of butterflies, which are in different sizes, postures and colors. They are flying around a larger butterfly. "Ruyi cloud" pattern, "Deformed Shou character (i.e., means longevity) with intertwined branches and flowers" pattern, "Deformed lotus flowers" pattern are painted on the mouth edge, shoulder and near foot respectively, and gold outlines string pattern is painted between each group of patterns. At the bottom, there are two lines of six characters in Regular Script "Made in Guangxu Period in the Qing Dynasty". The shape of this vase is elegant. The flowers and butterflies are vivid and delicate, and warm colors are used as the main tone. Especially pale pinkish purple, light yellow, pink, light blue, and light green are used in the painting, which adds a fresh and elegant aesthetic to the whole design. "Butterfly" and "more blessing" are homonyms in Chinese, implying lots of blessings and good luck.

234 Famille-rose Glazed Ornamental Vase with the Design of Hundred Bats and Two Dragons Play with a Pearl Pattern

Period Guangxu Reign, Qing Dynasty (1875 — 1908 CE)
Dimensions height: 39.6 cm; mouth diameter: 9.85 cm; foot diameter: 12.05 cm.
Collected by Beidaihe Cultural Relics Protection and Management Institute.

This vase has a flared mouth, an arc-shaped body, a long neck, abundant shoulders, a round belly, and a round foot. The whole body is applied with white glaze and decorated with famille-rose glaze. The front and rear themed decorations on the abdomen are respectively painted with an ochre dragon playing with pearls pattern, and ocher, yellow, blue, green auspicious clouds and flame cloud patterns are dotted around. The neck is painted with ochre-colored bat patterns throughout, with various auspicious cloud patterns embellished in between. "Ruyi cloud" pattern, "Shou character (i.e., means longevity) with intertwined branches and flowers" pattern, "sea water, river and cliff" pattern are painted on the mouth, shoulders, and near feet respectively, and string patterns are decorated between each group of patterns. A raised string pattern is applied at the junction between the neck and shoulders. The bottom of this vessel is marked with a two-line six-character year mark in red-colored Regular Script "Made in Guangxu of Qing Dynasty". The shape of this vase is stretched and elegant. The bats have different postures, graceful and lively. Cloud-dragons are strong and vigorous, powerful and invigorating. "bat" and "blessing" are homonyms in Chinese, the combination of bats and cloud-dragons pattern implies one's great happiness.

235 White Ground Glazed Bowl with the Design of Famille-rose Glazed Kui-phoenix Crossing Lotus

Period Guangxu Reign, Qing Dynasty (1875 — 1908 CE)
Dimensions height: 8.9 cm; mouth diameter: 20.8 cm; foot diameter: 8.8 cm.
Collected by Beidaihe Cultural Relics Protection and Management Institute.

It has an open mouth, a deep abdomen, an arc-shaped body, and a round foot. The texture of this bowl is delicate and fine, and it is applied with white glaze and famille-rose glaze. The interior is brightly glazed with plain white glaze. The exterior is symmetrically decorated with four famille-rose glazed Kui-phoenixes in red, yellow, green, and blue colors, which are crossing in vast interlocked branches and lotus flowers, spreading their wings and dancing in different lively postures. Brown string patterns are decorated on both mouth and foot rim. The bottom has six blue-and-white Regular Script characters "Made in Guangxu Period of Qing Dynasty" is placed inside in two lines. The pink color tone is soft and bright, and the painting is filled with colors with double lines, making it clear and colorful Kui-phoenix pattern is a traditional and typical pattern, which means "Peace in the world, and peace in all things".

236 Yellow and Green Glazed Bowl with the Design of Veiled Dragon Patterns

Period Guangxu Reign, Qing Dynasty (1875 — 1908 CE)
Dimensions height: 7 cm; mouth diameter: 14.04 cm; foot diameter: 7.17 cm.
Collected by Shanhaiguan Cultural Relics Protection and Management Institute.

This bowl has an open mouth, a convergent belly under the oblique body, and a round foot. The texture is dense and light, and covered by uniform yellow and green glaze interior and exterior. The interior surface is plain, the exterior surface is carved with dragon patterns and cloud patterns, and near the foot is carved with seawater, river, and cliff patterns. The carved patterns are delicate and beautiful, and the dragon's body is decorated with phosphorus flakes. Its body shape is curved and shuttles among the auspicious cloud. The bottom is painted with white glaze and signed with six blue-and-white "Made in Guangxu Period of Qing Dynasty" in two lines of Regular Script.

237 Yellow Ground Glazed Gallbladder-shaped Vase with the Design of Tri-color Glazed Two Dragons Play with a Pearl

Period Guangxu Reign, Qing Dynasty (1875 — 1908 CE)
Dimensions height: 33 cm; mouth diameter: 6.85 cm; foot diameter: 10.45 cm.
Collected by Beidaihe Cultural Relics Protection and Management Institute.

It has a straight mouth, a cylindrical long straight neck, sloping shoulders, a bulging and drooping belly, and a wide round foot. This vase has a regular, moderate thickness, fine and firm texture. The whole body is covered with thin, bright and delicate yellow glaze. The two sides of this vase are painted with purple and green two dragons play with a pearl. It is decorated with purple, green and white blooming auspicious clouds and purple flame clouds. The dragon shape is vigorous and powerful. The water ripples dotted with white color are applied near the foot. The bottom has six characters marked in two lines in blue-and-white Regular Script "Made in Guangxu Period of Qing Dynasty". The whole body is decorated with the REBAKING techniques of depicting and filling color. The depicted lines are slender and smooth, the filled color is slightly uneven, and the colors complement each other and are properly matched. Yellow color represents the morality of all living creating. Yellow was the exclusive color of ancient emperors. So yellow glazed porcelain was strictly controlled during the Ming and Qing dynasties, and this kind of vase is very rare. It is named because of its shape like a gallbladder.

238 Yellow Ground Glazed Famille-rose Kettle with the Design of Kaiguang Frame and "Wanshou wujiang"

Period Guangxu Reign, Qing Dynasty (1875 — 1908 CE)
Dimensions height: 11 cm; mouth diameter: 7.2 cm; foot diameter: 8.1 cm.
Collected by Beidaihe Cultural Relics Protection and Management Institute.

This kettle has a unique shape, and composed of a kettle body, handle, and lid. This kettle does not have a spout. This covered kettle has a short neck, oblique shoulders, cylindrical straight abdomen, and wide round foot. The texture is firm and pure white, applied with yellow ground glaze and famille-rose glaze. The surface of the vessel adopts a grilling flower technique, and the production is exquisite and meticulous. It comes with a bamboo hat-shaped lid with herringbone buttons standing on the flat top. The two sides of this kettle are equipped with a huge triangular handle. The beam of the kettle handle is slightly upturned, and the high point is level with the kettle mouth. Phoenix-tail-shaped curly grass concave pattern of grilling flower technique, which is vaguely seen on white ceramic clay body, and then decorated with safflower, green leaves, and various famille-rose glaze conbination patterns. Four large round Kaiguang Patterns are designed around the abdomen, and the four auspicious characters of "Many happy returns of the day to eternity" are inscribed in white glaze and red-colored Regular Script. The shoulders are decorated with two string patterns and Hui pattern. Near the foot is decorated with a lotus petal pattern. The caliber is roughly the same as the foot diameter. The bottom is covered with white glaze, and six characters in red color Regular Script "Made in Guangxu Period of Qing Dynasty" is signed in two lines. The whole kettle uses a strong warm tone and bright yellow as the ground. The color is soft, elegant, and bright. The complicated and cumbersome famille-rose glaze and grilling flower technique are perfectly matched, which is the icing on the cake. It perfectly presents the outstanding quality of this kettle, which is a masterpiece of the Guangxu period.

239 Blue-and-white Bowl with the Design of Eight Trigrams Kaiguang Pattern

Period Guangxu Reign, Qing Dynasty (1875 — 1908 CE)
Dimensions height: 6.6 cm; mouth diameter: 13.35 cm; foot diameter: 5.4 cm.
Collected by Beidaihe Cultural Relics Protection and Management Institute.

This bowl has an open mouth, a deep belly, an arc-shaped body, and a round foot. Bowl along the internal is decorated with diamond patterns in ribbons, and the center of this bowl is decorated with water ripple patterns. The exterior is decorated with double string patterns, and the belly is decorated with round Kaiguang patterns. The interior is described with eight trigrams, and between the Kaiguang patterns are decorated with egrets and auspicious clouds. The sea and river cliffs are drawn near the foot. The exterior of the foot is decorated with double-string patterns. It is signed blue-and-white Regular Script with two lines and six characters of "Made in Guangxu Period of Qing Dynasty".

240 Sacrificial-blue-glazed Ornamental Vase with the Design of Gold Outlines Elk and Landscape Pattern

Period Guangxu Reign, Qing Dynasty (1875 — 1908 CE)

Dimensions height: 36.7 cm; mouth diameter: 10.05 cm; foot diameter: 12.65 cm.
Collected by Beidaihe Cultural Relics Protection and Management Institute.

This vase has a flared mouth, a flat lip, an arc-shaped and slender neck, plump shoulders, a round belly, and a round foot. The whole body is covered with high-temperature monochromatic sacrificial-blue-glaze, and its glaze is smooth, soft, and clean. The exterior rim is decorated with lockrand gold Ruyi cloud patterns, the belly is decorated with gold outlines elk, and landscape pattern, and the neck and shoulders are decorated with raised string patterns. This kind of shaped vessel was first made in Yongzheng Period, it is praise highly by future generations, and it has been produced and used for ornamental, so it is called ornamental vase. The shape of this bottle is elegant and dignified, gentle and gorgeous. The blue tone supports the dazzling golden glaze and is extremely artistic charm.

241 Variable Glazed Garlic-head Shaped Vase

Period Guangxu Reign, Qing Dynasty (1875 — 1908 CE)
Dimensions height: 22.5 cm; mouth diameter: 3.8 cm; foot diameter: 7.5 cm.
Collected by Beidaihe Cultural Relics Protection and Management Institute.

This vase has a garlic-head mouth, a thin neck, abundant shoulders, a drum belly, and a round foot turned outwards. The whole body is applied with high-temperature Variable glaze, which is thick and smooth. A concave decorative band is applied around the shoulders. Red and black are the main colors, blending with each other. Beige and ochre color, which are excessively generated between them, become red glaze in the abdomen, head, and neck. It is bright light, which is beautiful and gorgeous.

242 Ge Kiln Small Vase with the Design of Rust-red Colored Branches and Plum Blossoms

Period Guangxu Reign, Qing Dynasty (1875 — 1908 CE)
Dimensions height: 18.6 cm; mouth diameter: 5.75 cm; foot diameter: 5.1 cm.
Collected by Beidaihe Cultural Relics Protection and Management Institute.

It has a flared mouth, a straight lip, a long neck, slopping shoulders, a bulging belly is gradually retracted and then turned outward, with double layers foot. The small vase is decorated with Ge kiln glaze on the whole body, and it is densely covered with cracking pieces. The abdomen is decorated with rust-red colored, dried branches and plums.

243 Black Color Ground Glazed Square Wooden-club Shaped Vase with the Design of Tri-color Glazed Plum Flowers, Bamboo, and Stones

Period Guangxu Reign, Qing Dynasty (1875 — 1908 CE)
Dimensions height: 49.7 cm; mouth diameter: 11.65 cm; foot diameter: 11 cm.
Collected by Beidaihe Cultural Relics Protection and Management Institute.

It has a round mouth, a straight neck, a flat folded shoulders, a straight belly to bottom, and a square foot. It has a firm and delicate texture, and the ground glaze is ink black and bright with pure and elegant tricolor. The interior is covered with plain white glaze, and the exterior is covered with black ground glaze, and leaving blank to fill in colors. Bamboo, plum, and stones patterns are drawn with green, purple, and yellow colors. The bottom is covered with white glaze, and signed with a blue-and-white pattern inscribed with the leaves. The plum tree is complemented by bamboo and stone, the old stem is winding and the new plum blossoms are in full bloom. Boldly using bright yellow color to embellish the stamens, and using black to set off the blossoming plum blossoms. Against the backdrop of black ground, it likes a gentle breeze swaying on a moonlit night, further highlights the quiet and noble quality of plum blossoms.

244 Yellow Ground Glazed Stool with the Design of Famille-rose Glazed Happiness and Longevity

Period Guangxu Reign, Qing Dynasty (1875 — 1908 CE)
Dimensions height: 46.7 cm; mouth diameter: 29.4 cm; foot diameter: 27.2 cm.
Collected by Beidaihe Cultural Relics Protection and Management Institute.

This stool is in the shape of a waist drum. The texture is thick, firm, and white in color. It is applied with yellow ground glaze, and decorated with green, pink, blue, pale pinkish purple, and other colors. The flat top surface is slightly collapsed, and the flat bottom surface is slightly arched as its foot. The ventral surface is divided into three areas, which is decorated with the theme "A myriad of Fu and Shou" (i.e., happiness and longevity) pattern in the middle. The four sides of the stool waist is decorated with a group of "Five bats offer longevity" patterns on opposite sides, and a set of pale pinkish purple hollow double-coin patterns on the other two sides. Surrounded by a number of peaches, "A myriad of Shou" (i.e., longevity), butterflies pattern. The theme pattern is decorated with a small white flower with drum nail pattern above and below. The auxiliary patterns in the upper area are tooth shaped patterns, drum nail patterns, diamond shaped brocade belt and longevity peach with Kaiguang frame, supplemented by convex nail patterns, and double leaves shaped patterns. The auxiliary pattern in the lower area is painted with deformed banana leaves with drum nail patterns. The middle of the top surface is hollowed out with coin patterns, with bat, longevity peach, and "A myriad of Shou"(i.e., longevity) patterns around the circumference. The exterior rim is decorated with brocade four Kaiguang patterns, and it is decorated with white ground glaze and red color flower patterns inside. This stool is applied with fine and gorgeous famille-rose glaze, which is outstanding in the rough porcelain industry in the late Qing Dynasty. The combination of patterns endows auspicious meanings. For example, the combination of bat and coin pattern means "Blessing is in front of you", the combination of bat and peach means "Happiness and longevity", and the combination of five bats and longevity peaches, means "Five bats offer longevity" and so on. Combining happiness, longevity, and auspiciousness, it expresses blessings and expectations for a better life.

245 Green Ground Glazed Covered Jar with the Design of Tri-color Glazed Magpie Stepping on Plum Blossom

Period Guangxu Reign, Qing Dynasty (1875 — 1908 CE)
Dimensions height: 20.4 cm; mouth diameter: 7.2 cm; foot diameter: 10.3 cm.
Collected by Beidaihe Cultural Relics Protection and Management Institute.

This covered jar has a paired mouth, plump shoulders, a bulging belly, and a recumbent foot. It comes with a bigger dome cover. The whole body is covered with green glaze, and leaving a blank area for painting. The theme decoration is magpies stepping on plum blossoms. On mountain side road, several flowers are blooming on some plum trees, and a pair of magpies are playing among them. The composition uses ochre to outline the branches and plum blossoms, bright yellow to describe stamens, ink color to paint with double magpies, and blue color to dye magpie wings. As a kind of "auspicious bird", the magpie is loved by people and is a symbol of auspiciousness. The plum blossom is also known as the "primrose". The design of magpies standing on plum blossoms means "announcement of good luck in real time", indicating incoming good luck and good fortune.

246 Famille-rose Glazed Bowl with the Eight Immortals' Ritual Instruments

Period Guangxu Reign, Qing Dynasty (1875 — 1908 CE)
Dimensions height: 7.5 cm; mouth diameter: 17.5 cm; foot diameter: 10.8 cm.
Collected by Qinglong Manchu Autonomous County Cultural Relics Protection Institute.

This bowl has eight edges. The mouth is octagon with outward rim. It has a round lip, the deep abdominal body is slightly arced, and the octagonal foot is outward. The texture is thick. The interior is painted with single turquoise-green color. Each side of the exterior is decorated with famille-rose glaze, respectively, with eight immortals' ritual instruments, that is, gourd, round fan, fishing drum, sword, lotus flower, flower basket, flute, and yin and yang boards, decorated with flowers and broken branches patterns. The foot is decorated with deformed sea and cliff patterns.

247 Bean-green Glazed Long Straight Necked Vase Covering with White Flowers

Period Guangxu Reign, Qing Dynasty (1875 — 1908 CE)
Dimensions height: 40 cm; mouth diameter: 6.7 cm; foot diameter: 16.6 cm.
Collected by Beidaihe Cultural Relics Protection and Management Institute.

This vase has a straight mouth, a long neck, a round belly, and a wide round foot slightly turned outward. The texture is heavy and firm, which is applied with bean-green glaze. Using lots of white four-season flowers as the theme on abdomen, it is surrounded by piles of white floral sprays and leaves among flowers.

248 Blue-and-white Glazed Jar with the Design of Ying-dragons Holding Lotus in Mouth as an Imitation of the Kangxi Period Style

Period Guangxu Reign, Qing Dynasty (1875 — 1908 CE)

Dimensions height: 31.9 cm; mouth diameter: 12 cm; foot diameter: 16.3 cm.
Collected by Beidaihe Cultural Relics Protection and Management Institute.

It has a paired mouth, a sloping shoulders. The abdomen is slightly bulging and the lower part is slightly convergent to the foot. The round foot is short, thick and strong. It is lack of lid. The texture of this jar is smooth and white, decorated with blue-and-white patterns, which is greenish and light. The belly is decorated with the theme of Ying-dragons holding lotus. Two Ying-dragons hold lotus, spread their wings, bend their bodies, and raise their tails. They walk through blooming lotus flowers and soar freely. The top and bottom are respectively Ruyi cloud pattern and water waves pattern and down respectively. The shoulders are adorned with brocade and four Kaiguang, and the eight treasure patterns are intertwined with lotus branches, while near the foot is adorned with flower patterns in a string. Six blue-and-white characters Regular Script "Made in Kangxi Period of Qing Dynasty" is imitated in three lines on the bottom. Ying-dragons, with scales and spines on its back, wings on its back, long branches of flowers in its arms, and feet on the clouds, is good at creating clouds and rain. It is the only winged creation spirit dragon in ancient mythology.

249 Blue-and-white Glazed Bowl with the Design of Dragons Chasing Pearls as an Imitation of the Kangxi Period Style

Period Guangxu Reign, Qing Dynasty (1875 — 1908 CE)
Dimensions height: 6.1 cm; mouth diameter: 11.05 cm; foot diameter: 4.15 cm.
Collected by Beidaihe Cultural Relics Protection and Management Institute.

This bowl has a flared mouth, a deep belly, an arc-shaped body, and a round foot. The interior is plain white glaze. The exterior body is decorated with two dragons chasing pearls head-to-tail, supplemented by flame cloud patterns. It is decorated with four sets of seawater, river, and cliff patterns near the foot. The exterior mouth rim and foot are decorated with lockrand blue-and-white string patterns. The bottom is decorated with a double column circle, with six characters in blue-and-white Regular Script "Made in Kangxi of Qing Dynasty" in two lines.

250 Green Ground Glazed Bowl with the Design of Purple Colored Walking Dragons as an Imitation of the Kangxi Period Style

Period Guangxu Reign, Qing Dynasty (1875 — 1908 CE)
Dimensions height: 5.25 cm; mouth diameter: 10.36 cm; foot diameter: 4.8 cm.
Collected by Beidaihe Cultural Relics Protection and Management Institute.

This bowl has a flared mouth, a deep belly, an arc-shaped body, and a round foot. The interior is plain white glaze, and the exterior is applied with green ground glaze and purple glaze, with two dragons chasing in the direction of head-to-tail, supplemented by simple cloud patterns. Near the foot is designed with seawater, river, and cliffs. The bottom is drawn with a white glazed double column circle, and six blue-and-white Regular Script characters "Made in Kangxi Period of Qing Dynasty" are placed inside in two lines.

251 Sacrificial-blue-glazed Plate as an Imitation of the Qianlong Period Style

Period Guangxu Reign, Qing Dynasty (1875 — 1908 CE)
Dimensions height: 3.65 cm; mouth diameter: 17.3 cm; foot diameter: 10.55 cm.
Collected by Beidaihe Cultural Relics Protection and Management Institute.

It has an open mouth, a shallow abdomen, an arc-shaped body, and a wide round foot. The texture of this plate is firm and fine, with a regular shape. White glaze shall be applied to the mouth rim. The interior and exterior are applied with sacrificial-blue-glaze, and the color is pure, thick and even. The bottom of this plate is applied with white glaze, decorated with a double column circle, and the blue-and-white Regular Script "Made in Kangxi Period of Qing Dynasty" are signed as six characters inside in three lines.

252 Light Blue-and-white Glazed Bowl with Bamboo Pattern as an Imitation of the Yongzheng Period Style

Period Guangxu Reign, Qing Dynasty (1875 — 1908 CE)
Dimensions height: 4.3 cm; mouth diameter: 9.45 cm; foot diameter: 3.45 cm.
Collected by Beidaihe Cultural Relics Protection and Management Institute.

This bowl has an open mouth, a deep belly, an arc-shaped body, and a round foot. The interior is white and plain, and the exterior is painted with two groups of blue-and-white understated double-lined bamboo patterns. It is drawn a double rectangular frame on the bottom, which is signed in six blue-and-white Regular Script characters "Made in Yongzheng Period of Qing Dynasty" inside in two lines. The blue-and-white color is clear and beautiful, and the bamboo lines are fine and neat. They highlight the upright, and elegant character of bamboo.

253 White Glazed Cup as an Imitation of the Yongzheng Period Style

Period Guangxu Reign, Qing Dynasty (1875 — 1908 CE)
Dimensions height: 6.06 cm; mouth diameter: 9.16 cm; foot diameter: 3.6 cm.
Collected by Beidaihe Cultural Relics Protection and Management Institute.

This bowl has an open mouth, a deep belly, a sloping body, and a round foot. The texture is firm and light. The whole body is covered with white glaze, which is solid and bright. It is drawn a double circle on the bottom, which is signed in six blue-and-white Regular Script characters "Made in Yongzheng Period of Qing Dynasty" inside the circle in two lines.

254 Light Blue Glazed Square-shaped Vase as an Imitation of the Yongzheng Period Style

Period Guangxu Reign, Qing Dynasty (1875 — 1908 CE)
Dimensions height: 24.9 cm; mouth diameter: 6.8 cm; foot diameter: 8.65 cm.
Collected by Beidaihe Cultural Relics Protection and Management Institute.

It has a slightly constricted mouth, an outward round lip, a short neck, flat shoulders, a round bottom, and a round slightly outward foot. It is in a shape of jade Cong vase. The vase is made of thick ceramic clay and covered with light blue glaze as a whole. The foot is wide and thick. The foot diameter is slightly larger than caliber. The bottom of this vase is marked with a two-line six- character inscription in blue- and-white Regular Script "Made in Yongzheng Period of Qing Dynasty". Because of the blue ground glaze, the blue-and-white glaze towards black in color.

255 White Ground Glazed Plate with the Design of Green Colored Dragons Chasing Pearls as an Imitation of the Qianlong Period Style

Period Guangxu Reign, Qing Dynasty (1875 — 1908 CE)
Dimensions height: 4.5 cm; mouth diameter: 18.1 cm; foot diameter: 11.15 cm.
Collected by Beidaihe Cultural Relics Protection and Management Institute.

It has a flared mouth, a shallow abdomen, an arc-shaped body, and a wide round foot. This plate has a moderate texture in a regular shape. It is applied with rich and smooth white glaze, which is close to greenish white, and decorated with green colors. Plate along the internal is decorated with a string pattern. The central part is decorated with a large string Kaiguang pattern, and inside is painted with a dragon chasing with pearl pattern, which is supplemented with thin flame cloud patterns. The exterior is decorated with two dragons chasing pearls on the white ground glaze, which are straight forward and head connected to tail. It is signed with six characters in blue-and-white Seal Script "Made in Qianlong Period of Qing Dynasty", located in three lines. The dragon pattern seems to be dull, and the lines are lack of change. Although the dragon pattern is showing teeth and claws, it lacks the inner mighty domineering.

256 Blue-and-white Ground Glazed Vase with the Design of Red and Green Colored Two Dragons Play with a Pearl as an Imitation of Qianlong Period Style

Period Guangxu Reign, Qing Dynasty (1875 — 1908 CE)
Dimensions height: 65.4 cm; mouth diameter: 15.6 cm; foot diameter: 19.7 cm.
Collected by Beidaihe Cultural Relics Protection and Management Institute.

It has a flared mouth, a long neck, plump shoulders, a rounded down belly, and a wide round foot. The texture is firm and light, applied with a light blue-and-white ground glaze, and supplemented with red and green colors. A raised string pattern is applied at the junction of neck and shoulder. The theme decoration is divided into two areas: the neck and the abdomen. Intervals with decorative Hui pattern belts and triangle pattern belts intertwined with lotus flowers. The neck is decorated with a dragon play with a pearl pattern, the abdomen is decorated with two dragons chasing pearl pattern. Two mighty dragons with four open claws, are glaring at the fire bead, walking among the ever-changing clouds, and the circumference is decorated with long white cloud patterns and red flame cloud patterns. It is decorated with yellow and purple color Ruyi cloud patterns on mouth rim, and green color dotted white sea river cliff patterns. It is covered with white glaze on the bottom, and six characters Seal Script marked "Made in Qianlong Year of Qing Dynasty" are signed in blue-and-white glaze. The blue-and-white glaze belongs to high-temperature under glaze color, which is different from the general low-temperature overglaze color of red and green color. It is more complex than carving and color filling techniques, and it is very rare. This vase is an excellent one in appreciating bottles.

257 High Foot Bowl with Tianji Cover in the Design of Red Colored Ying-dragons as an Imitation of the Qianlong Period Style

Period Guangxu Reign, Qing Dynasty (1875 — 1908 CE)
Dimensions height: 20.8 cm; mouth diameter: 15.7 cm; foot diameter: 4.3 cm.
Collected by Beidaihe Cultural Relics Protection and Management Institute.

It is divided into two parts: the upper cover and the lower bowl. The lid is an arc-shaped, with the top sculpture of a hollow auspicious bird as a button. The cock is designed as the cover button and the feathers are decorated with light red color. The auspicious bird is also called Tianji (i.e., cock over the sky), so it is called the Tianji Covered Bowl. It has a slightly flared mouth, a deep belly, an inclined and slightly arc-shaped body, and a straight tubular high round foot. This covered bowl has a firm and fine texture, designed in a slightly thin shape. Both of them are applied with red color on white ground glaze, which shows bright, smooth and pure white. The cover and exterior bowl are drawn with two red color bead patterns, each of which shows dragons flying toward fire beads, supplemented by fine flame cloud patterns. Both the interior cover and center of this bowl are signed in Red Seal Script "Made in Qianlong Period of Qing Dynasty" with six characters in three lines. According to the records of the Imperial Household Department of the Qing Dynasty, Tianji covered bowls were used as offerings for Buddhist temples, which preserved curiosity were very rare. This Guangxu Period product is realistic, no matter in shape, body enamel, or painting is slightly inferior to Kangxi, Yongzheng, Qianlong Period products. The red color is too rich and colorful and uneven, and faint colors and red color appear in some parts. The body glaze is slightly pale, but the defects do not hide the beauty, which is still a rare good product in this period.

258 Light Greenish-blue Glazed Vessel (Zun) with the Design of Chi-dragon Shaped Handles as an Imitation of the Qianlong Period Style

Period Guangxu Reign, Qing Dynasty (1875 — 1908 CE)
Dimensions height: 30.3 cm; mouth diameter: 13.75 cm; foot diameter: 17.4 cm.
Collected by Beidaihe Cultural Relics Protection and Management Institute.

It has a straight mouth, a round lip, sloping neck, sloping shoulders, a bulging abdomen, and a wide round foot. The vessel is made from moderate in thickness but firm texture, which is covered with smooth and clear light greenish-blue glaze as a whole. It has engraved patterns and decorations underglaze. The shoulders are decorated with flat Chi-dragon handles (i.e., ears). The abdomen is engraved with a loop of wide fluent pattern belt, which consists of Hui pattern (i. e., deforming from cloud pattern but look like a Chinese character "Hui") and imitative Copper decoration pattern. The neck and lower abdomen is decorated with banana leaf patterns upwards and downwards, respectively. The bottom is imitatively marked with a six-character in three-line in blue-and-white Seal Script "Made in Qianlong Period of Qing Dynasty". This vessel (Zun) has a light and elegant green glaze color, with a moist and soft glaze surface. Although this vessel is an imitation in Guangxu period, it fully expresses the vessel's (Zun) warm and restrained features. The quiet and deep trait is vividly expressed.

259 Famille-rose Glazed Snuff Bottle with the Design of Two Dragons Play with a Pearl as an Imitation of the Qianlong Period Style

Period Guangxu Reign, Qing Dynasty (1875 — 1908 CE)
Dimensions height: 8.1 cm; mouth diameter: 1.3 cm; foot diameter: 2.4 cm.
Collected by Beidaihe Cultural Relics Protection and Management Institute.

This bottle has a straight mouth, an outward round lip, a tied neck, plump shoulders, a long straight belly, and a round foot. It is applied with famille-rose glaze on white ground glaze. The belly is decorated with two dragons play with a pearl and flame patterns. It includes red, black, bright yellow, and tender green colors, which are bright but not soft. A four-character mark of "Made in Qianlong Period" is signed in Regular Script in red color on the bottom.

260 Square Green Ground Glazed Brush Holder with Tri-color Glazed Relief Carved as an Imitation of the Qianlong Period Style

Period Guangxu Reign, Qing Dynasty (1875 — 1908 CE)
Dimensions height: 21.85 cm; mouth diameter: 7.7 cm; foot diameter: 8.25 cm.
Collected by Beidaihe Cultural Relics Protection and Management Institute.

This brush holder is in the shape of a square column, with a square mouth, a flared round lip, a slightly bulging belly, and a square foot. The caliber and foot diameter are similar in size. The whole body is designed with carving craftsmanship, and applied with green ground glaze which is covered by tri-color glaze, and the colors are rich and colorful. The mouth rim is carved with yellow and purple interlaced Ruyi cloud patterns. The four sides of abdomen are designed as ridge rectangular frames, and the inside is convexly carved with yellow and purple inverted dragons holding curly branches. The upper and lower sides of the two dragons and surroundings are decorated with two large white and yellow flowers and light blue branches and leaves. Among them, two purple sacrificial-animal handles (i.e., ears) are decorated between the two dragons on two corresponding sides. The small rectangular horizontal Kaiguang frames near the foot is carved with yellow banana leaf patterns inside. It has a double layer platform square foot. The bottom is covered with green glaze, and the Seal Script "Made in Qianlong Period of Qing Dynasty" six characters are inscribed in three lines. It is in simple and elegant shape, with ingenious and unique composition, which is an exquisite carving product.

261 Biography of Waxberry

Shen Zhou, Ming Dynasty, Running Script.
Long scroll.
Paper scroll.
Dimensions longitudinal direction: 33 cm; transverse direction: 954.5 cm; full text: 426 words.
Collected by Shanhaiguan Cultural Relics Protection and Management Institute.

Shen Zhou (1427—1509), given name Qinan, he also went by the style name Shitian, Baishiweng, and Yutianweng. He was born in Changzhou (now Suzhou, Jiangsu). He was a famous painter, calligrapher, and litterateur in the Ming Dynasty. He, together with Wen Zhengming, Tang Yin, and Qiu Ying, was called the "Four Masters of the Ming Dynasty". He was the founder of the Wumen School of Painting. He was particularly accomplished in painting. He also worked on landscapes, flowers, birds, and figures, as well as characters, with outstanding achievements in landscape painting and flowers and birds. He studied calligraphy by Huang Tingjian, who was powerful and extraordinary. According to the "History of the Ming Dynasty", he "imitated the Zuo clan in literature, imitated Bai Juyi, Su Shi, and Lu You in poetry, imitated Huang Tingjian in characters, and was loved and valued by the world. He was particularly skilled in painting, and was rated as the first in the Ming Dynasty by critics".

This long Running Script, the "Biography of Waxberry", used personification to write a biography of waxberry. He wrote this essay with waxberry, expressed his feelings with the help of scenery, and expressed his mind straight. He described the simplicity of "honest Confucianism", free and easy of "lightly persistent, emphasizing slick and sly", feelings of "have talent but no opportunity to use it" in the mountains, and understanding the true meaning of open-minded "reaching" in life. The writing style of the Running Script is old, vigorous, and dignified. It seemed to be improvised and casual, but in fact, the characters were verve, exquisite, elegant and frank. It was signed "Shen Zhou" at the end without a year mark. It was affixed a seal carved of "Qi'nan", and other collector's in relief of "Qing Wan Cottage", "Zhang's Collection of Calligraphy and Painting", and "The Record of Calligraphy and Painting in Baishi Mountain House". A collector's seal carved in relief of "Mei Lin Pan's Family Collection".

Collected by Zhang Ruiting (1878—1944), equipped a toon wood box for this volume. The top of the box was engraved with the Official Script "Fine work of volume Biography of Waxberry, written by Baishiweng from Ming Dynasty, collected by Zhang Ruiting". One end of the box was engraved with the Official Script "Fine work of volume Biography of Waxberry written by Baishiweng from the Ming Dynasty", and carved with a square seal the Official Script of "Qing Wan Cottage".

262 Landscape Painting of Nuanxi River

Drawn by Zhang Fengxiang, Ming Dynasty.
Vertical scroll.

Paper scroll.
Light Color selection.
Dimensions longitudinal direction: 92.5 cm; transverse direction: 34 cm.
Collected by Shanhaiguan Cultural Relics Protection and Management Institute.

Zhang Fengxiang (1577—1657), was born near Luanhe, Hebei Province. "Nuanxi" is the name of the ancient Luanhe River. In this painting, the distant mountains and peaks are overlapped, with streams and waterfalls falling down. At the foot of the mountain, several cottages are hidden in the dense shade of the valley bank. The mountain stream flows through the village, and is connected to the bank by a slab bridge. There is a man on the bridge in a hurry. A boat is just off the shore, floating in the river, and the composition is clear and rigorous, and the ink color is appropriate. The pedestrian on the bridge and the boats on the water echo each other from afar. The quiet and indifferent life in the mountain village is full of interest. It is signed with "Imitated in a long summer of Bing Yin year, as Wu Mojing's painting, ask Shaoxuan to give suggestions, Zhang Fengxiang from Nuanxi". A concave seal of "longevity" and a seal carved in relief of "Seal of Zhang Fengxiang" are affixed.

263 Ink Bamboo

Drawn by Pan Dinglan, Qing Dynasty.
Vertical scroll.
Paper Scroll.
Ink wash painting.
Dimensions longitudinal direction: 83.5 cm; transverse direction: 32 cm.
Collected by Shanhaiguan Cultural Relics Protection and Management Institute.

Pan Dinglan (unknown birth and death dates), was born in Changning, Guangdong Province, with style name of Liutang. He was excellent in poetry, calligraphy, and painting, especially in painting, and also good at landscapes and figures. His representative works include "The Painting of a Journey to the North", "Be Ready to Start", etc.

This painting is a traditional freehand brushwork bamboo, which is very simple. Two green bamboos stand beside the stone, with several clusters of bamboo leaves. It is quiet and embellished, especially the small bamboos beside the stone, which have a kind of energy of self-improvement. It is only a few strokes to describe bamboo vividly, which gives bamboo a clear and ethereal realm and a spiritual quality of standing tall and upright. It was signed with "Pan Dinglan". The upper left is written in a concave seal with "Dinglan" and in a seal carved in relief with "Shichi". The lower right was affixed with "□□River□ Bai Gong Nan Lou".

264 Carp

Drawn by Shen Zishan, Qing Dynasty.
Horizontal scroll.
Silk Scroll.
Ink wash painting/
Dimensions longitudinal direction: 46 cm; transverse direction: 72 cm.
Collected by Shanhaiguan Cultural Relics Protection and Management Institute.

Shen Zishan (unknown birth and death dates). This picture shows two carps chasing and playing in the waves. One leaps out of the water, and the other dives enthusiastically, swimming and diving back to chase, flipping his fins and gills, swinging his tail, looming and lifelike. The picture seems full, but in fact, through the contrast between white phosphorescence and ink carp, the change of lines and the rendering of the environment complement and contrast each other in many ways, making the vision move and profound. It shows that fish are free and enjoy themselves in the water. They are skillful and ingenious. It was signed with "Shen Zishan". It was affixed with a concave seal of "□Shan".

265 Tiger in the Morning

Drawn by Gengshi, Qing Dynasty.
Vertical screen.
Silk scroll.
Color selection.
Dimensions longitudinal direction: 124 cm; transverse direction: 41.5 cm.
Collected by Shanhaiguan Cultural Relics Protection and Management Institute.

Gengshi (unknown birth and death dates). In this painting, a large and beautiful tiger comes creeping in the early morning sun among the grass and tussock. The tiger's head is bent slightly, and its eyes are bright. It looks forward as if it is looking for something. Shut its mouth and puff its cheeks as if there is qi in it. Its expression is alert, and angry without infuriation. Its movement is lifelike and straight out of the picture, just about "the tiger is looking down greedily, and its desire is endless". The composition is bold and full, and the shape is real and vivid, showing the strong, vigorous and atmospheric character of the tiger. The morning tiger facing us is quite like a king in the mountains. It was signed with "Geng Shi". It was affixed with a seal carved in relief of "Geng Shi".

266 Fine Brushwork Painting of Flowers and Birds

Drawn by Yun Bing, Qing Dynasty.
Vertical scroll.
Silk scroll.
Color selection.
Dimensions longitudinal direction: 141.2 cm; transverse direction: 45.9 cm.
Collected by Beidaihe Cultural Relics Protection and Management Institute.

Yun Bing (unknown date of birth and death). Known by her courtesy name Qing Yu, she also went by the style name Hao Ru, the nickname of Lanling Female Official, and Nanlan Lady. She was born in Wu Jin (now Changzhou, Jiangsu). She was Yun Zhonglong's second daughter, Yun Nantian's Xuan great-granddaughter, was a female painter who has won a deep family tradition. She was good at drawing flowers and fruits. She used pure color and wrote a poem after drawing. She was famous in Wuzhong. At the beginning of the Qianlong Period, the governor of Jiangsu, Jun Jishan, presented a painting of Yun Bing to the Empress Dowager, and was honored by Emperor Qianlong with his poem inscription.

This painting is fine brushwork and colorful. The picture shows that the old trees have new branches in the cave and there are two long-tailed magpies living on the flower branches. Under the flowers and trees, there are green grass and colorful butterflies, chasing each other. The painter created a harmonious and pleasant natural beauty far away from the secular vanity. Seeing this painting, a kind of inexplicable warmth comes to face. This composition is delicate and elegant, and its shape is stereoscopic and realistic, with vivid meaning. It is signed "Yun Bing Female Official" with two affixed seals (not clear).

267 Bamboo in the Rock

Drawn by Mochan, Guangxu Reign, Qing Dynasty.
Long scroll.
Paper scroll.
Light Color selection.
Dimensions longitudinal direction: 43.5 cm; transverse direction: 169.5 cm.
Collected by Shanhaiguan Cultural Relics Protection and Management Institute.

Mochan (1844—1911), known by his courtesy name Zhou Zhenyue, he also went by the style name Mochan and Xianshi. He was born in Beijing, and was a senior official in the late Qing Dynasty. He liked gold and stone, and was good at calligraphy and painting. In this painting, the lake stone stands in the middle, with several new bamboo and a clump of orchids hidden beside the stone. The stone is ugly but sensible, which is very strange and mystical. The young bamboos are interspersed with overlapping shadows, swaying in the breeze, and the dense orchids grow with the bamboo and stones. Bamboo, stone, and orchid show their own charm. At the end of the painting, it was signed with "On the Guangxu Period, Autumn of Guimao Year, the Taoist Cursive Script was written, brother of Renpu, who is a noble and superior adult, Zhuchu Monk from Yanjing, Mochan wrote in the Longevity Room". The end is affixed with "Mochan" in a concave seal, and a seal carved in relief of "Xi Chu monk returned from outside of Lou". The upper right is affixed with a seal carved in relief of "Fragrance outside of Lou", and the lower right is a concave seal of "Become attached to Hanmo".

268 Plum Blossom Painting

Drawn by Hu Jun, Qing Dynasty.
Horizontal scroll.
Paper scroll.
Color setting.
Dimensions longitudinal direction: 111 cm; transverse direction: 221.7 cm.
Collected by Beidaihe Cultural Relics Protection and Management Institute.

Hu Jun (1869—1909), was born in Huayang, Sichuan Province, known by his courtesy name Yulan, he also went by the style name

Zhen'an. He was a scholar in the 21st year of the Guangxu period, who was good at writing and calligraphy. In 1898, he was awarded to the Hanlin Academy in charge of editing. He has written dozens of poetry and prose diaries, and collected them into *Cangxia Pavilion Diary*.

The picture depicts two old-stem plum flowers leaning against the Taihu Lake cave stone. The branches are transversely oblique and straight, bending in the air. On the delicate branches, it was drawn red and white flowers, showing warmth and calm. White peonies, red flowers and green leaves grow next to the stone. The whole painting is dignified and graceful, vigorous and fresh, quaint and simple. At the end of the painting, the inscription of "Hu Jun, Han River in the autumn of Ding Hai Year" and a square seal were affixed.

269 Peony under the Pine Trees

Chen Banding, Modern.
a vertical scroll of painting.
Vertical Scroll.
Paper scroll.
Grisaille Painting.
Dimensions longitudinal direction: 134.6 cm; transverse direction: 64.3 cm.
Collected by Beidaihe Cultural Relics Protection and Management Institute.

Chen Banding (1876—1970), also known as Chen Nian, was a painter from Shanyin (today's Shaoxing), Zhejiang Province. He was good at flowers, landscapes, calligraphy, and seal cutting. He had published works such as "Chen Banding's Painting Collection" and "Chen Banding's Flower Painting Manual".

The inscription on the top left of the painting is "Fragrance is everywhere in the world, spring comes to the world. On the first day of the lunar month, Renyin year, Tomb Sweeping Day in March. Banding, an old guy of eighty seven years old". A rectangular seal carved in relief was affixed on the painting. A square concave seal and a square seal carved in relief are as a signature. A square concave seal was affixed in the lower left corner before painting.

270 Plum Blossom and Mandarin Duck

He Xiangning (Marked), Modern.
Vertical scroll.
Silk scroll.
Color selection.
Dimensions longitudinal direction: 113.6 cm; transverse direction: 41.9 cm.
Collected by Beidaihe Cultural Relics Protection and Management Institute.

He Xiangning (1878—1972), female, formerly known as Jian, also known as Ruijian, was nicknamed Shuangqing Building Owner. Her ancestral home was Nanhai, Guangdong, she was born in Hong Kong. She was an outstanding representative of the Left Party of the Chinese Kuomintang, a famous political activist, a pioneer of the feminist movement, an outstanding artist in the painting world, one of the main founders of the democratic revolution, and the wife of Liao Zhongkai, a pioneer of the Chinese democratic revolution. After the founding of New China, she served as a member of the Central People's Government, Vice Chairman of the Standing Committee of the National People's Congress, Vice Chairman of the CPPCC, Chairman of the Overseas Chinese Affairs Committee, Chairman of the Artists Association, Honorary Chairman of the All-China Women's Federation, and Vice Chairman of the Central Committee of the National Revolutionary Movement. She was good at painting landscapes, flowers, especially lions, tigers, deer, cranes and other animals. She had "He Xiangning's Collection of Poems and Paintings" to her credit.

On the top left, the Regular Script "Ms. Xiangning" was signed.

271 Lotus Painting

Yu Feichang, Modern.
Vertical screen.
Paper scroll.
Color selection.
Dimensions longitudinal direction: 131.4 cm; transverse direction: 33 cm.
Collected by Beidaihe Cultural Relics Protection and Management Institute.

Yu Feichang (1889—1959), Manchu, known by courtesy name Zhao, once used to be called "Xianren", "Wenren", "Laofei" and "Feian". His ancestral home was Penglai, Shandong Province, he was born in Beijing and lived for a long time. He was excellent at painting flowers and birds, and can draw freehand landscapes. He has published the "Selected Portfolio of Yu Feian's Fine Brushwork Flowers and Birds Painting" and so on.

This painting is light color freehand brushwork, showing a cluster of lotus flowers in full bloom. The process of the three life forms of bud, bloom and result is unfolded from bottom to top, revealing the true meaning of life. By using the method of "imitating people with objects", with ingenious ideas and a few strokes, the noble character of lotus, which is "candid, unbroken, emerges from the mud without being stained, and clean in water without being demon", is vividly rendered. A dragonfly flew into the painting from afar, and it seems that it is looking for a standing place where "tiny lotus leaf just comes out of water", which adds more depth to the content and meaning of the painting and adds a touch of ancient poetry to this painting. The lotus leaves change in intensity and become dry and moist. The white flowers and red stamens are lightly made up in plain clothes, which is a mixture of reality and emptiness. It focuses on their natural interest of growing and moving in the water, eulogizes the vitality of nature, and brings people a strong artistic appeal. From the top left, it was signed with "The cold and fragrant fragrance of flowers has quietly flown into the poet's sentence. Mr. Yi Pu is smiling. It was drawn two days before the Zhongyuan Festival in the Jia Xu Age, one of the four paintings of lotus beside Kunming Lake. Drawn by Feichang, YU, □" It is affixed with a seal carved in relief of "Feichang", and a concave round seal on the lower right corner.

272 "Beidaihe" Running Script Seven Character Poem

Guo Moruo, Modern.
Horizontal scroll.
Paper scroll.
Dimensions longitudinal direction: 65.6 cm; transverse direction: 135.3 cm.
Collected by Beidaihe Cultural Relics Protection and Management Institute.

Guo Moruo (1892—1978) , known by his courtesy name Dingtang, he also went by the style name Shangwu. He was born in Shawan, Leshan, Sichuan Province. He was a modern Chinese writer, historian and archaeologist.

The poem reads as follows:
Ground is covered with sweet potato seedlings which shows green color,
While sea waves are red all day long because of the rosy clouds.
Lighthouse is shining on the east mountain,
And the moon is faintly setting in the blue sky.

In the autumn of 1964, it was written for the Beidaihe Cultural Relics Institute.

273 Painting of Excellent People

Pu Xinyu, Modern.
Vertical scroll.
Paper scroll.
Light color selection.
Dimensions longitudinal direction: 113.7 cm; transverse direction: 33.8 cm.
Collected by Beidaihe Cultural Relics Protection and Management Institute.

Pu Xinyu (1896—1963) was known by courtesy name Ru, and the style name Xin Yu. He compared himself with Tao Qian. He was called "Master Xihuang" and "Xishan High-minded Scholars". He was born in Beijing, Manchu, Aisin-Gioro. He studied astronomy, biology, long scriptures and history, refined calligraphy and painting, and wrote the "Collection of Four Classics" and the "Collection of Western Mountains".

The composition of this painting is unique. The high cliffs are verdant, the huge rocks are sharp, temples are hidden in valleys, and the waterfalls are running in streams, pouring into the sky. In the close view, green trees shade the halls and buildings, and the pavilion stands beside the clear stream. The two scholars who met again after a long separation sit down in the pavilion and talk with each other, while the page-boy stands by. Deep mountains and ravines, ancient temples and terrace, landscapes and boundary paintings are unique and natural. The quiet valley, elaborately decorated with characters, conveys the secular interest of seeking success and visiting friends. In the upper right corner, was signed "Ancient trees leaning with stones, clouds hovering among mountains, excellent people sitting in the cottage, vessels consecrating to Zhouwen Emperor, drawn by Xinyu". It is affixed with a seal carved in relief of "Old descendants", and a concave seal of "Pu Ru".

274 Five Oxen

Li Keran, Modern.
Vertical scroll.
Paper scroll.
Ink painting.
Dimensions longitudinal direction: 136.2 cm; transverse direction: 66.2 cm.
Collected by Beidaihe Cultural Relics Protection and Management Institute.

Li Keran (1907— 1989), originally named Li Yongshun, was born in Xuzhou, Jiangsu Province. He was an outstanding painter in modern China. He was good at painting landscapes and figures, especially cattle. His works include "Li Keran's Collection of Ink and Wash Paintings Drawing for Nature" and "Li Keran's Painting of Cattle".

The upper part of the painting has a long inscription: "Five Cattle. Cattle, also have great power. Cattle usually bend down and are willing to work hard for common people, and work hard all life without taking credit for it. They are pure, gentle and kind, but stubborn. They move forward steadily without stepping into the air. It describes the sublime and imposing appearance. I have always respected its nature and loved its appearance, so I have been writing about it repeatedly. In 1962, it was drawn by Keran in Beidaihe." A rectangular seal carved in relief seal with the signature of "Keran". At the bottom right is affixed a rectangular seal carved in relief of "Dedicative cattle", and at the right side of the bottom is a square concave seal of "Old words must be removed".

275 Pigeon Painting

Drawn by Wu Zuoren, Modern.
Vertical scroll.
Paper scroll.
Color selection.
Dimensions longitudinal direction: 100.5 cm; transverse direction: 32.8 cm.
Collected by Beidaihe Cultural Relics Protection and Management Institute.

Wu Zuoren (1908—1997), male, born in Jingxian County, Xuancheng, Anhui Province. Famous contemporary Chinese painter and art educator. He was well versed in painting and poetry. It is published in Wu Zuoren's Painting Collection, Wu Zuoren's Art, etc.

In this painting, a pair of pigeons fold their wings and look at each other on their sides, looking forward as if to communicate with each other. There is no background, all blank. The painter intended to combine line drawing with Mo-gu to create changes and contrast in form. He used a few colored ink to draw the pigeons at one go. The unique appearance, unbridled modeling and simplified painting are thought-provoking. It is rare in the history of painting that the strokes are sparse but with integrated spirit. On the top left is the inscription "Zuoren, in 1961", with the seal carved in relief of "Zuoren's painting". From the seals, this painting should be the middle-aged composition of Mr. Wu Zuoren.

图书在版编目（CIP）数据

秦皇岛馆藏文物精品集 / 闫乐耕主编. —秦皇岛：燕山大学出版社，2024.4
ISBN 978-7-5761-0140-9

Ⅰ. ①秦… Ⅱ. ①闫… Ⅲ. ①博物馆—历史文物—秦皇岛—图集 Ⅳ. ①K872.223.2

中国国家版本馆 CIP 数据核字（2023）第 048561 号

秦皇岛馆藏文物精品集

QINHUANGDAO GUANCANG WENWU JINGPINJI

闫乐耕 主编

出 版 人：陈　玉
责任编辑：张　蕊　　策划编辑：张　蕊
责任印制：吴　波　　装帧设计：赵中极
出版发行：燕山大学出版社 YANSHAN UNIVERSITY PRESS　　电　　话：0335-8387555
地　　址：河北省秦皇岛市河北大街西段 438 号　　邮政编码：066004
印　　刷：河北文曲印刷有限公司　　经　　销：全国新华书店

开　　本：889 mm×1194 mm　1/16　　印　　张：20
版　　次：2024 年 4 月第 1 版　　印　　次：2024 年 4 月第 1 次印刷
书　　号：ISBN 978-7-5761-0140-9　　字　　数：430 千字
定　　价：580.00 元